A Walk Around the Horizon

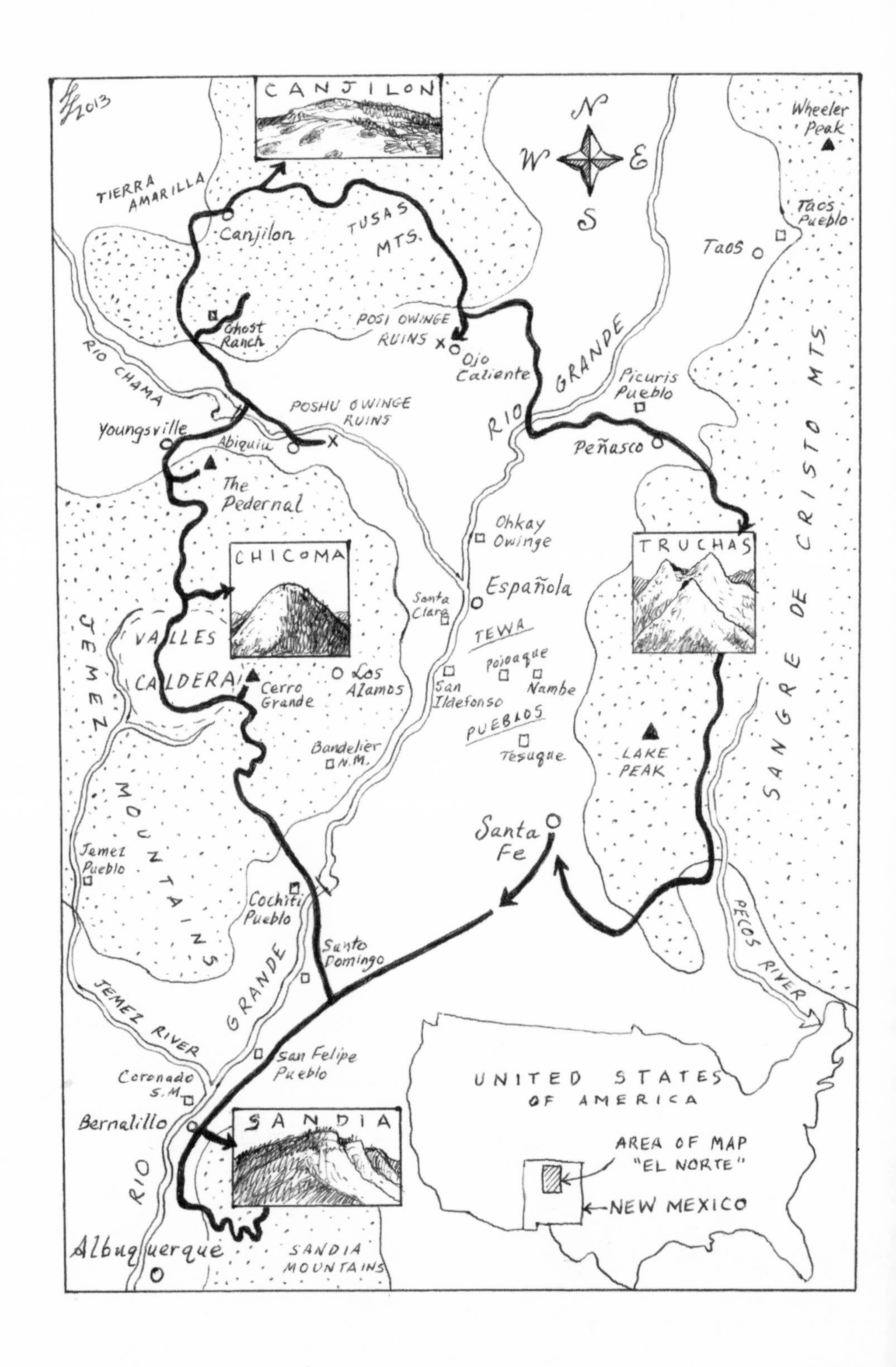

2013
CANJILON
N
W
E
S
Wheeler Peak
TIERRA AMARILLA
Canjilon
TUSAS MTS.
Taos Pueblo
Taos
Ghost Ranch
POSI OWINGE RUINS
Ojo Caliente
RIO CHAMA
RIO GRANDE
SANGRE DE CRISTO MTS.
Picuris Pueblo
POSHU OWINGE RUINS
Youngsville
Abiquiu
Peñasco
The Pedernal
Ohkay Owinge
CHICOMA
Española
TRUCHAS
Santa Clara
JEMEZ
VALLES CALDERA
TEWA
Pojoaque
Nambe
Cerro Grande
Los Alamos
San Ildefonso
PUEBLOS
Tesuque
Bandelier N.M.
LAKE PEAK
MOUNTAINS
Santa Fe
Jemez Pueblo
Cochiti Pueblo
PECOS RIVER
Santo Domingo
GRANDE
JEMEZ RIVER
San Felipe Pueblo
UNITED STATES OF AMERICA
Coronado S.M.
AREA OF MAP "EL NORTE"
Bernalillo
SANDIA
NEW MEXICO
RIO
Albuquerque
SANDIA MOUNTAINS

A Walk Around the Horizon

Discovering New Mexico's Mountains of the Four Directions

TOM HARMER

Tom Harmer

UNIVERSITY OF NEW MEXICO PRESS
Albuquerque

Printed in the United States of America
18 17 16 15 14 13 1 2 3 4 5 6

Library of Congress Cataloging-in-Publication Data

Harmer, Tom, 1947–
A walk around the horizon : discovering New Mexico's mountains of the four directions / Tom Harmer.
pages cm
ISBN 978-0-8263-5364-1 (paperback : alkaline paper) —
ISBN 978-0-8263-5365-8 (electronic)
1. Mountains—New Mexico. 2. Harmer, Tom, 1947– —Travel—New Mexico. 3. New Mexico—Description and travel. 4. Landscapes—New Mexico. 5. Mountain ecology—New Mexico. 6. Natural history—New Mexico. 7. Mountaineering—New Mexico. I. Title.
F802.A16H37 2013
917.8904—dc23
2013008671

BOOK DESIGN AND COMPOSITION: Catherine Leonardo
Composed in 10.25/13.5 Minion Pro Regular
Display type is Times Ten LT Std, Wilke LT Std, and Sabon

Contents

PART ONE

Where and Why 1

PART TWO

Watermelon 19

PART THREE

Flint 67

PART FOUR

Antler 135

PART FIVE

Trout 171

Epilogue 207

PART ONE

Where and Why

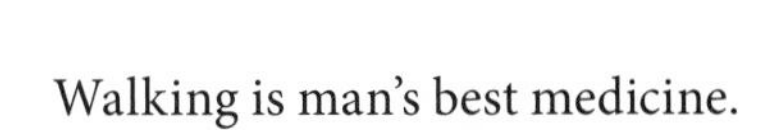

Walking is man's best medicine.

—Hippocrates, 300 BC

One

YEARS AGO, WHEN I first lived with my family in a Hispanic village north of Santa Fe, I became aware of four high mountains standing on the horizon in each direction.

Some of my neighbors, elderly men who scorned maps and compasses, taught me to use them as landmarks for locating myself in the high desert landscape. Jutting up from surrounding mountain ranges, they frame the visible limits of the vast and colorific Upper Rio Grande Valley of northern New Mexico from Albuquerque to Taos. I can still see old Eutimio "Timmy" Montoya, a retired *borreguero*, or sheepman, pointing out each one as he turned in a circle, naming them as he went: Truchas Peak ("Trout" in Spanish) to the east, Sandia Crest ("Watermelon") to the south, Chicoma Mountain ("Flint-Covered" in the local Tewa Indian language) to the west, and Canjilon Mountain ("Deer Antler," again in Spanish) to the north.

Such enigmatic and beguiling names attached to peaks everybody can see on a daily basis would seem to invite closer investigation. Yet only recently I learned that my Tewa-speaking Pueblo Indian neighbors regard them as the sacred peaks of the four directions—powerful and compelling deities whose other ancient names, besides "Flint-Covered," translate as "Shimmering," "Stone Man," and "Turtle." With one summit located in the Sangre de Cristo Mountains and another on the rim of Valles Caldera, both renowned wild areas in America's Southwest, who could resist an urge to make a summer journey out of hiking to the top of all four?

Turns out, almost everybody. A few Tewa men, religious leaders, still make a pilgrimage to rock shrines that have been kept atop each for almost a thousand years, but otherwise I was the only person I knew who was struck by the idea. And it wasn't just because I was being drawn to something from a much older time that persisted into the present. Following in the footsteps of Native pilgrims quickly became a passing fancy compared to the extraordinary idea itself—that I could set out from my home and walk the horizon in a grand circle, about 225 miles as the crow flies, in turn climbing each of the mountains that float above forested wildernesses few Americans have seen.

It seemed odd—even unlikely—that after spending all my free time over the past thirty years hiking and camping and scrambling up peaks in El Norte, as local Hispanics call the northern reaches of historic Spanish settlement, I never made it up these four. They've always been there, beckoning. On most outings, at least one of them was visible from a few to forty miles away, anchoring me in a known world and showing which direction was which. The more I thought about it, the more I saw it as an auspicious stroke of luck. I'd always dreamed of someday going on an extended solo backpacking trip in the Southwest, of leisurely exploring a great expanse of wild country on foot, and here it had been right before my eyes all along.

Then I wondered if I could actually pull it off. My last lengthy trek was a five-day crossing of Colorado's La Plata Mountains, a cold and rainy march over a twelve-thousand-foot pass under Sharkstooth Peak and down the long glacial valley of Bear Creek. It was a memorable culmination to a summer stint leading youth groups in a backpacking program of the City of Durango's Parks and Recreation Department, which focused mainly on trails in the Weminuche Wilderness of the San Juan Range. I probably carried a backpack for forty or fifty miles that summer and ended up in fantastic physical condition. But that was 1983. Now it was 2010, and I'd just celebrated my sixty-second birthday. I was still in fine shape thanks to decades in the chimney sweeping business, and I certainly knew my way around the mountains of New Mexico. Nevertheless, the journey I envisioned was way more ambitious than anything I'd pulled off since my twenties. Gone were the days when I could throw a few things in a knapsack and disappear into the mountains, living off the land and sleeping wrapped in a poncho wherever night found me, as I did in the bush along the British Columbia–Washington State border in the 1970s.

On the other hand, if I was serious about something this strenuous, it was probably now or never. I wasn't getting any younger, as they say. The passage of time has a way of eroding our shiny dreams. If the occasional weekend backpack trip in the mountains near Santa Fe was the most I had accomplished in recent years, so what? I could still do this, I told myself. And if it turned out to be my last big adventure, then hey, what better way to cap off a life gone to ground in this land of impressive scenic beauty than one last solitary promenade, full circle, around my adopted homeland?

My route, I figured, would bear a superficial resemblance to the Tewa spiritual pilgrimage, but I would go in a clockwise direction around the horizon, which was opposite the way they go. (Tewa friends insist counterclockwise movement is prescribed for nearly all their ritual actions.) And I would be in it for the journey, the escape into the outdoors, the immersion into the natural world, rather than the cranking out of trail miles or the bagging of peaks. It was true I looked forward to reaching the topmost point of each unfamiliar peak and gazing down on the miniaturized world I came from, and certainly the history, archaeology, and geology would have to be investigated along the way. However, as a lifelong student of natural history, outdoor survival, and Native practices in the wild, what most appealed to me was simply the process of discovery—those moments of surprise, understanding, and awe that come while finding one's way over the landscape. It would be the deep nature experience itself, prolonged to last most of a summer, that would make it all worth it. I heard myself mutter, "God oh mighty, yes! I'll do it!"

And there was a more urgent reason to go. The four peaks are home to a unique montane forest unlike any in the world—an amalgamation of familiar western conifers and associated broadleaf understory species mingled at most elevations with cacti, yucca, and other exotic desert- or drought-modified plants. As a consequence of converging biotic influences, a place where Rocky Mountain spruce meets Sierra Madre live oak and Great Plains bluestem meets Great Basin sagebrush, the high woods of El Norte are in big trouble. If global warming raises average temperatures by a few degrees, as seems to be happening, the rich diversity of this singular assemblage could shift northward into Colorado (or even Wyoming) in the next fifty years. Already, record-breaking droughts, insect plagues, and wildfires have wiped out or seriously diminished huge areas of woodland, and trees are disappearing in alarming numbers. Time was running out if I wanted to see it before it changed beyond recognition. (As it turned out, a swath of countryside that would take me three days to pass through would, a year later, be destroyed by a crowning forest fire.)

Once my mind was made up, I announced my intentions to family and friends, and even to my publisher. As I suspected, nobody I hiked with was up for joining me on a trip of this magnitude. Hoping to enlist at least a few fellow travelers on short legs along the way, I described some of the expected wonders to be experienced with the audacity and ringing conviction of a John Muir or an Adolph Bandelier—as if I, too, had hundred-mile rambles under my belt like those great nineteenth-century scholar-wanderers. Actually, since there were no foot journeys on public record of anybody circumambulating the peaks of the four directions, I had only the vaguest notion of what I was getting myself into. I decided some serious research was in order, which included asking locals, especially the only people who might know about a route such as mine, my Tewa Indian neighbors.

They live in six ancient and yet modernized "pueblos"—compact residential communities—surrounded by lands secured for each over centuries of conflict and accommodation with invading Spanish and later Anglo migrants. Each is really a sort of city-state within the complex and overlapping governmental structure that sorts things out in New Mexico. Three are located along the main course of the Rio Grande (Ohkay Owinge, Santa Clara, and San Ildefonso Pueblos) and three are on upstream tributaries in the foothills of the Sangre de Cristo range to the southeast (Pojoaque, Nambe, and Tesuque Pueblos). Except for the people of Nambe and Tesuque, whose view of Truchas Peak is blocked by intervening mountains and who identify nearby Lake Peak as their sacred mountain of the east, the Tewa have kept shrines on the same summits I hoped to visit ever since they migrated into this region from the northwest sometime around the twelfth century. (I had been to the top of Lake Peak many times. It wouldn't be on the itinerary.)

And not surprisingly, the Tewa I spoke to were vague about the details of their mountain pilgrimage. Only one elderly man, John Pesendo, the relative of a close friend, would actually discuss the route and the location of the shrines. He told me that tribal pilgrims nowadays go by pickup truck or horseback, at least most of the way, and that the purpose of the pilgrimage is to delineate the extent of their traditional homeland as well as to pay homage to their sacred landscape. At each shrine they leave offerings and prayers that not only renew their ties to the powers of creation but also solidify their sense of belonging to the landscape.

For the past thousand years, this mile-high semiarid basin, the upstream portion of a great rift valley channeling the Rio Grande southward, has been enticing migrating peoples to stay. Fleeing the breakdown of the Chaco Canyon and Mesa Verde culture centers to the northwest, tightly organized Pueblo Indian groups, including the Tewa, began descending headwater streams in stages until they were technically and socially capable of harnessing the great river for intensive irrigation agriculture. A few centuries later, Spanish forays from the south gradually coalesced into an isolated New World settlement that was able to thrive, like the first English colonies on the Atlantic coast, in the vacuum left behind by forced displacement and devastating population losses due to introduced diseases. Then a mere 160-some years ago a third migration began from the east after military forces seized political control in the westward march of the English-speaking United States. Only in the last fifty years has the land between the four peaks become as much an Anglo world as it has remained Pueblo Indian and Hispanic.

Natives and longtime residents alike easily identify the unique shape of each summit and speak of them as familiar features surrounding their homeland. Perhaps nowhere else but in the celebrated sunlight of high-altitude clear air where Santa Fe sits can you see far mountaintops in such intimate detail. Sandia, to the south, is a rounded oblong on the horizon like the outline of a watermelon lying in a garden. Chicoma, the highest summit to the west, has a more pointed profile, and although mostly forested, it has a pronounced and identifying bald area on the left or south side. Canjilon, to the north, is little more than a prominent high point on an elevated mesa. And on the east, Truchas is the highest of a cluster of classic alpine peaks carved by glaciers standing bare above timberline. But nobody I spoke to had ever been on top of more than one.

This is remarkable given the fact that there are roads almost to the top of three of them. Every summer, thousands drive the paved highway to a point on Sandia Crest to stand in the cold wind and look down on the city of Albuquerque baking in the hundred-degree desert below. A U.S. Forest Service road passes within a mile of the top of Chicoma in a heavily logged area of the Jemez Mountains. And a four-wheel-drive track accesses the ruins of the old fire lookout on Canjilon where herds of cattle wander the public range. Only Truchas Peak, the highest and most remote, requires wilderness backpacking skills to reach.

The informal canvas of people I spoke to revealed that, for the most part, Pueblo Indian people have been on top of Chicoma, rural Hispanic people have gone up Canjilon, Anglo backpackers have climbed Truchas, and city people of all backgrounds have driven up to Sandia Crest. Each mountain, it seemed, had come to "belong" to one of the identifiable groups that make up New Mexico's current cultural mosaic. And since Tewa pilgrims these days rarely visit more than the peak closest to their home pueblo, it wasn't likely that I'd encounter them as I walked the long way around all four mountains like I began to plot it on my worn and tattered AAA "Indian Country" road map (which originally opened like the crisp bellows of a new accordion, but now came apart like a sad and sagging origami project). Or that anybody would accompany me on much of the whole circuit. Vague pledges of joining me on this or that individual peak ascent began coming in. It was time to get real.

When I finally acquired detailed topographic maps and trail guides for the trip and began poring over them for possible routes to follow, I was stunned. I stayed up late one night going over every conceivable way I could figure to reach all four mountains, tallying up the miles on a pocket calculator with growing horror. My initial estimate of 225 miles measured with a twelve-inch plastic ruler on my trusty, if decomposing, road map suddenly doubled and then tripled on the ground. If stretched out in a straight line, it would be like walking from Albuquerque to Los Angeles, but with far more lung-burning ups and downs. Crushed, I impulsively tossed the road map into the flames of the fireplace. Quelling an urge to wake my wife and share my dismay, which might have tarnished her image of me as this grizzled and manly outdoorsman, I phoned an Indian friend, Scott Thomas.

"It's two o'clock in the morning, dude!" he snarled. But he didn't hang up. He and I had ranged the mountains together for almost twenty years—fishing the trout lakes, gathering medicinal plants, and hunting elk and deer. When I finished explaining how far the trip would really be, he said, "I don't understand what the problem is."

"I might as well hike the Continental Divide Trail from Mexico to Canada!"

"No, do that next, if you want," he said calmly. "But for this one, why not just hike the mountain parts, the national forest parts, and stitch them together by driving the lowlands in between?"

Of course. Why hadn't I thought of that? All four mountains are located in areas my Spanish-speaking neighbors call *montosa*, "mountainous, wild, well-forested" regions where each is a prominent height in a larger range. And these mountain ranges are mostly public land managed by three different national forests: the Carson, Santa Fe, and Cibola. Suddenly inspired, I took another look at my maps and saw it was the only logical solution. And, as an added bonus, it would allow me to cross hundreds of miles of private and Indian and Spanish land-grant areas without hoofing it along the shoulders of roads.

Scott interrupted: "Can I go back to bed now?"

"Yeah, thanks. I owe you one."

He chuckled. "I thought that's what you were planning to do from the very start."

"You did? Well, no. . . . And this way is much better. I'm relieved." Sleep deprivation was beginning to kick in.

"I couldn't see you going on a death march like that. You're not exactly the type."

"What type am I?"

"Well, if I had to put it in a nutshell, I'd say you're a throwback. Maybe not quite a Neanderthal, but definitely a hunter-gatherer." He laughed easily.

"How does that . . . ? I don't get it."

"Oh, you know. I've watched you out there. You sniff the bark of trees, study the shape of leaves, taste the water of springs, figure out the direction the wind is coming from. You'd be bored out of your mind walking down the side of the highway with cars zooming by."

That's right, I thought. Good old Scott.

It was still a long way to go, more than a hundred miles, and most of it would be at high elevation, around 8,000 to 10,000 feet, with long stretches even higher, including the ascent of Truchas Peak, which would take me up to a breathless 13,102 feet. This would be mitigated somewhat by the fact that living and working at around 7,000 feet, as I did, conditioned a person better than someone from sea level first arriving in Santa Fe. And the summits would not actually be all that hard to climb. Bagging all four in one season wouldn't exactly qualify me for membership in the elite community of technical climbers by any means. I'd still have little to say when brawny athletes in compression fabrics and clinking carabiners swapped tales of mind-boggling alpine ascents at the checkout line in the local REI store.

But that was not to say I wouldn't be exposed to possible danger. There were still lightning strikes on exposed summits, ticks, water-borne parasites, torrential monsoon rains, hail, summer snowstorms, hundred-mile-per-hour wind gusts, tree blowdowns, and mountain lions that kill and eat hikers. (This last has only been reported from California, Colorado, and Montana in recent years, but I'd seen three lions so far in New Mexico, one napping in the limbs of a juniper tree only a hundred yards from my house.) Not to mention bears, rattlesnakes, rabid coyotes, deer crazed by brain worms, and aggressive hoary marmots. (Marmots are large, shy, vegetarian rodents, yet the one I caught rifling a backpack I'd leaned against a spruce tree at Lake Katherine was so inflamed by the bag of trail mix I'd left open, it bristled and snapped and held me off for the time it took me to think of throwing a rock.)

Then there are skunks coming down the trail toward you who refuse to yield the right of way. And screams in the night that stop your heart and cannot be identified with the possible carbon-based life-form capable of producing it. Or snorts so close to the wall of your thin nylon tent that you remember all the convincing stories you've ever heard about the ghost of La Llorona wailing for the children she murdered, or the evil Indian doctor who lived by a black pond up Holy Ghost Canyon. Or the unsolved murder of hikers reported in western mountains every year.

For various practical reasons, most having to do with how cold it can get at night at higher elevations—even here in the Sunbelt—there is a very narrow window of opportunity for a mountain backpacking trip each year. It may be true that mild, sunny weather can occur at any season, even the dead of winter, but such events, often lasting weeks at a time, are not predictable. Nor is the depth of winter snow. The only way of being reasonably sure of above-freezing overnight temperatures and bare ground to walk on is to start out no earlier than July 1 and finish no later than September 30. I therefore blocked out the months of July, August, and September on my calendar.

Delving into books about the people and the mountains along my prospective path, I found a poem in *Songs of the Tewa*, translated by Herbert J. Spinden, called "Initiation Chant of the Kwirana K'osa" (pp. 86–87). A prayer about the wind that blows over all of us who migrated here—the air we breathe no matter who we are—it seemed to capture the feeling that my tramp around the horizon would celebrate:

For little people are we all, to be loved of the Gods
As far away as our Great Mother's sound of breathing
Reaches. Even to the Utes, Apaches, Navajos,
Kiowas, Comanches, Cheyennes, even to all of them!
To the Mexican people, even to them it reaches!

To the people of America, even to them the sound
Of our Great Mother's breathing reaches. So now
They are loved of the Gods and each by the other loved!
So that is why we hope to find our living here,
We mortal men!

Two

ALL WINTER THE four peaks loomed shiny white in a startling blue sky. In the Rio Grande Valley itself the snow didn't linger long—no matter how cold and snowy the storm, the sun usually returned the next day to warm and melt away inches of powder with a speedy Sunbelt ferocity. By June the high mountains were almost free of the stuff and the time to head out was approaching. Among everybody who knew me, it was more or less common knowledge that I would be gone the rest of the summer on a quest to walk around the horizon. My intention was to depart around the Fourth of July weekend. Most long backpack trips traverse a route that starts somewhere and leads to somewhere else. Mine circled completely around where I lived. I hadn't yet made up my mind where I should start—which would also be the place I would come back to in the end.

Then a helicopter crash and a midnight shootout in the mountains near Santa Fe brought home the reality of what can happen out there, beyond my familiar doorstep. I had completely forgotten about the helicopter that went down just below the summit of 12,622-foot Santa Fe Baldy the summer before. But a newspaper report of an official investigation into the incident came out just in time to remind me how mountain rescue attempts can sometimes go very wrong. Megumi Yamamoto, a twenty-six-year-old female hiker, was reported lost in the Hidden Lake area north of the peak—a steep, glacier-scoured alpine valley at timberline—and a search-and-rescue team was dispatched. Then a New Mexico State Police helicopter piloted by Sergeant Andy Tingwall was brought in to aid in the search. Accompanying him as spotter was Officer Wesley Cox. They located the woman, but due to poor communications with the ground team and disruptive disagreements between various unit commanders about how best to get the hiker to safety, the helicopter landed in the dark in extremely hazardous circumstances, picked up Yamamoto, and took off as a storm approached. The helicopter struck a ridge of rock and crashed, killing the hiker and the pilot, and seriously injuring Officer Cox.

Then on June 25, the weekend before I planned to start out, the *Santa Fe New Mexican* front page headline caught my eye: "Pecos Shootout 'Like OK Corral'—Witness to Campground Shooting Recalls Night That Left Several Injured." The article told about several Albuquerque families camping out together in the national forest having been the target of random violence. Conflicting accounts at least agreed that after most of the women and children had gone to bed, a poker game was still going on, and then two unknown men drove up in a pickup, got out, and stood around acting sketchy. When asked to leave, one pulled a handgun and tried to shoot a camper point-blank in the chest, but the pistol misfired. The poker players scattered from the light as the man ejected the bullet and fired off more than six shots after them. One of the campers returned fire and bullets flew back and forth in the darkness where about fifteen children were in bed in nearby RVs and tents. The attackers, one wounded in the shoulder, fled in their vehicle. One of the campers took a .40-caliber bullet in the arm. A sixteen-year-old boy was shot in the right calf and grazed in the right thigh. The initial shooter was in jail; the wounded camper's arm was so infected he was still in the hospital.

The Wild West was still wild, it seemed. The incident took place twenty-two miles from my home, along the route I planned to travel. I would not be carrying any weapon more formidable than a sharp camp knife. At least I'd be hiking in a region far to the north of the Mexican border where drug runners and recently mobilized National Guard units made mountains in that area even more of a war zone.

During the month of June I trained and built up endurance on day hikes near Santa Fe. A few days before departure, I pulled out all my backpacking equipment and saw it wasn't just worn and soiled, it was totally old school. Nobody in years except me and a few other holdouts had been seen in the Santa Fe high country carrying tubular aluminum frame backpacks with gear stacked high above our heads. Everybody else had newer *internal* frame packs with all their ultralight equipment hidden inside. I suppose it made me look hopelessly old-fashioned, like a Sherpa porter carrying supplies into a Himalayan base camp. The frame pack I decided to use, because it was the cleanest and lightest, belonged to my wife Theresa—the most recent heavy use it had seen was during her yearlong trek in the Andes of Bolivia and Peru just after college. And my one-man nylon tent had been passed on to me, well used, by a friend who'd departed to Los Angeles hoping to jump-start his acting career in 1995! But I had everything I needed, and it was all good-quality stuff. I was determined to make do.

The biggest problem seemed to be what daypack to bring along for side trips and summit ascents. None at hand weighed less than two and a half pounds empty. Theresa offered me the use of her teenage son Brennan's elementary school backpack from the nether reaches of a musty closet, which weighed only a pound. Unfortunately it was bright turquoise and lime green and sported a likeness of the cartoon dog Scooby-Doo surrounded by lavender fluttering butterflies. It was shockingly gaudy and awful. And perfect, I decided. A great conversation starter on the trail—as long as nobody got it in their head that I snatched it from some little kid hiking in the mountains. ("No, really, Ranger Rick. I traded Bobby four Snickers bars for it!")

In the end I spent the most time and money shopping for, repackaging, and weighing the mainly dried food I would eat along the way. Included were freeze-dried meals I could reconstitute with boiling water poured right into resealable packages, a commercial version of U.S. military MREs (Meals Reconstituted Easily? Mucky Rubbery Edibles?), which I hoped tasted better than the battlefield originals. In all, I spent less than fifty dollars for five days' rations, which was heavy on granola, dried fruits, and nuts (and Snickers bars). I kept paring down the load until I got the entire backpack, including two full water jugs, to weigh a manageable forty-five pounds.

Then a really big snag developed. Because I had a commitment from some people who wanted to join me on the Truchas Peak leg if I hiked it later on, I decided to start by climbing Chicoma and work my way north to Canjilon in order to get around to Truchas just in time for them to come along. But dry spring weather deepened into drought conditions by June, and a lightning strike north of Chicoma started a forest fire that closed where I planned to travel. Three days before departure, the South Fork Fire, as they called it, was only 50 percent contained and access could be prohibited well into the time frame I needed. Smoke from the fire drifting northeast made hiking in the Canjilon and Truchas areas inadvisable as well. All I had left was Sandia Mountain to the south.

I phoned the forest service ranger station in Tijeras and asked the lady who answered, Maria Varela, if there were any restrictions on hiking and camping in the Sandia Mountain Wilderness area, which constituted the whole north end of the range and my route over it.

"Oh yes, there is! That whole area is under Stage One fire restrictions," she said brusquely. "That means no open fires; only camp stoves are allowed. But that's about to change to Stage Two—no open flame of any kind. The order for it is on the district ranger's desk—as we speak—waiting for his signature."

I told her I wasn't planning on going until the Fourth of July weekend. "Won't things be better by then?"

"Oh no. Not at all. We will probably go to Stage *Three* by then—*full* closure, no entry allowed for *any* reason."

I hung up, stunned.

The woman had spoken to me like Smokey the Bear trying to deflect an arsonist gleefully bent on torching the national forest with illegal fireworks. Although I had no reason to doubt what she said as the official word (it later turned out that she was—as my mother would delicately say—*full* of it), I found it hard to believe that all doors were closed to me. Yet something seemed to be blocking my every move. It made me think of my old neighbor, Concepción (Sean) Fierro, who a few days before had driven up into the mountains to cut a pickup load of firewood. All came to naught because his chainsaw broke. After coming home empty-handed, he shrugged it off with what sounded like a Spanish *dicho*, or saying: "*Hombre propone, Dios dispone.*" It turned out to be his own translation of the Anglo proverb: "Man proposes, God disposes," which aptly described my situation, too. I had three days left before my scheduled departure and nowhere to go. Like him, I simply shrugged it off and went about my business. The next day, after work, I checked online at the public lands website for current fire restrictions. Nothing had changed for the Sandia Mountains; it was still okay for camping with gas stoves like mine.

That night, local television news reported a bear attack in the Sandias. A woman with children had been terrorized the night before in their tent. It was at a roadside picnic area frequented by bears, below Sandia Crest where no overnight camping was allowed. The mother called 911 on her cell phone and screamed she'd been clawed by a huge bear tearing its way inside. Officers arrived to find the family's food had been left out, both on a picnic table and inside the tent, a typical scenario with predictable results in bear country.

The next afternoon at an expensive downtown Santa Fe mountain-climbing store where I bought a small lightweight bottle to carry extra stove gas, I asked the clerk if he'd heard about any restrictions on camping in the

Sandia Mountains. Or at least I tried. He was a big muscled bruiser in his twenties with bushy black hair and beard, clearly a climber. He seemed bored and pissed off about having to serve me.

"Know about any restrictions—?" was all I got out before he interrupted impatiently.

"Yeah, but just no open fires."

"No, on *camping*. In the Sandias."

"There's no camping allowed in the Sandias!" he said, not trying to hide his contempt for my ignorance. "That's why that woman was mauled by the bear."

"But I thought it was okay—"

Again he cut me off. "No, there's no camping allowed in Sandia National Park."

Since there is no such national park, I realized my problem was simply that I was talking to someone who was either stoned or stupid.

I persisted, gently: "No, I mean in the wilderness. Backpacking, you know?"

"Oh. Hmm. Well, I guess you *could* if it was in the *wilderness*."

Then he shrugged and turned away.

I left the store with my bottle, smothering a laugh at the futility of asking anybody for information. Listening to the radio on the drive home, I heard a weather report calling for increased thundershower activity over the next few days. I studied the sky—clouds were massing in every direction. Could a moist monsoonal flow of air soon bring serious rain and lower the fire danger? At home, I stood out in the open and performed the *kwuntuká*, the Tewa ritual gestures for calling rain from the four directions that I'd witnessed at Pueblo ceremonial dances. It couldn't hurt, and it was from the heart.

The day before departure, I was able to confirm online that, indeed, weather conditions had changed. A plume of moisture from a tropical storm down south was making its way into New Mexico. Not only would the Sandias remain open but the forest fire mop-up near Chicoma would be completed in time for me to proceed on to the Jemez Mountains afterward, on schedule. Everything was unfolding in my favor.

Elated, I was almost in a frenzy to finish up last-minute details. In the afternoon I searched inside my wife's old pop-up camper stored out back, on blocks, for a durable plastic camp spoon. When I found it, I jumped outside and charged around to the front, not paying attention to how low the cab overhang was. My forehead struck the corner bracket with such force I was thrown to the ground like a sack of potatoes, where I moaned and kicked, bleeding like a stuck pig. As I began to recover from the dreamy horror of the concussion, my wife found me and knelt down in pity, rubbing me until the pain began to recede into a mere pounding headache. After washing up, the gash at my hairline looked like a tilted "Z," as if Zorro had carved his initial into my skin with a dull penknife instead of the tip of his sword.

I now had a huge bandage on my forehead. I looked ridiculous. The headache throbbed and I couldn't think straight. One careless moment and it all went to hell. How could I go on a long backpack trip with such a head wound? How could I not? Humbled, I went outside and watched a flock of ravens flying cartwheels in the gusting wind. Crows are present in El Norte, too, but are not as noticeable as ravens, which, as the largest and most playful of the *Corvidae*, are more like black eagles with cool and attitude. The glossy black birds began to land and roost in the tops of piñon trees as the sun set. I no longer lived in that same Hispanic village I first settled in, and here with Theresa in the woods east of Santa Fe the ravens sometimes flocked in the hundreds.

The 640 milligrams of aspirin I'd taken was starting to kick in. I felt better. I looked at the sky with new eyes. Thunderheads were firing up, lightning flashed, and faint thunder rolled in the distance. I was captivated in the vast silence. Only the very tops of the clouds were illuminated in the last rays of the sun, a gorgeous churning of white, buff, pink, and gold; a fiery spectacle of dragon breath and atomic power unleashed over the mountains in all four directions. There was no place more beautiful to my eye.

I thought about how my love of beauty was not merely a gratifying experience that heightened my appreciation of the natural world, but was an evolutionary adaptation that promoted the survival of our species. In the surprising and well-researched book *Deep Survival: Who Lives, Who Dies, and Why*, Laurence Gonzales wrote: "Survivors are attuned to the wonder of the world. The appreciation of beauty, the feeling of awe, opens the senses. When you see something beautiful, your pupils actually dilate. This appreciation not only relieves stress and creates strong motivation, but it allows you to take in new information more effectively." In addition, he said, recently discovered evidence shows that foraging in nature for things to use or eat results in higher dopamine levels in our brains. I could only hope that the genetically designed urges of my ancestors, which seemed so strong in me, would see me through, even wounded.

My cell phone rang. It was a new friend, Jimmy McNees, calling to confirm that he'd meet me at the Sandia Crest Overlook for the hike down on the last day of my planned trek over the mountain of the south. He said it was supposed to be dry that particular day, but the weatherman had predicted thunderstorms for each of the previous days I'd be up there—and heavy rain especially on Saturday. In an arid world where a little moisture made all the difference, this was good news.

I laughed in relief, and said, "Bring it!"

PART TWO

Watermelon

[The] most likely explanation is the one believed by the Sandia Indians: the Spaniards, when they encountered the pueblo in 1540, called it Sandia because they thought the squash growing there were watermelons, and the name Sandia soon was transferred to the mountains [east] of the pueblo.

—Robert Julyan, *The Place Names of New Mexico*

One

SANDIA MOUNTAIN STANDS alone on the southern horizon, a dark hulk, a singular immensity far above the tawny hills and layercake mesas.

At least that's what we see from the north, from Santa Fe and Los Alamos. The view is awesome. You look downward toward the lowland deserts, the hot south, the creosote bush vastness. And standing in the way is a rounded monolith of exceptional size and beauty that rises a mile into the empty blue sky above the Rio Grande Valley floor. Shaped like an ocean wave rolling westward, surf solidified at the moment of cresting, it's actually the northernmost end of a tilted fault-block range of mountains viewed almost in cross section.

The Tewa have been looking at it from this angle for a thousand years. What they think it resembles is embodied in their traditional name for it, Oku Pin, or Turtle Mountain. It does in fact look like the rounded hump of a turtle's back, and the ridge of lower Rincon Peak like the head extended from underneath the shell, facing west. This is their sacred mountain of the south, which is associated with the color red. From that direction come the ritually important scarlet feathers of the tropical parrot-like bird, the macaw, which they once obtained in trade from Mesoamerica.

Down through the centuries, the mountain must have appeared much the same as it does now. Approaching closer, it seems incredibly steep, a rugged rocky fortress with no easy access to the forested summit. Right at the very foot, at the old farming town of Bernalillo, the vertical west side looms up in a stupendous wall of pink and gray granite almost to the top, where white layers of limestone and sandstone cap the rim. The rounded backside slopes more gently to the east, but not by much, and is covered by thick forest. Narrow gorges and deep wooded canyons cut into the bedrock like steep chutes.

This is perhaps the view that the conquistador Francisco Coronado had when he wintered on the Rio Grande in 1541. His army's famous and fruitless search for the fabled golden cities of Cibola, which led him from the west coast of Mexico to modern-day Kansas and back, paused here for several months. Nearby pueblo ruins at Coronado State Monument could have been the lodgings his freebooters commandeered. Some 350 Spanish and 1,000 Indian soldiers, some of them veterans of the conquest of the Aztec empire only twenty years before, slaughtered the inhabitants of one local pueblo and forced the remaining communities to feed them until spring came. I'm sure the survivors, some of whose descendants are today the people of Sandia and Isleta Pueblos, were happy to see the invaders depart that summer as quickly as they had appeared.

Today, almost five hundred years later, the mountain I am about to climb is known to the outside world—if it is known at all—as the stunning backdrop to the city of Albuquerque. Nearly half a million people now live hemmed in between the still-pastoral Native lands of Sandia and Isleta, and most, I would wager, rarely give the frowning ramparts of granite a second thought.

But on a bright, clear, calm Friday morning before the Fourth of July weekend, the mountain before me is all I can think about. The drive down Interstate 25 toward Sandia Mountain takes only forty-five high-speed minutes. I'm driving my wife's new silver Toyota Yaris, nicknamed La Bala de Plata. It's much more a silver bullet than a can of Coors beer. Theresa, beside me, is in a sleepy hurry to drop me off and get back to work at her office in Santa Fe.

At sunrise, when I'd heaved my backpack in the rear hatch to set off, coyotes howled in the woods uphill from the house. A good-bye serenade. On the highway, I see a roadkill coyote that has been there for days. I point it out. It looks like a fur pelt glued to the pavement.

"It's a coyote," I say.

"Yuck," my wife says, looking away.

"It looks flatter today."

"Oh, wonderful."

"I guess he's becoming more one with the highway."

She is not amused. I'm heading off into the unknown, which startles the senses and surprises the mind out of its deep rut of habit. Everything is weird, lovely, fantastic to me. She is thinking about work.

We stop for the restrooms and more coffee at the San Felipe Pueblo Casino travel center. The hum of idling semis and glittering lights inside the Las Vegas–style interior are a shock to us early-morning visitors from the countryside. A chubby Indian man wearing a dramatic turquoise-bead necklace and pink running shoes offers me five dollars to give him a ride to Santa Fe. I tell him we're going the other direction, and besides, there's no room with my giant backpack filling up the rear of the tiny Yaris.

Thus we arrive at the foot of the mountain already in hot sunshine. Temperatures are expected in the nineties in the city today. The dirt road up to Tunnel Springs trailhead, which is rough and steep to begin with, has been washed out by last night's rain. Smelling the perfume of wet desert brush, we inch up the rutted grade, avoiding newly carved three-foot-deep chasms of mud. The forest service does its best to keep this road passable, but as usual, nature bats last. When we finally reach the old mine-shaft level at over 6,000 feet, we wave to a young couple in shorts, who are heading down with a pair of Great Danes to the residential area we passed through. At nine thirty in the morning, nobody else is up here.

The car splashes across a stream of clear water pouring from the mouth of the tunnel. In the deep shade of cottonwood trees, blue dragonflies hover and dart like tiny predator drones. A yellow flycatcher on a limb sees a bug fly by, takes off, and chases it through sun-dappled leaves. Just beyond, at the trailhead parking area, the arid mountain sunshine is blinding. We get out and look around. We're far enough up the mountainside to look down on the strip mines and scars of old smelters, or *hornos*. The well-watered slope below the abandoned mine, once a fish hatchery, gives off a marshy smell. Crickets sing in the rain-damp earth.

I'm so ready for this.

After a visit to the outhouse (which is painted a garish yellow inside, and among the graffiti I see Jason Sanchez has signed his name to a marking-pen depiction of a human skull staring at me at eye level), I stand my pack up against a signpost. I expect to spend four days traversing the mountain—up the back side, over the crest, and down the steep western side, a walking distance (including side trips) of just under twenty miles. I plan to reach the summit on the third morning, July 4, Independence Day. But who knows what will happen with monsoon storms coming? After a few words and a touching hug with Theresa, certainly the best of women, I shoulder my massive pack and shove off.

Immediately, I'm in another world. The trail hugs a boulder-strewn hillside as it descends into and crosses the sandy wash of Cañon del Horno. Last night's rain has left mud. Winding through tall stands of brush and prickly pear cactus, I find the gravel soil dotted with orange paintbrush blossoms. The trees are scrubby, resinous, tangled—either piñon pine or cedar-smelling juniper. A sign announces I've entered the Sandia Mountain Wilderness.

Going off into the wilds, if nothing else, always brings me back to my senses. The sights, the scents, the sounds of things become paramount, which is a nice distraction from how ungodly heavy the pack bears down on me. Fortunately the trail rises only gently as it heads due east along the base of the mountain, giving me time to get used to it. Along the way, the view to the northwest is hazy and gorgeous, the wide Rio Grande Valley with low cinder mesas beyond, the lone volcanic stump called the Cabezon on the far horizon, the dark uplift of the Jemez Mountains with the highest peaks shrouded in morning clouds. My anxieties have vanished and I feel instead a consuming joy. I have everything I need on my back to survive for days in Spartan comfort, and a whole mountain to explore. I'm the luckiest man in the whole world!

I listen to the vibrant cawing of ravens overhead. Around me I notice sticklike Mormon tea bushes, green snakeweed, lacy Apache plume brush. Rough eroded limestone boulders lie everywhere. A soft damp breeze blows from the east. I wonder idly if I have enough to drink in this heat to make it to Oshá Spring, my destination for today, another seven miles up the trail. I'm carrying two gurgling quarts, five pounds of water, and I can feel the extra weight of it.

The first mile is mostly level in order to skirt the base of a steep cliff where it meets the rolling foothills. In the morning glare above the tallest part of the cliff, I spot a redtail hawk circling in an updraft, its shrill whistle a sudden delight. The great hawk soaring in lazy circles disappears, but then reappears over a rugged side canyon, giving repeated piercing whistles. Each cry touches some unknown primordial part of me; I feel challenged by the great bird to wake up and be out here as true to the natural world as a hawk. Then silence. The side canyon is impenetrable brush and clumps of whiplike bear grass ascending steep banded walls of rock. From up there somewhere another voice speaks: a sweet descending series of whole notes, a canyon wren's nesting call.

The trail begins to climb as it passes around a headland overlooking the oasis-green trees of the village of Placitas far below. The name means "several small plazas" or settlements, and the historic Spanish farming communities that grew up there on the ruins of Indian pueblos were themselves recently inundated by Anglos. Placitas has become little more than a quaint bedroom community for commuters to Albuquerque, but it hasn't always been so tame. From my lookout, I can see a long knife-edge ridge called Cuchilla Lupe that marks the mouth of Las Huertas Canyon. On the other side of it, above the former gardens and fruit orchards that gave the canyon its name, is Del Oso Spring. Like the other references to bears in place-names in the Sandias—Bear Canyon, Oso Pass, Oso Spring—this was a locality frequented by the particularly fearsome grizzly bears that once were thick in these mountains.

It's the same all over the west. The black bear we're all familiar with is but a timid cousin in comparison with the holy terror that once routinely attacked and killed unwary humans. Naming a place "bear" or "oso" rarely had anything to do with black bears. It was a warning, a reminder of the presence of *Ursus horribilis*, a creature imprinted so indelibly on the consciousness of all early western Americans as a threat to life and limb that they were eventually exterminated by government hunters over most of their range. The last surviving grizzly bear in New Mexico was hunted down with dogs and killed in the 1930s.

The trail turns south and heads up a deep and steeply staircased canyon, where the real work begins. There are many striped lizards on the pathway. They seem to be eating the flies and gnats that begin to pester me. It's a steady uphill climb at last, making me sweat heavily. Once in a while a solitary cloud passes over, giving blessed shade. At the top of the grade, the trail levels off some, but I'm in an open basin of wide-spaced shrubby trees under a blazing sun. No wind blows and it's stifling hot. I keep going. So much sweat is pouring off my face that a drip rolling down my nose hits a fly trying to land and knocks it spinning to the ground. It rights itself and flies up again, joining its brethren in a cloud around my head, who probe mercilessly into eyes, ears, nostrils, and mouth. It occurs to me that I forgot to bring bug repellant. Swell.

Then the going gets steeper again, a steady uphill grind through a stately woodland of much larger trees. Views open up to the east and southeast, toward the Crest of Montezuma and the long gash of Las Huertas Canyon leading up to Palomas Peak. If I didn't need to get someplace by dark, I'd be all over this high desert landscape, this home to roadrunners, tarantulas, coyotes, rattlesnakes, and foxes (all of whom are probably snoozing in deep shade as the pilgrim plods by in sweaty progress). There are traces of old 4x4 roads and plenty of dead trees that were killed during the severe drought a few years ago. The detours I take to go around fallen trees are exhausting. I'm groaning under the weight of my pack. But I'm still elated to be doing this, a solitary traveler going up a mountain. This is who I am, I tell myself. After the tens of thousands of years that humans have carried heavy burdens as they walked over the land, this is what my body's made for. If I can still do this, I'm a man.

Switchbacks on the trail lead back to the west, zigzagging up and up to a red sandstone height where I look out to the north and see the steep dark summits of the Ortiz Mountains, and beyond to the Sangre de Cristos, the whole length of the sierra socked in by clouds. I find some shade and unbuckle my pack, lean it against a tree trunk. Have my first drink, my first snack. The silence is total. No sign of anybody else on the trail. I saw mountain bike tire tracks in dried mud, though—maybe from yesterday? In the heat and stillness, all thought fizzles out. I doze off.

Two

STILL IN THE shade, refreshed, I gaze off across the wide bright mountain world. To the east, miles away, I can barely make out a trail winding along just under the east rim of Las Huertas Canyon. I recognize the enclosed steel stairway of the tourist route to Sandia Cave. It was inside that deep limestone cavern in 1936 that archaeologists uncovered the remains of the oldest human encampment in North America. Chipped stone points and the bones of mammoth, mastodon, giant sloth, camel, and giant bison found there have been dated at around 10,500 years. Things then didn't look like they do now in these mountains. It was a lot wetter way back in the Ice Age, when the ancestors of Native Americans hunted the now-extinct megafauna and camped in that lofty shelter above Las Huertas Creek.

Back on the trail, giving it all I've got to keep going uphill under so much unaccustomed weight, I try to stay focused on the immediate moment. The long loop I've been following emerges from thick woods, curves around a boulder, and with no warning, the earth falls away into a startling void of empty air. I've been brought right back to the rim of Cañon del Horno, where I look almost straight down a thousand feet at the trailhead where I started. This North Crest Trail, as they call it, is not for the timid—for twenty feet there really is no trail, just a boot-wide curb along a tilted palisade of battleship-gray limestone. Balancing a top-heavy backpack, eyes glued to each step, I'm glad there's no wind.

Once across, protected by a wider ledge, I pause and look down again. The physical fear of danger sharpens my senses. I pick out one tiny car in the postage stamp–sized parking lot. The canyon is a stupendous vertical-walled gorge composed of layered sedimentary rock tilting to the north, downward, at a vertigo-inducing thirty degrees. The bottom is a steep gulch choked with fallen boulders and thick, dark vegetation. I go on, entranced by the breathtaking view. The trail skirts under the limestone palisade and heads deep into the upper reaches of the canyon in a roller coaster rise and fall, climbing over rockslide barriers and dropping down into isolated groves of trees. Like a drunken sailor swaying along a heaving deck, I walk a thin ledge at the top of each new layer of cliffs.

Though I'm still climbing, I'm deep under both canyon headwalls, where the air is still and moist. The gnats become far worse than the flies. Unseen birds trill from the shade of resinous piñon trees unmoving in the windless heat. And yet even here I can detect a faint grinding machinery noise coming from the far-off lowlands—the gnashing of civilization lapping around the edges of all wild places like this.

One after another, I come upon large trailside plants called yuccas, each a clump of rigid green spikes pointing out in every direction with needle-sharp tips waiting to impale the legs of hikers. I've been stabbed so many times in my life I give each one a wide berth as I pass. The popular name, Spanish bayonet, is apt. They come in many lengths and thicknesses, and these ones, with blades about two feet long and thick as my hand at the base, have each sprouted a vertical stalk as tall as my chest massed with green oblong fruits. If I had come this way some weeks earlier, I would have found them in bloom with large, lily-like, cream-colored flowers, which hang closed in daylight and open only at night when their pollinator, a moth, is abroad. The first Spanish explorers saw these succulent fruits as being like dates and called the plant datil. The common English name for this species, banana yucca, suggests what else they look like. Today, each of the small green bananas (which, from personal experience, taste bland and mealy even when fully ripe) is speckled with black dots. Upon closer inspection, the dots turn out to be black ants, dozens of them on each fruit. And they aren't moving. I can't imagine what they're doing. Waiting for the fruits to ripen?

Along the margins of each blade are curling fibers that Indians used to strip out for making things like baskets, rope, and sandals. I've found managing to just touch a yucca without drawing blood is not easy. I once helped a Navajo man dig one out of rocky ground with a steel bar and a shovel. He wanted the thick fibrous taproot that his wife used to make traditional soap and shampoo. We both bled from multiple puncture wounds by the time we were finished. Another time, when the earth was moist in the spring, I pulled a yucca plant from the ground by hand—a smaller, more narrow-leafed species with a three-foot-long creeping rootstock covered in reddish-brown bark. The raw roots smelled like herbal soap. Boiling thin pieces of root produced suds that I worked into my scalp and then rinsed out, resulting in darker, shinier, more manageable hair.

More deadfall trees block the trail. Clambering over tree trunks with a backpack is slow going. One right across the dry wash at the head of the canyon is a maze of stout, dry limbs tangled in bushes, but I figure if the mountain bikers can get their bikes through, I can muscle my load through. Marching steeply up out of the canyon, I finally reach Agua Sarca Overlook, elevation 7,600 feet, at noon. Here I look down yet more limestone cliffs into yet another deep canyon. I'm too hot and sweaty to care. All I notice is a pair of golden swallowtail butterflies skimming along above the scrubby trees at the edge. I tank up on warm water from a plastic jug and go on.

I begin to realize it takes ferocious physical stamina to keep climbing under such a load. My shoulders and back and hips are not used to the strain. I shift the shoulder straps to different positions, tighten or loosen the hip belt as needed to spread the burden around to different muscle groups. I'm determined to get used to this, get better at it. The work of it gradually becomes less conscious, especially when I take pains to be aware of what's around me—the newness of a part of the world I've never seen before.

Scarlet penstemons and white daisies line the path ever upward into thicker piñon-juniper woodland. Clearings are crammed with a bristling sticklike cactus called cane cholla, or as my Hispanic neighbors name them, *velas de coyote*, "coyote candles." An aged juniper tree, mostly dead, leans over the trail with limbs oozing bright orange witches' butter, a gelatinous life-form also called fire fungus. Skunkbrush sumac grows in the shadows beside spiny stalks of wolfberry. Sudden thunder booming away to the north makes me look up. A thunderhead is building over the lowlands, clouds churning high into the sky. When I look again later, a dark shadow of rain has been unleashed that blots out the distant Ortiz range, maybe twenty miles away. Where I am, nothing has changed; the hot sun bears down and sweat drips from my nose.

More switchbacks. I stop to catch my breath at rare shady spots. Take a little salt, drink more water. More distant thunder. In an opening I see the storm has moved on, trailing a curtain of rain northward beyond the misty outline of the Ortiz peaks.

In a sweaty lather I arrive at an overlook where a cool breeze blows at last. I'm at the upper Agua Sarca viewpoint, just over eight thousand feet. I find a place to sit at the brink of a thousand-foot cliff overlooking the Rio Grande Valley. The mountain above is much closer, incredibly steep and rugged, and thickly covered in a sea of green chaparral. The sky is an unreal blue. Below, the mountain falls away to the west with disorienting steepness. The town of Bernalillo lies spread out on the valley floor, far away, a bosque of cottonwoods lining the great river as it passes by on its way from the snowfields of the Colorado Rockies to the Gulf of Mexico. Looking north, I can see both Chicoma and Truchas peaks, two of my future destinations, but not Canjilon beyond. Too hazy and cloudy in that direction. All around on the horizon I see little cloudburst storms. Floating by at eye level, a small, perfectly round puff of cloud drifts northward, and below, the dark shadow of it moves across the flat yellow plain.

Absorbing so much of the wide world from such a height is astonishing, staggering, delightful. But a little unnerving. Closer at hand, a hummingbird comes to my sweaty red bandana lying on a rock. Blue and brown scrub jays fly out over the void. The bugs leave me alone for a while.

I shoulder the pack and go on for a half mile through dense woodland growing so close together I can't see far into it. But yellow wild flowers show up everywhere—gromwell, mountain parsley, creeping barberry. And on dull grayish cacti, a species of nearly spineless prickly pear, I discover giant saffron blossoms as beautiful as any garden rose. Before long the piñon trees disappear and it becomes true chaparral, impenetrable thickets of oak brush hacked back from a rocky right of way. I see my first high-mountain conifer, a thick-barked Douglas fir with a fringe of tender new pale-green needles at the end of each bough.

The transition from woodland to brushland is abrupt. All over the Southwest, plants grow in characteristic and recognizable associations that depend on the moisture of certain elevations to maintain themselves. In the simplest terms, this means the lowest elevations are open and dry and desert-like, and the highest are dense wet forests. In between are transitional vegetation zones, each one a little wetter than the one below. And nowhere are these successive bands stacked up more tightly together than on Sandia Mountain. From the desert grassland of the foothills, I had tramped up through increasingly taller and thicker woodland until I was now entering the mountain chaparral zone, a deciduous shrubland that would eventually, at higher elevation, give way to bands of increasingly wet coniferous forest.

Most people call the shrub zone just plain "oak brush" because the dominant species is Gambel oak, a typical wavy-leafed, acorn-producing oak. In deep-soiled canyon bottoms these oaks can grow into tall trees, but everywhere else—and especially on thin-soiled high mountain slopes like this—they form brushy thickets. Along with mountain mahogany and cliff fendlerbush, they provide the main browse food for deer in winter. The latter shrub, *Fendlera rupicola*, is more slender and delicate than either the stout oak or the brash mahogany, and at this higher elevation is in full bloom. The intricately spaced limbs with thin leathery leaves each hold up a large showy white flower of four petals in a sort of Celtic cross. Massed with dozens of blossoms on each bush, the sweet smell like a brushland jasmine perfumes the air.

Sitting down beside one, I eat a midafternoon lunch. The distant storm has disappeared and jet airliners glide low overhead on the approach to the Albuquerque International Sunport without a sound. I've seen nobody else up here yet. Half the water is gone. I see a horny toad eating ants. Invisible until it moved, the squat little reptile ("horned lizard" to taxonomical purists) is like a chameleon; it alters its skin coloration to match what dominates on the ground. This one is gray with black dots, which mimics the limestone, very different from how tan or reddish they look in the mountains near Santa Fe, where warm-colored granite prevails. After a rest, I push on yet again.

At a level saddle between two hilltops, I encounter the thickest and tallest oak brush of all. It closes in over my head until I'm shouldering my way along a winding green tunnel. On and on it goes, at once enthralling and claustrophobic. I've never seen anything like it before. In occasional openings, I stick my head out and glimpse the pointed tops of individual white fir trees standing up out of chaparral. In the shadowy passageway of green leafy branches, I come suddenly to a wooden post with a sign board. Unbelievably, this seems to be my turnoff, the Peñasco Blanco Trail, an even narrower and more overgrown tunnel to the left and my route to the only water on this side of the mountain. I can't even turn around with my pack on, nor can I see more than ten feet up either tunnel. Leaning my backpack against the signpost, I reconnoiter a short way ahead along each route.

Eventually I sit down on the trail and just listen in awe. I can hear wind blowing and birds twittering, but under the ceiling of shrubbery everything is perfectly still and motionless. Gradually what is close and immediate draws my attention. Indistinguishable brush begins to sort itself into individual leaf and twig and rock and flower. There is a miniature richness here that I had not suspected. Once adjusted to my new surroundings, I feel more confident. I lift my pack and move off with cautious care, slowly, following the new trail as it drops downhill. So few people travel this way, the brush closes in from both sides. I have to force my way through, scanning the ground ahead, utterly absorbed in not straying from the faint pathway.

Peñasco Blanco ("white rock bluff") is the local Spanish name for what Anglos call the China Wall, a hard, bare limestone seam that stands up out of the chaparral and winds along the side of the mountain somewhat like schoolbook pictures of the Great Wall. I'd seen it once, years ago, from a distance, but descending its namesake trail, I see nothing of it. Shooting down a sort of chimney-flue ravine underneath impenetrable chaparral, I rapidly drop over a hundred feet in elevation before turning sharply to the right, uphill again. Along the way, modest shaded openings appear under lone spreading fir trees where dark limestone boulders show in grassy glades. At one young tree, I pop a resin blister with my fingernail and lick the medicinal sap.

"Mmm, that's good," I blurt out loud. The sound of my own voice in the vast stillness is startling.

Hiking uphill again, the brush begins to open up. Innumerable side trails fork off, game tracks and rocky drainages that look no different than the old route I'm trying to follow. There are no footprints, no mountain bike tracks, not one sign of anybody going this way in a long time. It takes constant vigilance to scan every diverging opening and choose the correct one. Fortunately I'm pretty good at "reading sign," as they call it, and seldom lose my way. Having good pattern recognition helps, but the trick is really about paying attention. People who get lost are thinking about other things, not about what's right there in front of them. As Gonzales put it in *Deep Survival*, getting lost is a state of mind in which the mental map no longer matches the environment. What follows—called "woods shock" by search-and-rescue professionals—is an emotional survival response (panic, hurry, racing thoughts) that only makes the situation worse.

A rolling countryside of sun-drenched brushland opens up with plenty to see. Odd little "hop trees," none taller than a bush, have new yellowish fruit that look like the hops used to make beer. Mountain mahogany shrubs have formed seeds with curly wooly tails pointing straight up. Tiny white moths flutter among the leaves everywhere. A rare tall-stemmed mariposa lily has a single large, delicate white flower cup open to the sky. Among outcrops of ruddy marine sandstone are basins of rich black dirt sprouted with flowerbeds of blue flag iris, creamy white yarrow, and faded purple harebell.

Then the grade gets steeper. The last mile to Oshá Spring is serious uphill work at a time when I'm really beginning to drag. Clouds build overhead and the wind begins to blow. After an awful ascent up an open rocky stretch, I pass through a grove of ponderosa pine, the first sign of the mountain forest to come. The slabby cinnamon-colored trunks give off a scent of vanilla in the hot sun.

At the top of a crumbling yellow ridge, looking back the way I came, I finally see the China Wall undulating like ancient pale masonry through the rolling green chaparral. Here the trail is plain and clear, no way to stray from it. I hardly notice the gradual transition from brush to trees. Then I find myself in a forest silence so immense it swallows even the sound of wind tossing the tree tops. I begin to hear the wonderful, sad, flutelike calls of hermit thrushes. Ponderosa pines and white firs crowd so close that the understory trees—the spindly oaks and locusts—disappear, and thick duff underfoot muffles every step along a narrowing trail in an ever-deepening gloom of wilderness conifers.

I decide it can't be much farther to the spring. Alongside the trail I begin to see places where the duff has been freshly dug up. Some excavations are quite extensive and show large claw marks in the exposed black soil. The sudden ominous sign of a foraging black bear startles me from my daze of exhaustion. Reminded that I'm approaching the only spring around here for miles, I scan my surroundings more carefully. These are the wet green woods bears love, and with no sign of other people, I might easily stumble upon one unawares. After one last steep climb through dark massive trunks of Douglas fir, I emerge into the open daylight of a sloping meadow. I've hiked seven miles and climbed three thousand vertical feet to an elevation of just under nine thousand feet. This is where I expect to find Oshá Spring, so I'm relieved and drop my pack and gulp down the last few swallows of stale water in my bottles. Then I set off, instantly light and free, to search for the spring. It's not easy—the trail disappears among thickets and low groves of young trees, and the meadow stretches on and on with dry flats piled with boulder hillocks. Nowhere is there any surface water.

And everywhere I look I see startling eight-foot-tall *sebadillas*, or monument plants (*Frasera speciosa*). I stare at one in awe. Imagine a cluster of deer ear–sized leaves on the ground from which a single stalk shoots up over your head, whorled the whole length with drooping leaves and loaded with hundreds of greenish-white flowers—and so covered in bugs and ants and bees and moths, you can't touch it. The thing is too alien, too otherworldly to call a wild flower. Truly an old man of the mountains, it smells rank and fetid. The Indians smoke the dried leaves to gain strength and clear the mind after exhausting, mind-numbing journeys at high elevation. Something to remember if it comes to that, I tell myself.

An obvious footpath soon cuts left into a giant shadowy thicket of New Mexico locust trees, thorny and garish with clusters of lavender blossoms hanging from every limb. The way is overgrown with gooseberry canes and wild rose bushes sporting fragile pink flowers. Here I find the silent trickling pool of the spring, but not before my arms and hands are pricked by thorns from all three, as if exacting a toll to gain access to the precious place to drink.

Assured of water, I look for a spot to pitch camp. I'm delighted there's nobody else around—it's just me alone in the kingdom of the wild. In order not to crowd any bears making nocturnal visits to the only source of water in the area, I find a flat place about two hundred yards away, hidden in trees, and off the game trails radiating from the spring.

Before the afternoon light fades to evening, I go back and draw water. The spring wells up into a pond about the size of a Ping-Pong table and one foot deep, and a trickle flows a few yards before sinking away into the ground. The water is clear but the bottom is mucky. All I really want to do is strip off my clothes and lie in it, but just getting to the edge of it, my boots sink deep into black mud. Bathing would destroy it as a source of drinking water. When I was younger I'd drink straight from cool, clear mountain springs like this, but no more. Not after bouts of catastrophic dysentery. Now I use a hand-operated pump and filter contraption. Drawing water in through one plastic tube and out through another to fill my two bottles is an art I haven't quite mastered without hilarious incident, but this time all goes well. Forest birds bathe and drink on the opposite shore as I watch. I presume mountain lions come here to drink. The shy and stealthy cougar, puma, catamount—call it what you will. These lonely parts of the mountain are crawling with feline carnivores. I stay on full alert, listening intently.

Back at my campsite (which, as it turns out, is not easy to locate again), I set up my tent and stow things inside. Then I fire up the gas stove and boil water to make myself chicken teriyaki with rice, which I eat right from the steaming bag with a spoon. It's not gourmet, but it's not bad. After cleaning up at a distance from the tent, I stow everything a bear would drool over into a stuff sack, tie a small rock to the end of a clothesline rope I brought, and throw it over a high limb of a pine tree. Once I get it hoisted high and tied off to another tree, I'm free to lie around like an old dog, pleased and satisfied with how well things have gone, and marveling at my great good fortune to be out here in this wilderness solitude. At least until clouds of mosquitoes start taking me prisoner.

Inside the tent with the bug netting zipped closed, I lie writing in my journal until dark. Very faint distant thunder can be heard. A squirrel chatters in a high tree one last time. Darkness comes and the wind blows. My first day on the trail comes to a close with a tiny lamp turned on. I climb into my sleeping bag, utterly alone in the middle of nowhere. Tomorrow I will continue my journey up the great mountain of the south.

After lights out, I listen. There is a vast world of wind outside the flimsy wall of the tiny tent. When I focus on the wind alone, I hear it coming and going through the forest trees in great waves of sound that build and pass over and fade away. It mostly blows from the higher mountain above to the lower slopes below, but sometimes comes from other points of the compass. Sometimes it turns and sweeps over the tent in shuddering blasts. Sometimes it roars down distant forest slopes while it remains still around me. Always it seems like a living thing with its own volition, seeking in restless primordial motion for someplace else.

When it finally ceases, there is utter stillness. Then it begins to rain lightly, a steady, hour-long pitter-patter on the tent fly that puts me to sleep.

Three

THE MORNING IS cold and damp. There's just enough light in the tent to be sure night is fading. I open up and look out. A place feels different at first light, at dawn—the rawness of creation, the shapes of things emerging out of darkness. What I see is a clearing in a forest somewhere. A few stars still showing through a thin ceiling of overcast. Some *god-awful* wilderness wasteland to make me smile. Harmer Heaven.

After the deepest of sleeps, I'm reluctant to stir from my warm bedding. But then I catch the scent of coffee grounds in a bag by my head. In a flash I'm out, the nearly naked wild man of the mountains in a frantic tiptoe over damp pine needles far enough away to relieve myself, then stumble back in shivering. Once back inside my down bag, with water heating on the stove just outside the flap, I'm a happy slug, gazing off at the gradual brightening of the world into day.

By the time I sip my scalding-hot black medicine, the eastern sky is bright red. By the end of my second cup, the sun is glaring through the tent wall. One by one, hermit thrushes begin to sing their sweet sad call of the wild until there's so many, their flutelike whistling songs overlap in a heart-rending chorale. Robins join in cheerfully. A squirrel chatters in unseemly excitement. (Squirrels are clearly daytime people, I muse; none of that slinking about under the cover of darkness like predators.) A warm, humid breeze springs up. I am deep in the wild here, deeper into the lonely hidden reaches of this tiny remaining Congress-declared wilderness area than I will be at any time on my Sandia trek—and yet the city limits of Albuquerque are only five air miles away.

A perfect morning, it turns out. With only about four miles facing me before I get to Sandia Crest and make my next camp, there's no hurry. My forehead bandage comes off and I see my wound is healing nicely. I do a few things, slowly, like drape the wet rain fly over bushes, reel down the untouched food bag, and make a breakfast of granola and dried cranberries stirred in hot water. But mainly I sit on the ground and stare thoughtlessly at a beautiful mountain world in radiant sunlight alive with birdsong. Somebody has to do it.

In my idleness I recall the dream I had during the night. The images are still fresh but the situation seems odd. I was sent up into some wild mountains to look for a lost boy. Others had searched for him, but he'd gone feral and avoided them. I was expected to succeed because the other searchers just went through the motions and didn't really try to reach the boy, who was now afraid of people. I stalked close to him in thick chaparral where I could talk to him but not see him. I proved to him that I was a creature of the wild like he was but also a part of the larger world with everybody else. I convinced him to trust me and come back with me by talking to him—telling him that his ability to survive meant he was as much a beloved creation of the great forces as those mountains that hid and protected him.

In the light of day, with the sun growing fierce on my face, the argument I used with the boy seems ineffable and unlikely, nothing compared to the certainty I felt about it in the dream. Mulling it over, I begin to see the dream is really about me. The mature social adult me convincing the childish holdout rebel me (who was raised by wolves and prefers the solitude of nature) to come along and do life together. The two disparate sides of me—what the Jungians would call my ego and my shadow—working together now, to accomplish this mountain journey. Who says dreams aren't real? Not me.

Breaking camp drags on. I savor the lack of pressure. Taking my time, I reorganize how things fit together in the backpack, and load up more efficiently. Everything I need to live eventually swings up on my back, and I'm free to walk off to somewhere else in the world. It's a great feeling.

I really love this spring. Hidden away in a deep thicket, the wet soil around the pool is the only place at this elevation you can find certain edible and medicinal herbs, such as wood violet, Solomon's seal, and *oshá*. It's the iconic secret waterhole of ancient Indian travel, the elusive *ojo* of Spanish American cowboys. Thankfully they don't pasture cattle or sheep up here anymore, or it wouldn't look as pristine as it does. I've seen springs like this, trampled by the hooves of livestock, that were little more than barren wastelands of oozing muck.

Only a few small, unobtrusive oshá plants are to be found here, nothing like the gardens of tall robust monsters growing from perennial rootstocks under wet spruce forest higher up in the mountains of El Norte. A local species of lovage, or *Ligusticum*, which Indians all over the West call "bear root," this lacy-leafed wild parsley is prized for its sacred medicinal root that is dug up, dried, and used in myriad ways. A proven cold remedy, chewing a little of the odorous root also increases respiratory capacity, valuable in enduring sweatlodge rituals and hiking at high altitude. My Hispanic neighbors swear that carrying a piece of the root keeps rattlesnakes away. I have some in my pack and bite off a bitter chunk to suck on as I pack up my full water bottles.

At about ten in the morning I'm back on the trail climbing steeply upward from the meadow into mountain forest. An owl hoots far back in the timber. Fresh droppings and hoofprints reveal the presence of unseen deer. The thin air above nine thousand feet makes me pant. At a trail junction, I take the northern leg of the Oshá Loop Trail. My choice is based on the fact that it's extremely hot already, with few clouds overhead, and this route follows north-facing slopes, which (I hope) means heavier forest, taller trees, and thus more shade. Plus, the grade is easier. According to the map, a mile and a half of walking will regain the North Crest Trail after only a six-hundred-foot climb in elevation. Piece of cake.

Of course, there's another ascent after that, but one thing at a time.

There's plenty of shade, but the climb is still hard work. The backpack is freshly massive and dreadfully heavy, especially with both water bottles refilled. Since there's nothing to be done about it but get used to it, I chug on. And besides, the world is beautiful up here. Old-growth pine forest gives way to Douglas fir and whispery groves of trembling aspen. I rub my hand on the smooth white bark of a shimmering aspen, and it comes away covered with a creamy powder—the Native skin treatment for prickly rash. Once on the north-facing slope, above another outcropping of the China Wall, I find myself in the dark, cool depths of tall timber as I'd hoped. But the trail unaccountably goes up, down, sideways, every which way—until it dawns on me that it leads from one forest clearing to another as if following an old herdsman's track from one pasture to the next. Each clearing has a berry patch, but none of the gooseberries, currants, or raspberries are ripe. Each grassy opening is also surrounded by huge old-growth fir trees—some of the biggest trees I've ever seen in New Mexico. A few are long-dead snags with black bark peeling off in long, curved slabs. And ringing each glade is a sunny understory of slender Rocky Mountain maple trees draped with pendulous stringers of new winged fruit.

Alongside the trail itself, the trunks of trees are blazed at regular intervals. Reminders of an older era when trails through the woods were marked by boy scouts chopping the bark of trees with hatchets, most have closed with regrown scar tissue, but some are still visible, like upside-down exclamation points. I come upon fresh bear scat, flies busy on it, and poke it apart with a stick to see what's been on the menu. Bits of nylon tent? Human bones? But no, it looks like mainly salad—greens and roots and bugs and grubs. Things you find rooting around in damp soil and decaying logs. Bears really are *of the earth* as I've heard old Indians say.

Big tree trunks have blown down across this trail, too, which require brief but gnarly bushwhacks to get around each obstacle. More like hiking in the Canadian bush than the arid Southwest, the ascent through the north-slope forest is so dank and musty I'm startled by a sudden view out to the world beyond—clouds scudding over brilliant, tan desert flatlands far below. Then a steep series of switchbacks through second-growth forest, smaller trees growing up in dog-hair thickets around fire-blackened stumps, and I pop out into the open, sucking air and pouring with sweat in the hot sunshine. I'm at the edge of a huge swath cleared through the forest, a giant firebreak about fifty yards wide running horizontally across the mountain slope, with a dark wall of unburned old-growth fir forest above it.

The trail crosses it in dazzling high-altitude sunlight. The swath is overgrown with locust brush in pink bloom, the thorns tearing at my clothing, the pea-scented flowers perfuming the air. Bees and swallowtail butterflies seem stoned out of their tiny minds as they weave erratically amid the cornucopia of blossoms. At the upper edge, at a trail junction, I turn around and the view is staggering, magnificent—the entire east side of the Sandia range like a rumpled green carpet sloping away toward the Great Plains. The scene is vast beyond imagining, and all my grinding effort for the past day and a half is suddenly worth just this extraordinary moment. Sweeping my eyes from left to right along the horizon, I can see the Jemez range hidden under dark growing thunderheads; the Sangres aglow in clear, limpid sunshine; Rowe Mesa and the endless flat plains under an iron noonday sky; and to the south, one big rain cloud forming and coming this way over the spine of the Manzano Mountains.

Realizing how close I am to the crest itself, I charge off with a second wind, hoofing it up an overgrown and hard-to-follow trail as the slope starts to level off. In the scrubby open woods of Douglas fir and limber pine, reminiscent of timberline (but not), I see blue sky through wide-spaced trees ahead. I grow excited and breathless in the thin air at just under ten thousand feet, impatient to reach my goal.

Then at another trail junction, I regain the North Crest Trail, which is so heavily traveled by hikers and cyclists it resembles a wide dirt freeway through the woods. I'm reminded that I still haven't seen another person since early yesterday morning. It can't be long before I do. I can hear the wind roaring ahead, but not feel it. The trail winds through open grassy flats and young thickets of fir. I press on into a shadowy grove of aspen trees, pale trunks swaying, millions of soft green leaves hissing in the blow overhead. And then I step out into the open at a bare expanse of flat limestone. Here the world seems to end in a terrifying drop-off—Sandia Crest at last.

The site is marked by the eroded remains of a tree trunk about five feet high upon which someone has attached a dream catcher—a hoop crisscrossed with webbing decorated with colorful seashells and starfish. Other shells dangle from ribbons and plink against each other in the huffing wind like a tangled wind chime. Leaning my pack against the snag, I cautiously approach the edge for a look down. There's no barrier or railing, only a wall of dry wind holding me back. And what a dizzying depth below! Sheer cliffs and granite crags in endless succession shoot downward into Del Agua Canyon. Jumbles of complex geological formations narrow to a spur ridge leading out to a lower rocky peak—I'm looking *down* on the head of the mountain turtle, Rincon Peak. I'm a mile above the flat valley floor beyond, and it feels similar to looking down one side of the Grand Canyon, except greener, the almost vertical walls thickly covered with aspen and oak brush most of the way down.

Near to the left is North Sandia Peak, a ship-like prow of tilted limestone another five hundred feet above me, the slope up to it a solid mass of aspen trees swept by undulating waves of wind. Far out on the western horizon is the dark conical shape of Mount Taylor, an extinct shield volcano eighty miles away that broods over vast lava-capped plateaus extending to the north and south. To the right of that is the Cabezon, floating like a barely visible fireplug in the mist under dark rain clouds.

I hear a strange sound—click, clack, click, clack. Suddenly someone comes striding into view along the Crest trail. A tall gray-haired lady with a daypack and aluminum hiking poles zooms by without a glance in my direction. I have to call out to get her attention. She can hardly be bothered and stares at me with ferocious displeasure. She appears to be in her seventies. Grinning like an idiot at the shocking richness of human interaction, even with a complete stranger, I stammer shyly that I've been alone in the woods for almost a day and a half and she's the first person I've seen since I started up the mountain.

"Almost a day and a half?" she says, incredulous. Then barks dismissively, "You'll get used to it!"

I have no idea what she means. Used to being alone? Used to seeing people again? She waves and turns to go.

"Wait! I mean, excuse me, ma'am." I want more of a conversation than that. Not clear why. It dawns on me that she thinks I'm new to backpacking, to being alone in the wilds. And she, fresh from driving up from the city and hiking in to get away from people, resents my intrusion. I try to seem less insistent and make it about asking for information, saying, "Did you come from the Crest House?"

She'll have none of it. She glares at me. Lifting one pole and jabbing it toward me in exasperation, she says, "Young man, I have no time for chit-chat. You have your whole life before you. You'll be fine!"

"Okay. I guess I will, of course. Thanks," I say. She obviously sees right through me, though her eyes can't be very good or she'd know I'm not young.

"Look here," she goes on unexpectedly. "You're speaking to someone who is all alone in the world. I'm quite familiar with your predicament, your situation, though it seems to me a bit premature. Nonetheless, I have too much on my mind, having just been diagnosed with cancer, and I'm sure I've never been all that good at, how shall I say, suffering fools gladly?"

I nod, speechless. She pauses to think, two fingers pressed to her temple with the quizzical air of a retired professor of literature.

"Let me see, now. Oh yes. Would you like my advice?" Without waiting for my reply, she swings a pole around and jabs at the scenery around us. "Be sweet and smooth and in love with the world and everything in it! Take my word for it. Too soon you weaken and a light goes out forever!"

Without another word, she's gone. The rhythmic click-clack of her poles fades away. That went well, I think wryly. Only later, on the trail again, do I fully grok the veritable nugget of crazy wisdom I received from an unlikely mountain sage.

Four

EXPECTING HORDES OF day-trippers along the main route following Sandia Crest, I'm pleasantly surprised by how few people I meet climbing the last mile to my lunch stop at the top. There's nobody at first, the way up entering by degrees into the highest, wettest forest zone, but never quite leaving behind the twisted scrubby brushlands that face into dessicating desert winds blasting over the summit. Gambel oak, ninebark, wild rose, wild yellow pea, and snowberry give way to stunted, storm-twisted, fat-trunked aspen and subalpine fir.

In every open glade are more tall sebadillas standing off by themselves like disheveled homeless people, and stands of enormous oshá plants with delicate, green feathery foliage topped by sprays of tiny white flowers. And what are these shockingly iridescent orange flowers I've never seen before? Then it dawns on me they are a high-altitude species of western wallflower, which blossoms yellow lower down. Wild flowers pop up everywhere—pale-yellow sky pilots, white violets, purple monkshoods, yellow cinquefoils, magenta penstemons, pinkish paintbrushes, even pale-blue Jacob's ladders.

The trail winds back into tall forest behind North Peak where the shade is blacker and the silence deeper. The first spruce trees I see are all dead—solitary giants that let in sunlight to the forest floor where elderberry and brush maple have sprung up. Higher up, living spruces begin to dominate among the subalpine fir; the forest closes in again. The damp earth sprouts thickets of baneberry, the shade-loving and precious medicinal *yerba del peco*, whose poisonous root is dried and extracted for alleviating women's monthly cramps. The flowers (that later become evil-looking poisonous berries) are now just formed into oval cream-colored puffs above the broad palmate leaves, standing high in the pallid light among ferns and fiddleheads.

Dashing abruptly into my botanical solitude, a young, tan, blond guy in shorts and shades jogs past. Behind him follows a similarly dressed woman. Both of them ignore my waved greeting. Behind them comes a party of less athletic women, each in brightly colored tights, wearing elaborate face makeup, and smelling of perfume. Their scent is so striking, I wonder who they hope to attract. Bears? Some young boys race by, screaming. Clearly I'm approaching a busy urban entry point—the parking lot is a little more than a mile away.

At an overlook just beyond North Peak, I dump my pack and stare in awe at the view. The famous Needle stands like a giant rounded skyscraper straight out from the crest in empty air, blocking the view of most of the city of Albuquerque spread out below. Bare white limestone headlands thrust out of forest over the void with wind-shorn thickets on top. Hermit thrushes sing endlessly. A huge dark thunderstorm blots out the world to the southeast.

I sit and eat lunch, famished. A solid wall of spruce-fir-aspen forest stands behind me, trees sailing in the wind. Hikers stream past. Two men stroll up, each with a bottle of water in hand, and stop at the view, talking loudly. They are dressed in casual street clothes and running shoes. I hear one say to the other, "I can make just about anywhere work for me."

"You mean you think if you got lost you could survive up here?" the other guy asks.

"Yeah, I know I could."

"How do you figure? Because you grew up on a farm?"

"Yeah, you know. Like the song says, 'A country boy will survive.'"

"Oh, come on! That song is such a crock. A fat, beefy, angry country boy without his beer and his pickup—he's going to survive out here? Hopefully not long enough to reproduce!"

They both cackle with laughter and depart.

From there, the trail leads gently uphill along the edge of forest from viewpoint to viewpoint. I am above ten thousand feet at last, and will be staying at this elevation for two nights. At a grand promenade of flat rock protruding out over a vertigo-inducing emptiness, the abyss is nearly straight down four thousand feet to what appears to be a parking lot full of cars. Checking the map, I locate it as the Juan Tabó trailhead, my ultimate destination and my way out of the Sandias. The trail down to *that* must be one hell of a descent! An involuntary tightening of my sphincter muscles makes me back up from the terrifying attraction of the drop-off. Unmarked on the map, I dub my location Itchy Butt Overlook.

Clouds build darkly and thunder rolls from the south along the mountain chain. The storm that has been a blip on my radar for so long begins to gather force overhead. I scramble off to find a campsite, remembering the weather report that predicted heavy rain up here today. Below the trail, back under tall swaying aspen and fir, I search about and find a flat spot. The deep leafy duff is easy to mold into a bedding surface (the air mattress has developed an unfixable leak), so I pitch my tent, string up the rain fly, and stow everything inside. Flashes of lightning and continuously booming thunder sweep overhead. Tightening all the lines as fat drops of rain begin to fall, I barely get myself inside the tent before angry black clouds open up in a deluge of rain. At 3:30 in the afternoon, I burrow into my sleeping bag as snug as a bug in a rug as all hell breaks loose. Heavier and heavier waves of rain pour down amid brilliant lightning and pounding thunder. A battle of the mountain powers rages on, but I fall asleep.

An hour later I wake up to robins singing and the patter of raindrops dripping from wet trees. The storm has passed. It's sticky and humid inside, and the tent has leaked in one corner. After bailing out and mopping up, I crawl forth into a cool wet world of forest, the sun already shining through the tree trunks again. Wind blows in the canopy of aspens above. Two nearby dead ones clunk together rhythmically, like a boat against a dock.

Throwing some things into my daypack, I write a list of things I need from the store and head off to the Sandia Crest House at the parking lot. Without the heavy backpack I'm suddenly light as a feather, head high, bounding along the trail with a spring in my step. Fresh after torrential rain that left puddles I easily leap, the air is cold and mist hangs in the forest. Then at each viewpoint the wind blows hot and dry in the blazing sun. And on that wind come snatches of a faint dull roar—the groaning of the great city below.

In no time the pathway forks around a wooded hilltop covered in electronic towers, and taking the back way, I hear the distant sound of cars zooming up the Sandia Crest Highway. Brand-new cell phone towers gleam through the trees, and steel cables run across overhead, anchored in the woods below the trail. Windowless buildings appear with strange humming sounds coming from within. At a clearing, a power line supplying electricity to run all this gadgetry has been cut through forest straight as an arrow down the east slope of the mountain for miles. And as if all such disturbance to the wet wilderness wasn't enough, the trees come to an abrupt end and I step out onto a huge sloping asphalt parking lot steaming in the hot sunshine. My boots clump on pavement as I make my way through parked cars and throngs of people in a kind of daze. A large party of East Indian people on a holiday outing go past me speaking loudly in their own sibilant language. Others in their group yell from a lookout above the gift shop; those near me shout back and laugh uproariously. I notice by contrast the Americans talking quietly in hushed groups. The cultural difference is striking: transplanting what works on the teeming streets of Calcutta to the silent wide-open spaces of the Southwest.

Inside the gift shop, drifting about aimlessly among the overpriced tourist crap and babble of voices, I'm quickly on sensory overload. Eventually my bush-sharpened senses begin to dull amid the competitive jostling of well-dressed bodies. Some people look askance at the dirty, smelly, unshaven guy with a lime-green Scooby-Doo daypack looking like he wandered in after getting lost in the woods. The young lady at the cash register, in particular, stares curiously at me as I stand for long minutes before a glass case of what appear to be ordinary useful items.

"Can I help you?" she finally asks. "Double-A batteries? Why, yes—we do!" she says, enunciating slowly in a Texas twang as if being especially helpful to the mentally challenged.

She seems barely eighteen and yet displays remarkable concern and patience as she locates and piles up on the counter the various things—batteries, plastic poncho, candy bars, bottled water—that I request with gradually improving verbal skill and growing confidence. Here at last is someone who wants to talk to me; never mind that I'm a paying customer. Once the cash goes into the till, she really lets down her hair.

"So, y'all been camping? I thought so. We don't get that many like you in here anymore. That's why we don't have much. Just all these trinkets and pots and Indian blankets, you know? So listen, did you hear about that woman and her kids who got attacked by a bear just down the road from here? You did? Well, guess what? I actually saw that bear when I drove up to work that very same morning! It ran right across the road in front of me! No, for reals. I kid you not. And it was barely larger than a cub! *Just a baby!*"

She pantomimes the mother screaming about it later to the cops, a vicious snarling bear snapping its teeth at her and her kids, quoting her as saying, "Omigod! The bear was huge!" Then adds ironically, "Yeah, a huge *Chihuahua* maybe!" We both laugh.

"And then they had to go and kill it," I say sadly. Game and Fish officers trapped the bear and took it to an undisclosed location where it was "put down," according to the news report I heard.

"Well, they have to, if it attacks somebody," she says with a shrug.

"But it doesn't seem right, does it? I mean, the lady had food out everywhere, on the picnic table, on the ground, in the tent. Seems pretty stupid to me."

She sighs. "Yeah, it doesn't seem fair. Just a little cuddly baby bear."

"Why do we have to make things safe for the stupid ones, anyway? Every time they try to make the wilds safer it's just bad news for the wildlife."

Her eyebrows lift. She laughs but looks embarrassed.

"No, I mean it," I say. "There should be a line that if you cross it, like that woman did, you're on your own. She just got scratched anyway. Scared to death, maybe, and you can be sure she'll never do that again. Why do they have to trap the bear and kill it?"

"Well, so it won't get a taste for it, and go after you in your tent next?" she says brightly.

Before I head back to camp, I saunter up to the tourist lookout along a paved walkway that comes out on a raised and fenced-in platform with informational signs and benches. A young Hispanic couple occupies one bench, openly making out as if I'm not even there. Lips glued together, they radiate languid teenage sexual infatuation rather than passionate love.

Ignoring them, I'm stunned by the view—without a doubt the most spectacular yet, a full 360-degree look at almost everything in New Mexico. I turn in a slow circle, drinking it all in. Mountains as far as the eye can see to the north, Great Plains to the east, desert mountain ranges to the south, and nothing but mesas beyond Mount Taylor to the west. And from here the sheer west wall descending to Albuquerque is even more ruggedly studded with spires and pinnacles and chutes than I ever imagined. An arid mountain world washed by rain, crisp and clear, illuminating the distant aerial tramway, a mere glistening dot climbing invisible cables.

And here I get cell phone reception at last. A strange feeling comes over me as I listen to messages from people who don't know where I am. Then one from my friend who will descend with me from here to the bottom of the mountain the day after tomorrow, a message of final enthusiastic confirmation. I call and chat up my wife. She, too, confirms our arrangement for her to pick us up at the trailhead. All goes according to plan so far.

The skinny lovers have stood up and join me lingering at the rail, but barely glance at the view. Another Hispanic girl comes up from the gift shop, the first girl's friend. As they gab away animatedly, the boy drifts away. I hear the girlfriend ask the other, "Why don't you like him?"

The new girl shrugs, and says, "*Ese huevo quiere sal.* [That egg needs salt.] Look at him! He's just a big nothing without you!"

On that note I, too, drift away from the unfolding telenovela drama and back into the blessed silence of wet forest. On the hike back, new wild flowers seem to have just bloomed in the aftermath of the rain. I come upon a huge woodpecker hammering on a dead spruce tree. The air smells coastal, fragrant with coniferous purity. I meet nobody along the way. At sunset, giddy at the glow of golden clouds on the horizon, I arrive back at my tent hidden in the lonely timber.

After the candy bar and fruit juice I consumed at the lookout, I'm not hungry, so I hoist my ditty bag up a tree and turn in. Tomorrow, the Fourth of July, I have the whole day to explore the remote highest reaches of this giant tilted mountain and to see if I can find the ancient shrine the Tewa people use when they pray and make offerings to this god of the south. Alone in a tent on the ground in the dark I fall asleep in the cold stillness under billions of glittering stars.

Five

Day comes early, the sun barely up but shining horizontally through the gaps in trees from out over the plains. I'm amazed to discover I've slept for ten hours. I make coffee kneeling on a piece of plastic on wet rotting aspen leaves, beside a lone lacy green oshá plant that seems to have grown six inches taller overnight. The yellow beams of sunlight grow blinding, brilliant, illuminating an outdoor cathedral of mature aspen and fir, tall wooden columns holding up a swishing canopy forty feet above.

Still not hungry and with nothing pressing—camp stays where it is until tomorrow morning—I wander off to explore. Drawn to the open air and light of the crest, I hike out onto the broad half-mile curve of rimrock at Itchy Butt Overlook, which I saw yesterday, but which is even more incredible in the early morning light. At about 10,500 feet, about even with far-off North Peak and a little below the array of steel towers, I walk the magnificent shelf of rock like the deck of a seagoing tanker. The whole wide world to the west is as impressive as the view from the Crest House lookout, but here there are no guardrails, just a running edge of bare, hard sedimentary rock falling away into a black abyss the sun won't reach for hours. The mountain casts a shadow far out beyond the city, still glimmering with streetlights below. I decide this would be a perfect spot to watch the display of Independence Day fireworks when they light up over the city tonight.

The wind casually yanks at a person close to the edge like this, making you prop your legs more firmly, study the surface you stand on, perhaps vaguely note the presence of marine fossils embedded in the sandpapery limestone. There's an eerie attraction to the empty void before you. Being so close to certain death you either love the thrill of it or back away with a sick fear, wishing you'd thought to bring adult diapers. Either way, once back from the imminent danger, you notice again how warm the sun feels on your face, how pine-scented the wind smells tossing the bushes with seashore gusts. Farther back, underneath Douglas firs pruned by winter blizzards into a leaning hedge, you find fire-blackened circles of rocks on flat dirt clearings where people have camped in the endless moan of wind. You stand at a high point and discover not a cloud anywhere in the endless blue vault of sky.

Back at camp, starving, I cook breakfast and eat sitting on a log. Last night's skipped item on the menu, freeze-dried beef stew, reconstituted with boiling water, tastes enough like the real thing to fill me up (everything tastes better with an outdoor appetite). As I spoon it from the steaming packet on my lap, enormous delicate mosquitoes hover in the still-cool air around me. Only a few actually land on my face. They float about in such slow motion it's almost pathetic how easy they are to smack away.

After camp cleanup, I load the daypack with food, water, map, rain gear, flashlight, heavy warm shirt, and notebook, and head off for the day's trek to the summit, North Sandia Peak, which is the highest point on the crest as viewed from El Norte. It feels like I'm not carrying anything on my back. I decide to make a closer inspection of the crest itself along the way. The main trail stays back in the forest between viewpoints, but I forge right up to the brushy rugged ridgeline and make my way slowly along it, observing everything close up in a sort of exalted reverie like a hunter looking for sign.

Cruising along traces of game trails, I look down vertical rocky chutes into labyrinths of ledges and pinnacles, hanging gardens of wild flowers, and bonsai trees growing from cracks. Big, old, twisted, wind-blasted firs and pines grow from dark grottoes below and sprawl with trunk-sized limbs along the rock edge. The way follows fresh deer tracks right through these diminutive treetops hanging with fresh, pitchy evergreen cones—the long and pointed yellowish ones are limber pine and the purple ones with green three-pointed tongues are Douglas fir. After so much rain, the forest smells are pungent. I can detect individual tree scents by species, wild flowers by unique perfumes. Even the yarrow blossoms, which barely smell at all, give off a rank creamy odor in the wet air.

Great hogbacks of mossy rock block the way through a murmuring leafy jungle of low aspen, driving me back down to the trail where I continue on and pass many hikers. The happy hordes are out—it's the Fourth of July—and I take pleasure in the cordial company of other morning people tramping along. The smiles and greetings, the dogs racing up to sniff my crotch, the shouts of kids—"Mom, come here! You gotta *see* this!"—or from one boy zipping up his pants as he emerges from the woods, "Well, there's five pounds I won't have to carry back to the car!"

Back on the curving half-mile rock shelf at Itchy Butt vista point, this time following it all the way around until it intersects the trail again, the wind has become fierce in the sunlit heat of the lowlands. The desert city glitters in broad daylight on an otherwise brown and empty land. Heated arid-brush smells rise up from below with bits of fluff, dried leaves—even tiny birds shoot up on the wind over the brink. And out in front, lit up in sunshine, is the huge dome-like bulk of the Needle, a dark granite mountain in and of itself. One glance and you know only technical climbers ascend its cliff walls. The immense size of it becomes obvious when I see, partway down, a large cave-like alcove, the kind cliff dwellings are found in, and realize it is so huge it dwarfs the tall pine tree growing from the floor of it. I can't see the feature the climbers call the Prow beyond it, but away to the north is the Shield, a three-thousand-foot sheer wall of bare maroon granite, startling to behold, dropping at only a slight angle from vertical all the way from North Sandia Peak to the brush and tumbled boulders of Juan Tabó Canyon. If you went over that edge, you'd fall for a long, long, long time.

A group of three black, glossy ravens appear, sailing out over the void. I watch as they tuck their wings and plummet downward, forever, until they are black dots, and then float back up, cawing raucously, never beating a wing, obviously playing. Hummingbirds pause sometimes for minutes in the uprush of air.

The updraft is so strong and steady, Sandia Crest has for decades attracted hang glider enthusiasts who jump off and soar on days like this (but usually from over by the parking lot). Nowadays you see mainly paragliders, hardy souls floating under a curving canopy like a parachute. I once picked up a hitchhiker, a bearded, baby-faced dude who told me he'd hang glided off this mountain many times and urged me to try it. He said the best ride he ever had was from Sandia Crest, a silent sail all the way east to Santa Rosa, where he landed in a cow pasture, a distance of about a hundred miles. I now contemplated what it would take for me to run off the edge of this cliff with only a light fabric and aluminum framework to hold me aloft in the wind. Clearly a sport for those with nerves of steel. My hitchhiker told me you don't actually need to run, just lean out over the brink and push off. Yeah, right. That makes it much easier.

North Sandia Peak stands out alone from the crest, a wooded headland about a mile and a half away, beckoning. It's the only summit peak not easily accessed by a forest service trail, and the route up, I've been told, though well traveled, is steep, rugged, dangerous, and in places hard to follow. Based on what John Pesendo told me and what I've seen up here with my own eyes, it's the most likely place to look for the Tewa shrine. He didn't use maps or know the English or Spanish names for many features, but it has the right shape. And in any event, it's the last lonely high point on this mountain range, the only one with an unobstructed view north to the other peaks on my pilgrimage, and my destination for today. As I head off toward it, breathing in the crisp air, the day glorious and bright beneath a wide blue sky, I find it hard not to entertain the giddy thought that I am embarked on the finest adventure I've ever attempted.

A mile of leisurely walking brings me to the shoulder of the peak looming up. Here I leave the Crest Trail and follow a narrow track along a treacherous hogback of crumbling rock. At a hot sunny spot out of the wind, I unexpectedly get a whiff of myself. I've forgotten until now how three days on the trail coats your clothing with a rime of dried sweat and dust, and your body starts giving off the scent of some wild animal. I've brought along enough socks and underwear to start fresh every morning, but without a bath or enough water to wash more than hands and face it begins to seem pointless.

Upward I climb, a strenuous ascent using both hands and knees in spots, clambering up a sharp, smooth knife-edge of ridgeline (called a *cuchillo* in New Mexico) where there is just enough width between tilted slabs for a worn pathway. The track disappears across bare rock, and at each higher ledge, I rest, panting. Along the margin of fractured rock that leads up at the edge of the woods, the trees become little more than shrubs, twisted and flattened into mat-like tangles of spruce and fir and aspen. At one grim spot, I look down both steep sides of the mountain at once, a fall to the left or right equally deadly.

My eyes are drawn to what looks like a large black volcanic rock sticking out of the ground beneath a copse of trees, which seems a striking anomaly on a mountain made of sedimentary and granitic rock. But on closer inspection, it turns out to be a massive meteorite embedded in soil so deep, thick tree roots encircle it. I'm seeing only one square foot of a much larger chunk of stellar debris. The rounded surface is a mass of rusty-orange metallic squiggles, clearly solidified molten nickel/iron ore from the sky.

Higher up, the tilted edge is less steep but still climbs. The track at times swings inland behind a screen of fir trees—huge, squat, storm-broken, and long-limbed conifers, like on West Coast beach walks behind rows of shore pines—where calm and shade prevail, shielded from the wild and terrific huffing of wind in the blinding brightness beyond. At a break in the trees, I get a clear view of the faraway Rio Grande, which has turned a muddy color since yesterday, no doubt a result of flash flood runoff after the colossal thunderstorm that went over yesterday. Today it's the Rio Browno. (Or as they say in Spanish, Rio Puerco. This word for "pig," when used as an adjective, means "dirty" or "soiled" in the Southwest, or in the case of a stream of water, "muddy.")

I come upon a stratum of grayish limestone embedded with inch-thick chunks of pink quartz, a weird and amazing sight. Then a grove of limber pines, each tree with new resinous green cones *and* flowers giving off puffs of yellow pollen into the wind. I've never seen both on the same tree like that.

Usually a tree flowers, then later fruits. How can there be both at the same time? Can't quite figure that one out. This mountain is yielding one eye-opening marvel after another.

The last slope to the summit is rolling and park-like—grassy wild-flower meadows and stunted groves of trees. As I kneel panting in the shade, drinking warmish water, marveling at the four-foot-thick trunk of an ancient Doug fir with monstrous limbs going up only fifteen feet to a wind-sheared canopy, I hear a noise. Three hikers go by ahead without seeing me—two men and a woman, college-aged.

I follow them up to where the land tops out on a tilted, mesa-like summit. The very tip-top is at the far end, where the hikers have stopped to eat lunch on the remains of three old concrete footings (ruins of an old tripod fire lookout tower). Hanging back from their noisy excitement, I drift around on outcrops of solid country rock, a sere yellowish limestone crusted with auburn lichens, and gaze off at the world beyond. At first it's too much, too endlessly huge and wide to fathom from such a height. The wind is icy but I'm flooded with warmth from a sun that has never seemed so near, so blinding, in such a strangely dark and ultraviolet sky. On the brink of the north face, the light is more from behind me, perfect for viewing the faraway homeland from which I have always previously looked this way, at this mountaintop.

With the earth spread out below to the northern horizon, certain features draw my attention. Traces of snow on Truchas Peak. The Rio Grande emerging from White Rock Canyon. The three prominent peaks of the Jemez range: Nacimiento, Redondo, and Chicoma. I see the river meandering like chocolate milk among the bosques and the Keres-speaking pueblos at the foot of tongue-like lava mesas. I see the hills where my home is located. Letting my eye wander up the broad valley of El Norte, over the miniaturized and flattened towns, the tawny, crumpled landscape, I pick out Canjilon Mountain above all the hazy northern mesas.

Back at the south face, a vulture soars past at eye level, wings held out, rocking. Then one by one, three more vultures circle slowly up from a thousand feet below. My eye follows the line of the river through green woods and the grid of Albuquerque streets to the farms beyond, until it disappears in the far hazy south. In my oxygen-starved thoughts, sacred peaks and vultures and precious flows of water in an arid land seem somehow connected. Breathing deeper, I circle around the summit and see the other hikers still lingering at the very high point.

Continuing my idle exploration of the summit area, this time studying the ground before me for sign of an old Pueblo shrine, I drift around on bare rock and through scrubby timberline spruce woods. In a matter of minutes and quite by accident, I find it. It has the usual horseshoe or U shape, a wall of rocks about three feet high and six across, but in this case hikers have scavenged some of them for use in nearby campsite fireplaces. The basic outline is still there, the back wall fairly intact, the side walls less so, and the imprints of large slabs recently carried away still showing in the ground. Most of it is conveniently overgrown in thorny bushes. Sighting across the open end, I see it definitely faces north over the eroded remains of a dirt mound, the altar.

Standing there in bright light and wind, exultant with the fever of discovery, the delight of real accomplishment, I am suddenly humbled by the reality that this is an age-old shrine where feathered prayer sticks were placed. That this site is every much a living remnant of ancient America as the stone ruins of villages or the panels of petroglyphs that are scattered over this land. And that nowadays when rain priests come here to pray and make offerings to direct the blessings of Turtle Mountain to the Tewa towns to the north, they go down in the woods and hide them underground where non-Indians like me won't disturb them or take them home as souvenirs.

The three young hikers suddenly appear, moving with casual athleticism in shorts and Tevas, following another of the many trails crisscrossing the area. They've bagged the peak and are heading down. To them, what I'm standing next to is little more than a pile of rocks in the bushes. I step out and talk to them. They are students at the University of New Mexico; one man is from Germany. They all seem so nice and talkative and impressed with the wonder of the mountaintop that I mention there is a rock shrine up here that is special to the Indians of the area. The girl ignores me and wanders off to sit by a bush covered in hundreds of orange ladybugs. The Anglo guy laughs. He has the beginnings of an unruly mouse-hair beard.

"Oh, look. She found another village of ladybugs!" he says. He looks at me. "She hates bugs, can't stand them. Those are the only kind of bugs she lets crawl around on her." He watches her hold an arm up, absorbed in the dozens of insects crawling on her bare skin.

Ladybugs, the familiar, beetle-like, golden-shelled garden predators, gather in swarming clusters of hundreds, sometimes thousands, on plants and bushes on mountaintops all over the Southwest during the summer. Among other purposes, they gather to mate, clearly something on this guy's mind. I want to warn him not to plant his longings in a girl so indifferent and self-absorbed, but know it's useless.

The German guy begins to hold forth in excellent English, barely accented and with the precision of an academic expert, on the subject of Indian sacred sites, but quickly runs out of steam. They are plainly not interested, as I suspected, and change the subject. We three males drift irrevocably over to where the girl sits transfixed by the bugs crawling all over her. She looks up at her boyfriend in what can only be described as carnal bliss.

I take my leave and circle around to the topmost point, now deserted. Standing on the flat concrete footings where a striped chipmunk races warily about, nibbling on food crumbs dropped on the ground, I see the three hikers heading far down the mountain. I'm alone again, on the very western point, with vertical cliffs falling away on both the north and south sides. I notice the cliff facing the north is only about forty feet high and at its foot is a sloping forest of tall trees. A wooded trail drops off the end of the point and leads down to a series of ledges. I scramble down to a truly scary overlook. I seldom have problems with heights, but I shrink back with queasy fright from how the wind from behind tries to push me over the drop-off. A hundred feet straight down are the pointed tops of conifers.

Angling around the mountain on a game trail, I skirt the base of cliff where it meets dense sloping forest. I find two small caves and then a third. It doesn't look like much, but once inside, I'm surprised it opens up into an immense chamber with a flat floor extending far back into the mountain. Forty feet back by the dim light of my flashlight, it narrows, and I—always uneasy underground—lose interest and turn back. The musty air is freezing. Old candle stubs and a rock fireplace seem somehow malevolent. Outside again, I discover old rotten boards to one side. The cave has obviously been used as a shelter in the past, but I'll never spend a night in it.

From there I continue onward and upward, slowly and laboriously struggling back to the top of the cliff through tossing thickets of aspen, grateful to be back in the wind and sunlight. The sun is lowering to the west; it's four o'clock and nobody is on the summit. Time to head back, I tell myself.

I make my way to the rock shrine again. A limpid golden light suffuses everything. There are no deep thinkers at high elevation, but my feelings are sharp. I'm filled with inexplicable wonder simply to be here atop the first objective of my journey. By coming up here I had hoped at least to get a glimpse of this land through the eyes of my Tewa neighbors. I now stood gazing north over their shrine at our shared home world spread out beyond.

I had come in the same spirit as Colin Fletcher, the great walker, who said in *The Man Who Walked Through Time*, his book about hiking lengthwise through the Grand Canyon: "If you want to know how a cliff-dweller felt, go live in his cliff." Here I was, standing where they stand, seeing what they see. What, I ask myself, is the proper thing for me to do?

I abruptly feel moved to speak out loud to the mountain, to the awesome silent vastness of the wide world of which I am but a tiny part, a pinpoint of awareness. What I say is lame, of course. I give thanks for my long life, my strong body, and for being trusted with the knowledge of what is still here on this summit. I leave my own offering on the horseshoe of rocks.

"This is from me, this man still wandering around in the mountains," I say.

At that moment a flock of blue Stellar jays flies up and lands in nearby trees, calling out as if in response with a piercing *shook, shook, shook, shook!* A Canada jay zooms over, crying out with a sound like mewing laughter. A raven perched on a dead snag starts cawing endlessly. I listen, fascinated by all the voices of those who live in the open air and who have come unexpectedly to this high peak to speak out as I have.

Six

LATE IN THE day, after strenuous exploration at ten thousand feet, the lure of dinner is irresistible. The descent from North Peak seems to take only minutes. The main trail appears and I stride with ease among the forest trees standing along Sandia Crest bathed in warm yellow sunlight. Ravenous for something to eat, I nibble on the white blossoms and tender leaves of wood violet, a sweet and earthy-tasting salad green. At every turn in the trail are majestic conifers I had not noticed when I came this way before, standing out in a golden afternoon glow made even more dramatic by the black shade of forest behind.

Not that any of them are all that tall. Too much desiccating wind from the desert below, and perhaps more important, too much wind shear in the winter—ice crystals blasting away at anything living that stands above a snow-encrusted canopy. But many of these singular trees are very old.

The most immense of all is a Douglas fir with a trunk *six feet thick* that stops me in my tracks. I stare at it in wonder. Deep furrows in the bark have split open, revealing vertical layering: centuries of thin accretions to the protective husk surrounding the trunk, including layers of charcoal from the wildfires it has withstood. The many-forked upper limbs are as thick as my body and are clotted with massive scars and stumps of lightning strikes the tree has survived to continue holding up a low canopy of wind-pruned green. It has to be at least eight hundred years old and yet tops out at a mere twenty-five feet.

Scientists using tree-ring dating on core samples drilled in trees on Sandia Crest have found a limber pine that sprouted in AD 416 and a Douglas fir from AD 995—more than a thousand years old. If the grizzled monster standing before me is, say, just eight hundred years old, it was a seedling first sending its roots deep into the rocky soil around the thirteenth century. It was a centuries-old veteran of winter storms by the time the first Europeans laid eyes on Sandia Mountain. It means this fir tree has been alive on this very spot of earth for so long it makes my own brief time under the sun seem like the blink of an eye.

Back to camp. More things I didn't notice before: My way down into dank woods to the tent goes over innumerable slippery logs and through a pure stand of "twisted stalk," a knee-high acre of the stuff, each plant having glossy green leaves on a zigzag stem—and each now dangling with a single white lily from each leaf axil. How could I have missed a million tiny white blossoms, even facing downward? It seems impossible. They must have opened in one day's sunlight after heavy rain.

Everything in the tent is undisturbed. The lowering sun shines through ranks of trees and the glade is quiet except for the whisper of aspen leaves. The ground has dried out. Before long I'm sitting on an aspen log impatiently waiting for my spaghetti with meat sauce to "cook." Freeze-dried, pre-cooked food resembles nothing more appetizing than dog kibbles before boiling water is added and the bag is sealed and set aside. I look at my pup tent and all my camp gear spread around on the ground like it always is at mealtime and realize this is the new normal. This homey, familiar mess is the quotidian (if mobile) world I now dwell in.

Oops. Opening the food bag too soon, it tastes like Italian-seasoned mush. I wait some more. Finally I eat the hot meal, not all that good, but filling and necessary. I accept it in the spirit of sacrifice for a greater good—less weight I have to carry on my back. After cleanup (bear country trail guides all urge backpackers to keep a "spotless" camp—to which I respond, "Hey, guys, it's the ground, for God's sake! How would you know if you missed a spot?"), my bag of bear bait goes up high into a nearby fir, and I wash up before closing everything else into the zipped-up tent.

Ready for the evening's entertainment—viewing the city's fireworks celebration from the crest—I carry a few things with me back up to the trail again. Aware that I'll be returning to camp after dark on a moonless night, I pick a certain boulder near my turnoff as a landmark and stand there memorizing its shape until I'm certain I can recognize it by the beam of a flashlight. After the damp chill of deep woods, I'm amazed to arrive at the first overlook where a hot afternoon desert wind still hammers the wall of mountain. It feels twenty degrees warmer.

The crest is lit up in a whiskey glow and the far horizon dims to a magenta haziness. In the weakening solar glare, I feel the creeping cool of night approaching. With a tee shirt and long-sleeve thermal shirt on (I brought no jacket or coat), I use the emergency rain poncho I purchased at the gift shop as a windbreaker. Shiny red and no thicker than a plastic garbage can liner, it works well, making up for lack of insulating capacity by molding tightly to my upper body like an extra skin.

Studying the flat valley floor, I see cars moving as slowly as ants along Tramway Boulevard and Interstate 25. I see every detail of Sandia Pueblo's hotel and casino complex spread out for miles amid irrigated golf greens on otherwise dull brown, sloping desert cut by snakelike sandy arroyos. Out on the West Mesa the cones of extinct volcanoes are like dark blips, mere pimples—blackheads on the earth's face from this distance. Lit by a lowering sun, the curving river and city buildings shine, especially the cluster of downtown skyscrapers, which cast long, tapering shadows across the east side.

Seed fluff flies upward on the ceaseless wind from dry lands below. It is the wind of the sea, or of the open plains, except as I watch, enormous vultures shoot past, rocking on spread wings, at sixty miles per hour. A friendly hiker stops and we talk. He points to his house twenty miles away on Albuquerque's far southwestern side. He tells me anecdotes of mountain climber friends attempting to scale the formations before us—the Needle, the Prow, the Shield—how some were stranded when night fell before they could get back down, and others clung precariously while waiting out sudden thunderstorms that swept over them.

With the sun almost on the horizon and miles-long shadows stretching across the lowland world, I make my way to Itchy Butt vista point. The great shelf of bare limestone is empty of people, but not for long. The friendly guy I just spoke to, Jim, shows up with a friend, Steve, from Houston, Texas, who has carried his professional photography gear, including a folded tripod, from their car at the parking lot.

"Hey, again," I say.

"Oh, it's you. We were looking for a place with a good view to shoot pictures of the fireworks over the city," Jim says. "And this is by far the best. But we thought this was so remote that nobody else would be here."

"Me, too," I say.

With Jim's assistance, Steve sets up to photograph the coming sunset. Absorbed in the complex process of assembling all the pieces into a standing array of technological gadgetry, they are somewhat unresponsive to my cheery, gregarious conversation. I have to remind myself they're fresh from the city below and not at the end of day three spent on a mountaintop. I move off to the side, at the brink, and look out again. The dome-like top of the Needle juts up dramatically in front of the city beyond. Backlit by the sun and about a half mile away, it has two concave areas facing us that are in dark shadow and that look like the eye holes on a skull. Or even more like the eye holes on Darth Vader's helmet, in the movie *Star Wars.* I point it out to Jim and Steve. They howl with laughter at the resemblance, and Steve takes pictures of it.

The air grows colder and the wind blows more fiercely. I find a place back from the edge, shielded by a tree trunk, and watch the sun set. Above the horizon the brilliant gold ball slips behind a thin lilac layer of cloud—the only cloud visible in the sky over a vast darkening earth. The Rio Grande glimmers like the shard of a mirror.

The sunset seems to take forever.

Jim and Steve carry the camera stand and luggage a hundred yards farther north along the rim for a more unobstructed view. The sun emerges from under the cloud like a molten blob of gold and with majestic ease gradually dips below the horizon at a point between the Cabezon and the San Mateo Plateau. The Cabezon, Spanish for "Big Head," has never looked more like a giant skull protruding from the earth. (It was named by the Navajo, who consider it the head of a giant monster killed by the hero twins of myth—the Malpais lava beds near Grants are the monster's congealed blood.) The last orange glare spreads out in a bright liquid line and then disappears. The wind falls to nothing and a pink glow lingers above the horizon. In the unadorned silence, many tiny birds fly trilling up over the crest and into the forest behind me for the night's roost.

Then in the gathering gloom of dusk that follows, the wind returns, blasting even more vengefully than before. Jim and Steve come back and set up on the very brink of the drop-off, aimed down at the city where street-lights start to appear. In the night wind Jim still wears shorts and a tee shirt as he helps brace the tripod legs with loose rocks. He says he's a distance runner and doesn't even feel a cold wind like this. He claims he often runs up the La Luz Trail to the crest and back down to the city to train for marathons, and "sometimes just for the fun of it."

More people show up: a short, quiet muscular man in his forties and his two sons—a boy about eight in a tee shirt and glasses, and another about seventeen or eighteen, bare-chested with dreadlocks down his back and an elaborate wooden-bead necklace around his neck. They, too, thought they'd have this place to themselves to watch the fireworks. We all laugh over having the same idea. The newcomers head off to set up a camp for the night in the trees behind the overlook, but soon the younger boy returns and plays distractedly on the very edge of the cliff. He hums and talks to himself, picks up rocks, dangles his legs over the brink. And it's getting darker by the minute. He's like a shadow off by himself at the edge of the void. I grow nervous and wonder if I should say something. But then father and older brother join us and seem unperturbed by the boy playing along the edge. So be it, I think.

Almost fully dark, the wind grows stronger with wild moaning gusts. I don gloves and a wool toque to stay warm. Everybody else puts on a jacket or windbreaker, even Jim, still with legs bare. Within ten minutes I realize a winter parka would not have been out of order.

Distant tiny flashes of light signal fireworks going off in the city below. A mile down and five to twenty miles away amid the twinkle of a well-lit urban area, the varicolored explosions are not much to see. After a while, things really get going, silent bursts of light popping up all over the city in continuous flashes. It looks like CNN coverage of Baghdad or Kabul being bombed as viewed from the air. The father and older son give up and go back to camp.

The boy says, "My dad thought the fireworks would be going off at eye level." He sounds disappointed.

"We're too high for that," I say. "We're a mile up."

"It doesn't seem all that exciting after all, does it?" Jim says.

Steve, clicking photos, says, "Yeah. After all we went through to get here!"

Nothing more spectacular shows for about half an hour. Then finally we see globe-like flashes at Balloon Fiesta Park—the "balloon glow" of rising but tethered hot-air balloons illuminated by gas-fired jets. Immediately the most unbelievable fireworks explode above them. Huge, shocking blossoms of multicolored light appear, one after another, above lines of car headlights pulled over on the interstate. There are no sounds of explosions from this distance, but the pyrotechnic creativity is visually awesome. The father and older son return at the sound of our excited shouts of amazement. We *ooh* and *ahh* in childlike wonder at each more complex and dramatic burst.

"Happy birthday, America!" I yell, and the others send up their own cheers.

For a while at least we forget about the very different USA, out there under a dark sky, that some of us can't quite fathom or accept or unreservedly love the way we did as children. We agree we are seeing the best fireworks display in all of New Mexico.

During a lull the father is revealed as a veteran hang glider. His boys clearly revere him, and it's hard not to be impressed by his reticent, carefully chosen words delivered with deliberate slowness. He tells calmly of flying off from this spot and landing hours later in a church parking lot in the Northeast Heights of the city. He explains with technical detail what he had to do to make it all the way to Balloon Fiesta Park, which he said was about fifteen miles away, and which included circling upward some two thousand feet above takeoff before heading west, in order to glide that far. He said that even so, sometimes he'd fall short and have to land in the old airstrip south of the casino.

No wonder he's so casual about his boy playing on the edge of the drop-off. Any mother present would have been long since reduced to a moaning wreck by the boy's fearless indifference to life and limb. As it is, with only males present, the testosterone is palpable in the breezy way we laugh and are held spellbound by the father's descriptions of jumping off into the void. Like his two sons, we know who has the biggest balls on the mountain tonight.

More fireworks light up the sky. The climax is awesome—a prolonged and concentrated series of multiple starburst explosions with trailing secondary fiery effects. Delayed booming can faintly be heard on the wind. Abruptly it all fades to nothing. At once, we are freezing. Father and sons retreat to their camp. Steve says he has over a *thousand* shots—he had the camera on "continuous" toward the end. As Jim and Steve pack up the camera equipment, we smell something in the campfire smoke swirling around.

"What's that? Popcorn?" Steve asks.

"Shit. I'm starving," Jim says. "Let's go."

"Hey, you mind if I hike back with you guys as far as the turnoff to my camp?"

"Sure," Jim says. "Is that flashlight all you've got?"

They both have headlights on, brilliant LED lamps strapped to their heads, which make the beam of my flashlight seem yellow and dim. We haven't needed or used them before this because the light cast by the city has been enough to see by on the open ledge. The last time I wore a head lamp was on my hard hat while on a forest fire crew twenty years before. Theirs are vastly brighter and more effective.

Shivering and anxious to be off, I wait for them to finish loading up. The Big Dipper and Cassiopeia's Chair glitter in the northern sky. I take one last look at the city below, at the tiny flashes of fireworks still going off. It looks like a giant psychedelic cabbage patch. Then I fall in behind the two guys as they take off at a dogtrot. On the Crest Trail everything is different—a forced march in pitch-black timber, eyes on the illuminated ground before me to keep from tripping. We're almost at a run headlong in a dark rushing world.

Their car is in the parking lot a mile beyond my camp, and I hear snatches of their voices making plans for when they get to Albuquerque—a sports bar on Central Avenue where the food is good. Eventually the boulder looms up and I call a halt. We shake hands all jolly and cracking jokes.

Jim says, "Hey, this could be the first of a new annual tradition!"

Steve says, "Yeah, and we could all have nicknames!"

And before I quite catch on that they've already worked this out, Jim says, "Yeah, and yours could be Scooby-Doo Man!"

Hooting along with them, I wave good-night. Picking my way downhill through utterly unfamiliar forest, I take a wrong turn and have to backtrack before finding my tent at last. Away from the wind, the moist air is fragrant with resinous fir and the sweet balsam of aspen. I jump in my sleeping bag. All is still and serene in the deep woods, but I can hear the ceaseless roar of wind at the crest, fifty yards uphill. It feels like falling asleep behind a beach dune, listening to the sound of surf crashing ashore.

Seven

IN THE WEE hours of the night I'm startled awake by truly titanic winds scouring through the tall trees and clawing at the tent fabric. Ferocious gusts continue well past dawn. I sleep only fitfully until six thirty, when I heat water for coffee without getting out of my warm bag, the Primus stove blazing just outside in the lee of the tent flap. Not a bird sings in the first rays of eastern sunlight shining through the trees—the wind is that extreme and relentless. (During my visit to the Crest House I saw a sign with a sobering warning: Lowest recorded temperature on Sandia Crest, 32 degrees below zero. Highest clocked wind speed, 117 miles per hour.)

Daylight reveals the surrounding trees swaying and creaking continuously. There isn't a trace of a cloud in the sky, and as I sip scalding hot coffee, the air feels charged with a wintry chill. Wind rules the world and hardly anything can be heard beneath the roar of the canopy overhead.

With little time to get myself over to the parking lot and meet my friend for the hike down the mountain, I finish the coffee in a series of gulps and climb out. There's no more water, so I don't cook breakfast, just strike camp and load up. The wind tears at everything, making me chase after an empty stuff sack that bounds away like a tumbleweed. Once down, the tent is impossible to fold up properly so I just wad it up and jam it into the backpack.

Excited to move on, get going again to somewhere else, I'm just as strongly struck with nostalgia at leaving this place that now seems so familiar. The frame backpack hoists up considerably lighter with less gas, food, and no water, but feels uncomfortably heavy on my shoulders all the same, especially on the uphill stretches through moss-shrouded forest with dancing dapples of horizontal yellow sunlight. The wind chill makes the air seem freezing, but I'm moving; I'm a well-oiled machine marching along under a thirty-pound pack. And I'm ready to get on with this last leg of crossing the great mountain of the south—which according to the map is a drop down eight miles of endless switchbacks to the desert city below.

In no time I pass the row of cell phone, radio, and television towers, the humming building that I now see has the letters KNME on it—the public TV station in Albuquerque—and arrive at the parking lot. It is empty of all but a few parked cars. Nobody is about. I'm a few minutes early for my rendezvous and discover to my dismay that the Crest House doesn't open for another hour. There is no public water source. Out in the open, the crisp, clear, beautiful morning unfolds on top of the world. The unblinking sun barely tempers the cold wind of outer space.

My friend drives up in a black Toyota RAV4 with his wife and a friend. Jimmy McNees hops out in shorts and a blue Hard Rock Hotel tee shirt. We shake hands, grinning.

"Omigod! It's freezing up here!" he howls.

"Did you bring a coat?"

"Nope. It was warm in Santa Fe when we left—in the sixties. I guess it's been so long since I've been up here, I forgot it was this high up!"

His wife Carolane and friend Barbara are dressed the same. After a quick hug hello, they stand shivering, shocked by the cold. Neither have been to Sandia Crest before, so I urge them to go with me to the lookout, about fifty feet away, and see the incredible view before they head back home. Barb makes it as far as the ramp up to the overlook before gasping and running back to the car. Carolane makes it to the top with Jimmy and marvels in delight at the wondrous 360-degree view of New Mexico.

After our good-byes, Jimmy and I make a quick decision not to wait until the gift shop opens for me to buy bottled water. He has a liter of "performance water" in his fanny pack and says he'll share. We both want to get moving and get out of the wind, so we bolt off, me leading the way down a rugged mountain trail that quickly drops off the crest into the protected stillness of forest. But the sun isn't high enough yet to shine down the steep west face of Sandia Mountain. It's all shade at first. Jimmy soon rubs his hands together and stamps his boots to stay warm. At every spot where the sunlight hits the trail, we stop and stand moaning in the relative warmth of direct sunlight.

The trail heads southward under the limestone wall of the crest, following a natural line of descent through heavy spruce and fir. We make slow progress, talking about everything, cracking jokes, pausing in awe at the views into shadowy gorges where we see the switchbacks of the trail far below.

Jimmy is an excellent hiking partner—cheerful, curious, quick to laugh—but as an amateur photographer fresh from community college courses and carrying a new Pentax camera, he dawdles over every shot that strikes his fancy. A clump of scarlet penstemon in a spot of sunshine holds his attention for a half-dozen close-ups from every possible angle. With his short-brimmed felt bush hat and broad, sandy mustache he looks like an intrepid English botanist/explorer, or like a European tourist on holiday. He is not amused by me making this observation and turns his camera on me to document the pitifully soiled and bedraggled mountain pilgrim he finds himself stuck with. He tells me he had a big breakfast and plenty to drink in preparation for the day's hike. Commiserating with me not having anything but coffee this morning, he offers me a granola bar. I decline. All I've had to eat for days is granola and trail mix and dried fruit and nuts and freeze-dried packaged food, I say. He tells me how on lazy Sunday mornings he lies around reading the newspaper while his wife cooks him his favorite: pancakes with ham and eggs. Really rubs it in.

"You're killing me, Jimmy!" I burst out.

He takes pity on me, suggesting that when we get to the end of the trail at the bottom where my wife will pick us up, we can go to a restaurant and he'll buy me anything I want.

"Now you're talking!"

The trail comes to an impassable barrier, a short cliff, which has been circumvented by an ingenious staircase of steep concrete steps descending a wide crack. Below that, the forest is even wetter and gloomier along shelf-like terraces of exposed sedimentary bedrock. We arrive at a saddle where the rock turns into solid granite, the faulted, upthrust intrusion from deep below the earth's surface that forms the rest of the west face downward. Here the sun shines full from overhead and we take a break, lounging in animal bliss, warm at last.

Lean and panting runners come up the trail dressed with less on than Jimmy, and fly past. In response to shouted questions, some reply that, yes, they often run up and back down the sixteen miles of steep, torturous trail like this. One white-haired old man with massive calf muscles sprints past uphill, and ten minutes later comes running back down. After he disappears down the trail ahead of us like a young gazelle, I turn to Jimmy with a disapproving shake of the head.

"Now that's just *too* fit, if you ask me!"

"I know!" he says with an incredulous look. "How in the world do they do it? They can't be seeing very much of their surroundings. It's just like a giant StairMaster for them, is all!"

Trying to hide my envy, I try to sound reasonable: "Well, there are many different kinds of addiction. What else could it be?"

The few people we meet coming up the La Luz Trail in the first mile turn into a stream of people, then a torrent—more people running or hiking up a wilderness trail than I've ever seen before in my life. It is Monday, July 5, a holiday in the big city below, and by the time we make it to the bottom, we will have seen about two hundred men, women, and children go by. And surprisingly, the women and girls will outnumber the men and boys by a ratio of about five to three!

The most difficult part of the descent is some two miles of crossing back and forth down a talus slope of loose angular rubble rock beneath a towering pale granite formation known as the Thumb. My legs ache from the strain—especially my calves and ankles—and I often set down my heavy pack to rest and wait for Jimmy to catch up. He is spellbound in the gorge, shooting endless photos. From the spruce-fir-aspen forest near the top, we enter the mixed conifer forest of Douglas fir, limber pine, and white fir. The drop is so much quicker than when I climbed up, and we are soon among ponderosa pines and tall Gambel oaks, starting to hunt out shady spots to rest as the heat grows and the air dries out.

We pass two women, each about twenty, sitting together in deep shade and drinking from water bottles. They look flushed and sweaty in their stylish outback outfits. After we go by, they get up and quickly pass us, heading back down.

"Too much for you?" I ask.

"Oh, that's where the really rough part starts," one girl says with a shrug. She points at her friend's footwear. "And she's only got those tennies on."

The other girl pipes up brightly: "Yeah, I took one look at all those rocks, and I said, 'In these shoes? I don't think so!'"

At the base of giant pink granite cliffs with still about five miles to go, the trail begins to loop around onto more arid south-facing slopes. The granite underfoot becomes paler—a speckled tan color—and we cross deep ravines of oak brush, mountain mahogany, and cliff fendlerbush. At the first piñon tree we are dropping fast into the hot high-desert zone. After so much recent rain, the brushlands smell like wet chaparral. Most of the trees are widely spaced ponderosas and white firs. Fresh mint-green wormwood, or *estafiate*, grows in carpets beneath thickets of white-blossoming mock orange.

At noon, halfway down at 8,400 feet, there is not a breath of wind. The sun bears down on us relentlessly. We seek deep shade to rest, and drink almost all the liquid in Jimmy's bottle. Two older men hike up, and one quizzes me about my external-frame backpack. He prefers the older style, too, and wants to see how I rig my sleeping bag, tent, mattress, and daypack on the outside with hooked tension cords. I notice his fancy carved wooden hiking stick and ask him where he got it. He says Washington, D.C., and brandishes it over his head, crowing, "I got it to fight off politicians!" The other guy, speaking to Jimmy behind my back, snickers about my Scooby-Doo daypack.

"You got a problem with Scooby-Doo?" I ask.

"What did you do? Steal it off some kid on the way home from school?"

We laugh and part ways. Refreshed, Jimmy and I go on. We descend into thickets of Apache plume and chamisa. Black-and-white and rust-red towhees, a kind of large, ground-feeding sparrow, hop among the dried leaves of unusually thick chaparral. We pass the very last mountain conifer, a stunted white fir in a dry gully, and there is no more shade to be found. The heat is terrific. My only consolation is that I am walking downhill.

Replaying in reverse the same elevation life zones I passed through when climbing the mountain, we drop from forest to brushland to woodland to open desert grassland in a matter of a few hours. More switchbacks appear, this time zigzagging down steep south-facing slopes with tall canes of cholla cactus sporting bright magenta flowers. Jimmy stops in the brutal sun to photograph them. Every turn in the trail seems to present us with a foot-long lizard lying in ambush for flies on the sandy ground. We come to the lowest granite on the mountain, a white feldspar/quartz mix with specks of mica and black biotite that decomposes like the layers of an onion into rounded boulders sitting on glaring gravel hillsides. Cicadas whine in the hot brush and grasshoppers flee before us. We see the red tile rooftops of a housing subdivision far below, at a canyon mouth we are approaching.

At a trail fork, we find a bit of shade under a piñon pine and drop to the ground, sweating profusely. People are still streaming by uphill, but nobody is running—not in ninety-degree heat. We finish off Jimmy's bottle. Gnats swarm our faces, probing into eyes, nostrils, ears, open mouths. A scrub jay lands on a nearby bush with a wingspread splash of bright blue. Jimmy laments his inability to photograph what we both saw.

"What a picture that would have made!" he says.

"Maybe we can ask the bird to come back and do it again," I say in my heat-stroked daze. A feeble attempt at humor elicits a feeble laugh.

We heave up and go on. For the umpteenth time Jimmy offers to carry my heavy pack for a while—to spell me, give me a breather. Not sure why, I refuse again. It's a part of me now, and wouldn't feel right.

Along the canyon bottom to our left, we see the fluttering green tops of cottonwood trees and hear the echoing trickle of a stream. Thoughts of fresh cold water dance in my head. Despite the temptation, we hurry on the last half mile. I told my wife we'd get to the Juan Tabó trailhead around noon and it's already two o'clock. Almost on our last legs, we plod through the giant boulders and riot of wild flowers just above the parking lot. Theresa steps out from the shade with a smile and a sweet hello.

"We made it!" Jimmy says in relief.

"You guys are really sunburned," she says.

"Yeah, but—we made it!"

We load everything into her Yaris, and Theresa speeds off down the winding mountain highway. She has only a few swallows of warm water left in a bottle. Jimmy and I kill it. She says she's been waiting there for hours, reading mainly, and that every group of people that hiked down and arrived at the trailhead before us said the same thing we did. We look at her, exhausted, not comprehending.

"They all said 'We made it!'"

A half hour later, seated in the dark, cool bar area of the Range Café in Bernalillo, I down a glass of ice water and another of ice tea before the food arrives at the table. Famished, I make quick work of a platter of beef burritos with green chile, rice, and refried beans. The pleasant return to the comforts of civilization and dreamy conversation with intimates nearly puts me to sleep in my chair.

Outside, strolling the main drag of Bern-town in hundred-degree heat, I see Sandia Mountain looming above, a forested island in the sky. I pick out North Peak, where I found the shrine, and study the faraway features I clambered around on. It feels like a dream. It's hard to believe I started this morning in freezing wind and cold wet forest up on Sandia Crest. And then I look north at the hazy peaks of the Jemez Mountains, my next destination, where I will climb Chicoma Mountain, the sacred peak of the west. But not right now. Now we have to drop Jimmy off in Santa Fe.

That night, after a long luxurious bath, I tumble into bed at eight o'clock and sleep for eleven hours straight through.

PART THREE

FLINT

Mas sabe el diablo por viejo que por diablo. (The Devil knows more because he's old than because he's the Devil.)

—Northern New Mexico dicho,
equivalent to "Experience is the best teacher."

One

ON JULY 15, ten days later, I arrive back in Bernalillo at noon to resume my expedition around the horizon. The temperature is already ninety-three degrees and the Rio Grande is running lower, not so flooded but still muddy. Before driving the link that connects my way from Sandia to Chicoma (from Watermelon to Flint), I've decided to stop in at Coronado State Monument, on the west bank, to ground myself.

With one mountain under my belt, I have a better idea what to expect. Tested, seasoned, ready for more, I climb out of my pickup truck feeling confident, lighthearted, welcoming the blast of heat. Native desert grasses and brush cover the sandy flats around the ancient adobe ruins of Kuaua. Baking in the relentless sun, only snakeweed and winterfat, low shrubs growing in clumps, are still green. Everything else is sere and lifeless, or turning into straw like the Indian ricegrass. Surprisingly, I see several cottontail rabbits hopping around in the glaring midday heat.

The campground here is a favorite of retirees on the road. On a high bank above the great river, where it sweeps by in a broad curve, the shade trees and colorful, rustic picnic table shelters are hemmed in with motor homes and travel trailers. I assume the electric generators are humming to keep the refrigeration blowers going inside. Roughing it in comfort, I would guess. Beyond massive green cottonwood trees lining the far shore, Sandia Mountain rises up through wavering heat layers, an indistinct blue shape under the shadow of a dark silent thunderhead.

Inside the visitor center, in a rear room, the Museum of New Mexico has provided a reproduction of one of the kiva murals found here during the archaeological excavations of the 1930s. In the same dim coolness you would expect in an underground ceremonial chamber like a kiva, the images march along the walls in procession: fish and birds, deities and rainbows, sprinkling rainfall and corn plants, lightning and masked dancers. The paintings are staggeringly beautiful. Unlike petroglyphs and pictographs, which they resemble, these images have depth, solidity, color, background, and movement.

Who knew the inside walls of kivas were the real canvases for the religious artists of the Pueblo people?

The frescoed ceiling of the Sistine Chapel was no more a labor of love and awe than this, and the depictions of nature speak to me far more persuasively of the ultimate origins of life than two guys in flowing robes touching fingertips in the clouds. There is none of the exaggerated self-importance of humans, just an elegant and sophisticated representation of the natural world under the care of godlike beings.

The official brochure given free to the public reports the words of an Indian visitor from nearby Santo Domingo Pueblo, who said, "These pictures around here—they are everything that we believe. They show us how to live. To us, these paintings are everything to live for."

The kiva mural reminds me forcefully that I'm not alone in worshipping nature as the source of all life, or in regarding the natural world as beautiful and good for us. Beyond that, I don't have any big answers, any ideology or doctrine, and I'm suspicious of people who do. Certainly the big answers to life might be found in giant metropolitan cities, in cars racing down highways, in electronic gadgetry consuming our attention, or even in the pleasure of our comfortable homes (or motor homes). But such things are ultimately all derived from nature, made out of nature. Only *out there*, in the vast empty solitude, under the open sky where the wind blows, have I been able to see myself in something like proper proportion: not the giant of the earth for which all good things are intended and taken for granted, but a creature as mysterious as a flower, a pebble, a coyote, or a mountain—and no more important than any one of them. It's a monumental discovery to realize that the natural world from whence we spring is really, in the end, all we have. And I personally cannot get enough of it.

Whoever originally painted these kiva images must have felt the same thing.

But then screaming voices break my reverie. I emerge back into the busy front area of the visitor center where a uniformed female docent is helping a giggling blond-haired boy, one of a group of elementary schoolchildren on a field trip, try on the replica armor and helmet of a Spanish conquistador. There's a Disney-like air of pretend in the room, and the trivializing of historical conflict feels jarring.

Exiting to the outdoors, I stand beside the ruins. This may or may not be the ancient Tiwa pueblo where Coronado and his troops wintered in 1541—despite naming this place for him, nothing has been found to prove his presence conclusively one way or the other. Blooming purple thistle and orange globe mallow line the edge of a restored village foundation. Otherwise there's not much to see but bare dirt. Beyond the dry plain to the west looms the huge Santa Ana Star Casino with the fresh-mown greens of its golf course spread over rolling hills. The commercial menace of the place is palpable, but so too is the reassurance of growing economic parity for the people of Santa Ana Pueblo in the local marketplace. From the south I hear the roar of heavy traffic on U.S. Highway 555.

Itching to get going, get back up into the high country, I head up Interstate 25 with my loaded backpack on the seat beside me. My destination, the Jemez Mountains to the northwest, is a much larger range than the Sandias. The wide-spaced peaks look dark in the noonday sun under classic anvil-shaped thunderheads. I feel drawn inevitably toward them, the raw elements of stone and sky in an outer world that is more real to me than this human-made one.

The drive takes about an hour. Beyond the black volcanic plug called Toe Rock, the mountains loom larger and closer on the left. To the right is the long sierra, the Sangre de Cristos, stretching away to Colorado, also blanketed with clouds. Recent rain has extinguished all the wildfires. There is no trace of smoke. At the San Felipe Pueblo exit I can see more rain already falling on the highest peaks of the Jemez—thin, darkly transparent curtains veiling the blue-sky summits of Redondo and Chicoma. On a hot, dry day like today, it's easy to see why the mountains are revered for capturing and passing to the lowlands the precious gift of water. I can't wait to get up there again—into the forest, the thin cool air, the damp mossy banks of icy streams.

At the Santo Domingo exit, I get gas at their station, a tribal enterprise known for the cheapest gasoline near Santa Fe, and then head directly toward the mountains on a two-lane highway. Crossing a high-desert plain, the view is enormous in every direction. Skinny Indian horses and horned cattle move across a parched grassland, while up ahead, falling showers blot out whole areas of mountains.

Within view of the immense earth-fill dam above Cochiti Pueblo, I see a dust devil swirling enigmatically across a plowed field. The lower peak, called St. Peter's Dome, sits atop vast burned areas stretching away northward toward Los Alamos. Most of the world ahead is under dark rain clouds, which make the sunlit pale-orange cliffs and mesas shine with lucent starkness, framing each canyon mouth. Far up Cochiti Canyon, my route into the mountains, rain is falling in the forested headwaters.

I've chosen to go this way to avoid the crowds. The more popular routes westward into the Jemez Mountains follow trails to the north of here, through Bandelier National Monument and the Dome Wilderness, eventually reaching the national forest high country close to the city of Los Alamos and the sprawling National Laboratory famous for developing the first atomic bomb. Those trails are loaded with hikers in the summertime, and subject to the usual restrictions on where you can camp and what you can do on lands controlled by the National Park Service. Trying to find a quieter, lesser-known, less invasively controlled and monitored way up (Bandelier has undisclosed remote-area video cameras), I discovered Cochiti Canyon—lined for six miles by an old mining road that is usually closed to unauthorized vehicles by a locked gate. Known only to a few and well watered by a mountain stream, the canyon road is hooked up to trails that lead up onto the Pajarito Plateau and the peaks beyond. It should be perfect as a quiet, hidden route into a busy part of the Jemez country.

To cross the whole of the Jemez range from south to north is about three times farther than my crossing of the Sandias. Essentially a collapsed stratovolcano of immense proportions, the Jemez Mountains have historically been under a patchwork of public, private, and Pueblo land ownership, and as a result, the peaks ringing the vast crater, or caldera, do not have any through trails to speak of. To devise a continuous route that climbs Chicoma, the mountain of the west, I've had to break the journey up into three phases. The first will be this three-day initial ascent up Cochiti Canyon, onto the broad Pajarito Plateau above, to the top of Cerro Grande at the rim of the caldera. The second phase will be the crossing of Valles Caldera itself, to the north rim. And the third will be the ascent of Chicoma Mountain, the highest of the ringing mountains, followed by a hike along the north rim and down Cañones Creek into the redrock lowlands beyond.

Driving the highway behind Cochiti Dam gives me the creeps. The surface of Cochiti Reservoir is hundreds of feet above my head, and the dam leaks, of course. Across the highway from water ominously seeping through the earth-fill dam, the Cochiti Pueblo herd of buffalo rests in the sun on a river-bottom pasture, oblivious. Before construction of the dam in 1975, the Rio Grande periodically flooded, destroying whole villages and neighborhoods downstream. The Pueblo of San Felipe, for example, was washed away completely in the late 1800s and was rebuilt on the other side of the river, on higher ground.

The gravel road up into the foothills is rough and dusty through miles of rolling uplands thickly covered with juniper scrub. It approaches tall, jutting sunlit cliffs of pinkish-orange tuff—solidified volcanic ash in horizontal layers hundreds of feet thick, honeycombed with rounded pits, holes, and passageways like pumpkin-colored Swiss cheese. This is the tip end of Horn Mesa. Cave dwellings carved in the porous rock in prehistoric times are visible at the base, the remains of homes built by the ancestors of the various Rio Grande Pueblo peoples who inhabited all these canyons, farming along the mountain streams. Frijoles Canyon in Bandelier a few miles north was the heaviest populated and contains the most ruins, but signs of the Ancestral Pueblo people are everywhere in the Jemez Mountains.

Then the road drops down into a canyon and runs alongside Dixon's Apple Orchard, lush, leafy trees in rows hung with green apples, the locally famous Champagne Golden Delicious. The orchard was developed on the long narrow floodplain of the Rio Chiquito, the creek that runs down Cochiti Canyon and provides the water for irrigation. Where the canyon narrows, I find the trailhead in a wonderful oasis of tall cottonwoods and ponderosa pines. The locked gate is at an elevation of about six thousand feet, and just as I gear up to hike off, thick rain clouds close in overhead. Instantly the shade tempers the burning edge of a high-desert afternoon, but it's still hot.

Things look different here compared to the Sandia foothills. The ground is a soft white clay embedded with stream-rounded rocks and boulders, and everything is volcanic in origin—the soil from ash and pumice, the stone composed of dark basalt or brilliant orange tuff or pastel rhyolite or shiny black obsidian. The slopes are wooded with the same live oak and juniper and mahogany, but mostly other species of shrubs and cacti and yucca. The east-facing wall of Horn Mesa frowns overhead with shadowy caves and fissures and weird, unlikely pinnacles—columns of rock formed by erosion that are called hoodoos by rural westerners.

I shoulder my pack and head off. Only a few people have vehicular access to the washed-out, rutted, two-track route I now start up. My hike this afternoon is just a matter of following the old road up to the vicinity of Pines, a once-booming mining settlement but now ghost town about six miles up the creek. I carry only a quart of water. I'll draw more as I need it from the creek with my filtering device. The pack is much lighter but not just for that reason—the memory of the crushing burden I staggered under going up Sandia Mountain has also led me to replace some items with lighter gear and reduce the sheer volume to a bare minimum. Outfitted with a leaner, meaner cargo on my back, I'm amazed and gratified by the difference it makes. Hiking with unexpected ease along the roadway as it climbs gently back and forth into dry, eroded white pumice hills, I soon forget the pack is even there.

Once into sloping woodlands of piñon and juniper, the road swings toward the narrowing of Cochiti Canyon upstream. White pumice gravel gives way to light brown volcanic cobblestones. Gnats rise up to meet me in the cooling breeze. The blessed clouds grow darker overhead, and distant thunder rolls. The view is awesome back across the baking plains to far hazy mesas and black volcanic cones. I'm exhilarated to be off on the trail alone again, happy to admire the splendor of a new landscape, convinced there is nothing better than this wandering on foot over the earth.

Thunder continues to mutter in the north, over the high mountains. The grade is easy, even as the road approaches cliffs of a rich red-brown rock, narrowing to a dark chasm. Rocky crevices are crammed with a wrinkled pad cactus called "old man's whiskers," covered so densely with long, hair-thin white spines you can't really make out the succulent shapes underneath. I'm high above the tall pine forest that surrounds the orchard homestead in the canyon bottom below, tramping along an old, eroded road cut that I see heads for a gap in the wall ahead. Directly across on the west side of the canyon is a narrow neck of land, a tenuous connection between the lower and higher parts of Horn Mesa, where a faint trail switchbacks down shadowed pine woods to the creek below. It is the only easy access to the isolated, flat-topped potrero of lower Horn Mesa, which is about even with me across a vault of air swimming with darting swallows. I hear the sound of an orchard tractor working below, and then a clip-clop of hooves from farther up the road. Around a bend, a rider on horseback comes toward me.

Both are sweaty and covered with dust. Under a battered felt cowboy hat, the man's face is aged and wrinkled, but his eyes sparkle with intelligence and warmth as he reins up and shakes my hand without dismounting. A kindred spirit, I think. Another lover of the mountains, he rests in the creaking saddle exchanging pleasantries with me. His horse, a scarface Palomino with sleepy eyes, sniffs my backpack with a foamy muzzle. The man is Florentino Vigil, a retired forest ranger from Peña Blanca—a nearby Hispanic farming community—who has been riding since sunrise, he says, on trails he's known since he was a boy herding sheep in the mountains.

He looks off across at Horn Mesa—where I was looking when he rode up—and asks me if I know what happened up on top "in the old days, long ago."

I say I do.

After the initial colonization of New Mexico by the Spanish led by Juan de Oñate in 1598, an uneasy accommodation with the Pueblo Indian inhabitants grew more difficult to maintain. Religious persecution and the impossible requirements of feeding a growing population of outsiders eventually led to the Pueblo Revolt of 1680, which drove the Spanish out for twelve years. They returned in 1692 under Diego de Vargas, who used the tactics of playing one pueblo against another to achieve what some historians have called a relatively "peaceful reconquest." It was anything but. In 1693, military campaigns were directed against several pueblos that refused to submit, among them the people of Cochiti, many of whom had fled to the top of Horn Mesa. The Spanish attacked them in their town atop the mesa, and all the men captured were executed. The women and children were distributed as slaves. Today, 317 years later, the ruins of their homes on top are little more than crumbling rock walls and mounds of dirt littered with fragments of painted pottery. They had used that same trail I could see across the canyon to come down for jars of water and to farm corn and beans—where now is all apple orchard.

"That's right," Florentino says. "And my ancestors, the first Vigiles, came to New Mexico right about then. I don't know if they were conquistadores or not. But anyway, I think it is important to know your history. To face the facts. We all live in peace here now, even the Anglos."

With a tip of his hat, he rides off.

Two

I TRUDGE ON farther into the narrows of Cochiti Canyon a hundred feet up from lime-green box elder trees along the Rio Chiquito. The road passes through a tiny *puerto* or notch of lichen-encrusted boulders, and threads along inside a shadowy gorge. Canyon wrens sing from the cliffs overhead and a delicious breeze funnels coolly through. I'm sweating, of course. At the high point I see the canyon opens wider again upstream, and the road drops down into it. I stop and pick a handful of wax currants, dry and tasty red fruit also known as coyote berries. I can hear the rush of the creek below but cannot see it. Great rugged, pock-marked cliffs of dull volcanic rock in various shades of brown and pink rise up hundreds of feet on both sides. Unreachable caves and crevices and ledges abound.

Ponderosa pine forest fills the bottom of the canyon ahead. Deep shade beckons. Onward I stride to the distant sounds of echoing thunder, the chirping of crickets, the melancholy cooing of *tortolitas*, or mourning doves. I smell the scent of rain mingled with dust and dry chaparral. Let it storm all it wants! I've got everything I need on my sweaty back. The way drops down into a sweltering, still jungle of Gambel oak and box elder among the huge cinnamon-orange trunks of pines. I find a lava rock overhang beside the road where friends told me they sheltered from a pouring rainstorm a month earlier. Then I come to where the road crosses the stream, a wide pool of clear water that vehicles easily ford. I have to find a way across upstream to keep my feet dry, leaping on boulders like stepping stones across a tinkling brook. Here, under the deep shade of alder trees, I plod through damp stands of rank, green streamside vegetation—cow parsnip in stinky white bloom and poisonous water hemlock, an herb that many people mistake for the medicinal oshá, sometimes with fatal consequences, and which I soon discover grows along the banks of the creek all the way up.

The road turns sandy and easy, a stroll up a shady lane only gently going uphill beside a musical mountain stream. The ponderosa pines are truly enormous, towering high overhead. Great boulders have fallen from the heights and stand like houses back in the woods. The overall impression is like the hidden canyon bottoms of the Sierra Madre in Mexico, a mingling of forest and lush, subtropical riparian woodland walled in by desert-scrub mountainsides.

In the dampest, shadiest woods I also find spreading thickets of native wild ginseng, a rare and lovely slender shrub with robust leafy layers of foliage held up in the pallid light. Related to oshá and cow parsnip, *Aralia racemosa*, or "spikenard," as it's known in the herb trade (a name I find too hilarious to use myself), looks like a miniature ash tree at first, with long, sweeping compound leaves composed of many serrated leaflets as rounded and pointed as aspen leaves. But abloom with greenish-white flower umbels that smell spicy like ginseng, it can only be *Aralia*, a woody perennial whose fleshy, oily roots I've dug up and dried and used for their chemically active ability to relieve the worst chest-cold symptoms. An Indian herbalist I know once referred to it as "mountain Mucinex."

At the second stream crossing, a fresh breath of cool air flows over me. The hillside rocks still feel hot to the touch from before the clouds blocked the sun, and away from the creek, the humidity is as blistering as a sauna. I'm really hoping for rain.

More and more wild flowers appear alongside the road: scarlet penstemon and giant yellow coneflower, yarrow and gromwell, purple aster and wild geranium and yellow primrose. They are the flowers of the forest at much higher elevation than this, reaching down fingerlike into this deep, moist canyon.

At the third crossing, deep pools of cold water tempt me to soak my overheated body in relief, but I'm too close to the road to strip down. A car might come by, although none have so far. Only the wind high above and the sound of birds calling invisibly from dense undergrowth intrude on the perfection of the silence around me. I pass tall poison ivy bushes amid stalks of crimson parasitic pinedrops. The solitude is deceptive. On dry flats are old, sandy campsites with blackened fireplace rocks. Then a half mile of private land, with four old, weather-beaten summer homes set back from the road but nobody home.

Yet another crossing of the creek—a deep ford with fresh, wet tire tracks emerging—but the stream itself barely trickles to and from a still puddle with water striders poised on the limpid surface. I'm miles up the canyon and yet the creek seems to be drying up. The damp dirt banks are covered with leafless green horsetail stalks, the silica-rich plant picked and used by pioneers to scrub pots and pans. Looking forward to a spring I see marked on my map, where I plan to fill up on fresh water, I pass the mouth of Medio Dia Canyon on the left. The word *mediodía* means "noon" in Spanish, and Florentino Vigil, whose ride took him in a loop that came down this side canyon earlier today, told me why: "It is so steep and narrow the only time the sun shines down to the bottom is in the middle of the day!" Beyond, the main canyon narrows again, tan cliffs closing in like walls, but so straight I can still see for miles up it. The clouds thin, and the sound of thunder fades farther away. So, too, fades my hope for a cooling rain shower.

I pass great towers of rock to the left, capped with spire-like hoodoos, some of which have toppled in slabs down the slopes. The creek inexplicably starts running again, splashing noisily alongside the road. I finally locate a hidden pool to soak in, with tiny trout and mossy boulders, unseen from the road. A cloud of flies and gnats attacks me fiercely as I strip naked and stumble over slimy rocks to a basin of cold, clear water formed by a tiny waterfall. After the initial icy shock of going under, I'm in heaven, bobbing in roiled, silty ice water, gazing up through hovering hordes of mosquitoes at the green layers of leaves overhead. To one side is a tall, dark Douglas fir, the first I've seen. Climbing the bank numb and dripping, I hardly notice the insects. Refreshed and renewed, I dress, heave up my pack, and go on.

Another stream crossing. This one is the biggest ford pool yet—thirty feet long and a foot deep, with a log waterfall above it and another below it. Beneath a tall gallery forest of cottonwood and pine, the banks are hidden in willow brush. At a noisy place of foaming waters in deep shade—a good place for a mountain lion ambush—I jump warily across. A little farther on, at a quiet spot where I sit on a rock and rest, a Stellar jay floats down silently and lands on a dead branch a few feet away, looking me over without fear. It has a charcoal-black crested head and blue feathers covering a tough, crow-like scavenger's body. The jay's interest feels like a good sign, a denizen of the mountains checking out the newcomer laboring up into its world. It flies away just as noiselessly.

Along the road there's an enormous spreading Gambel oak unlike all the low brushy ones I've seen. Fifty feet high, it grows like a gnarled ancient tree of the English countryside, casting an impenetrable black shadow on the rocky ground. Around the next bend, I see the sheer canyon wall on the east side shoot up thousands of feet. The crevices and hanging gardens and fluted chimneys of pale-orange rock remind me of Zion Canyon in Utah. Hermit thrushes sing from high ledges where I see faces—the grotesque shapes of eroded hoodoos. I see a monkey face, a lizard face. One is like the profile of a man, a frozen human likeness so real my hackles stand up.

It feels lonely up here. I expected the road to be only lightly traveled, but the lack of anybody at all besides the horseman, don Florentino, seems improbable. The road curves around a narrow spot where the cliff comes down sheer and vertical to the bottom. I can see up cracks and ravines to high dry pour-offs and beyond—to the very top of the mesa where the trees are just tiny dots. No thunder has sounded for some time, and patches of blue sky begin to show. A cooling wind blows in swaying pines. The canyon widens into broad riparian woodland, and beside another old campsite I find a tall fir tree chopped down with an axe, the tip end of it also chopped off and missing. (Unfortunately a common sight in New Mexico forests, it is the incredibly wasteful way some people acquire their Christmas tree every year.) In a dank, swampy area I find the nameless spring hidden in thick brush, the surface of the water floating with parsley. After drinking my fill and topping off my jug, I discover ripe raspberries mixed in with stinging nettles where the ground is wet around the spring. Very carefully I pick and gobble down all I can find.

After lunch, the flies and gnats swarm my face. Hiking onward, I accidentally discover that if I hang my yellow bandana over the top of my hat and down the back of my head, the bugs leave me alone. It amazes me. In the spirit of objective scientific inquiry, I pull it off and see what happens. They instantly return to whining attack. I drape it back on and they vanish. My heat-fried brain struggles to grasp how this could be happening. Theorizing feebly (they are repelled by the color yellow or the flapping of loose cloth or the concentrated smell of my sweat) leads to nothing. Eventually I give up and simply enjoy the freedom it provides.

Fresh deer prints show at each muddy stream crossing. In the cooler air that flows down the canyon, I start to make good time. More wide, grassy meadows appear, surrounded by tall, stately ponderosa pine trees. The higher I go, the lower the walls on both sides become. Finally there's a long view up to the end of the canyon where a huge white "tent rock" formation sits, a smooth, rounded prow of solidified volcanic ash coming to a sharp point on top. It marks where the canyon forks, with Pines Canyon to the left and Spruce Canyon to the right. Before I see any sign of the ghost town, I come to a trail taking off abruptly to the right, my destination for the day. From the willows along the creek it heads steeply up a rocky bluff and disappears into open pine forest. And it has rained here, the sudden fresh smell of wet pine needles strong in the air.

Exhausted by hiking in the heat, I ease out from under my pack and check the map. I've ascended more than 1,000 feet to an elevation of around 7,300 feet, covering a distance of six miles in five or six hours (which is slow for me). The Rio Chiquito is still running, which is important because tomorrow I will have to fill both my jugs and climb six miles to the next water at Alamo Spring, elevation 8,800 feet. In fact, the stream here runs from one deep, clear pool to another, where I can see trout darting away from my approach.

After making camp and eating a cooked meal in the early evening light, I rest with my back to a pine tree in the deep silence. Idly throwing weightless pebbles of white pumice into the creek, I watch them float away like popcorn. I see an eagle lazily soaring in the updrafts, circling upward toward the high country. As it turns, glinting in the sunlight that still shines high above, it reveals the yellow sheen of a mature golden eagle, the bearer of Native prayers to the sky beings in this mountainous world.

Then a huge hawk perched in the top of a dead pine tree calls out with a long, piercing cry, repeated with measured gravity every minute or so. When I get up and stroll closer in the dwindling light, a rabbit darts across my path. Supper scared off, the hawk flaps up and away, still crying out shrilly. A big buteo, perhaps a redtail, it circles slowly upward on the same air currents the eagle followed, finally disappearing over the east rim—the way I'll be heading in the morning.

Three

A LATE START this morning. During the night I heard a car coming slowly up the road and saw headlights go by. After a drowsy breakfast (the previous day's hike remembered like a feverish dream from the hours of low-grade heat prostration I had to recover from), I see a blond guy in his thirties striding along the creek with a fishing pole. He seems anxious about something, distracted, but he's the first person I've seen up here so I greet him with a friendly "hey." He stops and talks to me, but his smile seems forced.

"You catch many fish in this creek?" I ask.

"Oh, yeah. Lots."

"What kind of trout are they?"

"Cutthroats, I think. None of them are very big. Just large minnows, really. But they sure taste good. I roast them on a stick over the fire."

"Do you live up here?"

He tries to answer but makes a face instead—a look at once pained and startled.

"Are you all right?"

He grimaces. "I just had an attack of diarrhea."

"No, really?"

"Yeah, it's all down my leg, inside my pants."

I suddenly smell it. He drops his pole and waddles uncomfortably toward the creek. Grateful that I've already drawn my water for today's hike, I see him disappear behind willow brush and hear him splashing in the stream. It's the only way he can clean up—I'd do the same thing. I feel sorry for the poor guy. Eventually he comes back, humiliated but relieved, a pitiful fellow human being with his jeans sopping wet, and picks up his fishing pole. I try to think of something to say to cheer him up, but I don't want to put him on the spot, make him feel worse than he already does. Fortunately he sees the humor of the situation.

As he slogs off wetly to resume fishing, he says with a snort, "Damn, now I'm gonna get a bad case of diaper rash."

Suddenly inspired, I call after him: "Hey, buddy. You got a permit for planting those brown trout in the creek?"

I hear his cackling laughter from the willow brush.

The hike out of Cochiti Canyon climbs steeply up switchbacks on a washed-out forest service trail deeply incised into soft, pale pumice bedrock between harder layers of pyroclastic rock forming vertical cliffs. Covered in dry oak brush and jack pine, the slope is rugged and the grade daunting in the hot sun. The back-and-forth under a heavy pack is backbreaking work. I see the faint track of a dirt bike that went up sometime before yesterday's rain. Higher up, the ground turns damp underfoot from what must have been heavier rain yesterday. As the long canyon bottom opens up below, the views are dramatic, encompassing more and more of the surrounding mesas and canyon walls the higher I go.

The trail swings around a brushy point and tops out on level ground, where it then turns into a delightful footpath over soft, sandy dirt across an open ponderosa pine flat. Turning inland, I cross grassy parklands dotted with bracken fern and head up a gently sloping valley. The canyon fades behind as I enter an upland world of silence and solitude. The motorcycle track turns back—only my own footprints show on the trail. I'm climbing into an area of remote and seldom-traveled side valleys and deep ravines that lead onto a fingerlike mesa of the Pajarito Plateau above, following a trail used for thousands of years by Indians hunting game animals. It has no name, just as the spring had no name, and the mesa on top has no name, which is possibly why so few pass this way. Obscurity is often the best protection for wild places. There's plenty of logging and mining and livestock grazing going on in the Jemez Mountains, but here I find myself entering an untouched open forest of giant old-growth pine and fir, crossing open flats with deep swales of tall, green grass, marveling at the pristine quality of a secret landscape I didn't know existed.

A lean-to stands beside an immense tree trunk, an old pole framework for a tarp or brush shelter, but with no sign of recent use. A striped chipmunk sits on a downed log chewing seeds, watching me go by. Half the log has been torn open by a bear, no doubt seeking tasty grubs and termites. (Yum!) Nearby is a rotten stump left in pieces. Fresh bear tracks in the soft dirt make me instantly more heedful of my surroundings.

The trail becomes an eroded groove a foot deep, climbing a gentle grade into a colonnaded pinery with nothing but wild flowers as ground cover. A single cloud floats over in an empty blue sky, and a breeze springs up under its shadow—blessed cooling on a hot day. I'm drinking lots of water to try and stay more hydrated than I was yesterday. I find a big owl feather on the trail, perhaps from the tail of a great horned, fluffy around alternating bands of brown and yellow, but don't pick it up. It feels like a bad omen, a warning of danger ahead, and sure enough, I soon see more fresh sign of a bear along the trail, and seemingly minutes-old clawed footprints heading the same direction I'm going. I become even more careful and aware.

At a saddle, a breezy opening atop a ridge where the trail drops down the other side, a sound of something big in the bushes slows my steps. A young bear, black as charcoal, jumps up with a startled huff and looks me over. I freeze for a moment, gradually start breathing again, and keep my eyes on it, staring back into beady brown eyes forty feet away. The bear clacks its teeth nervously, warning me. It seems reluctant to leave the shade of a white fir where I presume it was napping. My heart pounds furiously in my chest, but I don't move. After a few minutes of standoff, the bear ambles clumsily away, then breaks into a run downhill in great, loping muscular strides that are beautiful and terrible to see.

Once the sound of bear crashing through woods fades away in the distance, I breathe a sigh of relief. Then I go look where the beast first jumped up. All the dead trees on the ground have bark clawed off and pieces of wood torn out. My feeling of exploring an empty wilderness—empty of people anyway—is confirmed and heightened by the presence of the bear. And since it ran off into the next drainage ahead of me, there is a real possibility of encountering it again. I search around for something to use as a defensive weapon and find a stout dry branch that I can swing around like a club and whack on trees and bushes to warn the bear away.

After dropping to the bottom, the trail goes up another sloping valley with a flat floor, and into even heavier timber. A plant called skyrocket gilia grows on stalks as tall as I am and leans out over the sunlit trail, brushing my bare arms. Tiny, iridescent green hummingbirds dart about, nosing into the scarlet blossoms shaped like exploding firecrackers. Rolling hills hem in around the smooth sand path lined with chokecherry brush. So many wild flowers are in bloom—yellow black-eyed Susans, lavender bergamot, orchid-purple flower balls of Rocky Mountain bee plant—that honeybees fly everywhere and crowd in gangs on nodding flowertops, buzzing deliriously in the presence of so much nectar. Dozens of orange fritillary butterflies flutter amid the bees, competing for position at the feast.

I round a bend and look up over the tops of trees. A big reddish stone battlement juts out from the side of a forested mesa. To the right is a dip in the skyline, the point where the trail tops the mesa less than a mile away. Off to the left of the trail I see through the trunks of pine and fir a wide flat cove about a half acre in extent surrounded by eroded pumice hills, and in among the trees are tall tent rocks or hoodoos or mysterious narrow pillars hidden in the shade. I turn aside to investigate. I find four rock formations about twenty-five feet tall, shaped like flat wedges about five feet thick, and spaced evenly about thirty feet apart. From the side they are circular, sharp-edged, and made of some kind of brownish rock I don't recognize. It feels weird seeing them standing parallel to each other in a row as if sprung up from the thick duff and pine needles. They look like flying saucers that crash-landed in formation, all four tipped on end, half buried in the ground, where they have been decaying as the forest grew up around them. Or like the huge, eroded dinner plates of an ancient giant stacked in a dish strainer of tree trunks.

Spooked by something so unlikely, I feel alone and exposed in a place that seems haunted, like an abode of malign spirits, and back away. Get the hell out of there.

Relieved to clamber through forest over a low ridge back to the trail, I'm startled by a big black hawk shooting through the trees at eye level. I recognize it as a rarely sighted northern goshawk, a large accipiter that hunts secretively in the high forest. Hearing the sound of a squirrel chattering in alarm, I forge ahead excitedly to see what's going on. At a sharp turn in the trail, about four feet up a fir tree, I see the hawk diving at a red squirrel that is frantically trying to keep the trunk of the tree between them. Around and around they go, the squirrel leaping from limb to limb in a race for its life and the goshawk swooping and darting in relentless acrobatic attack. I'm surprised each time the hooked beak of the hawk barely misses. Suddenly aware of my presence, the hawk gives up its meal and flies away silently through the forest. I pass the tree and see the reddish squirrel perched on a high limb, stunned and panting.

Up over the next dry saddle, I drop down into a deep damp ravine where the trail winds like a sandy arroyo under the shade of whispering aspens and steamy thickets of Rocky Mountain maple brush. With clouds closing in overhead, the morning is turning oppressively hot and humid. The shade, at least, is cooling, and the dirt banks on each side of the narrow pathway, in places waist high, are still moist from yesterday's rain. Deadfall trees block the trail; the way through becomes more difficult.

I hear a sudden commotion ahead in the thick brush, but it's not the bear. A family of mule deer who have been resting in deep shade bolt up and leap away, crashing through the underbrush in all directions. None have antlers, most are yearlings and fawns, and all have smooth, reddish short-haired summer coats. One, an old doe with patches of bare skin showing—the matriarch—doesn't run. She stands stock-still, staring at me as I hike slowly by on the trail fifteen feet away. She's like a statue—only her eyes move, tracking me. Maybe it's too hot or she thinks I don't see her. Either way, it's not the usual way deer act. Then I see other, younger deer standing frozen on the hillsides like lawn statues, all of them staring at me. It's comical. And it confirms my suspicion that few people ever pass this way. It's like a wild animal sanctuary, and makes me wonder what I'll see next.

Farther on, I hear a Stellar jay calling from up ahead and pay attention. Jays often announce the presence of large animals. But nothing's moving in the brutal heat. Only me, the two-legged one, disturbing the midday rest of wild creatures. The ravine I'm hiking up turns rocky with dull, dark, clunky basalt. Wolfberry, a plant that looks like the pyracantha used in Southwest landscaping and loves rocky places, lines the trail with thorny reddish stalks. The grade grows even steeper. The forest trees are all white fir, and many have fallen across the trail.

Then all at once it starts to rain. No lightning or thunder from the dark overcast, just a wonderful shower that instantly refreshes me and fills me with joy. As it slows to a steady sprinkle, I feel a surge of strength and pick up speed, smelling the cool misty air scented with mountain conifers. The trail climbs over successive exposed layers of different kinds of volcanic bedrock, some yellow, some maroon, and some creamy gray with embedded dots of glossy black obsidian. Some of these have eroded out and lie along the trail like gemstones—what rock hounds call Apache tears.

I come to a place where huge trees have blown down across the ravine in a windstorm. Somebody using a chainsaw has cut a way through the lowest dead logs. In the sawed end of one, the woodcutter used the tip of the chain bar to carve the letters "AL." I'm quietly thanking Al for all his good work when I suddenly freeze at the sound of something breaking and clattering farther up the trail.

After waiting and hearing nothing more, I creep forward, scanning the wet woods ahead. Eventually I see it: the same black bear is twenty feet up a dead snag, precariously holding on and using shiny black claws to peel away a strip of thick bark with a sound like a ripping gunshot. I can hear the animal's snuffling breaths as it licks up tasty grubs. I watch, motionless and enthralled, in the light rain. Apparently catching scent of me, the bear suddenly rockets down the tree trunk, wiggling through springy maple branches that douse it in a spray of water droplets. I get glimpses of it—young and powerful, yet weighing more than I do—running wildly up the ravine.

I follow the trail carefully as it skirts above on the left side of the ravine. When I hear the bear panting, far uphill on the opposite side, I bang my club repeatedly on dead logs and tree trunks to keep scaring it off. The bear's direction of flight is away from where the trail leads, so I figure that's the last I'll see of it.

Silence returns and the rain stops. The trail crosses one last wet ravine and starts up steeply toward the top. Bare bedrock is exposed like rubble cemented into the matrix of an ancient ash flow. The slopes become greener—grassy openings between groves of aspen swaying and swishing in the wind. I pass through a towering forest where no fire has disturbed the growth of giant fir trees in centuries. The trail rut grows deeper, in some places a waist-deep, V-shaped channel with difficult footing that slows me down under my heavy pack. Huge boulders stand off alone in the trees. A rock squirrel dashes across ahead of me. In a white cutbank I discover a glossy black boulder of pure obsidian, a foot in diameter, bulging from the friable tuff. A little farther on, I am treated to a rare sight: a dark red cinquefoil flower beaded with silvery raindrops.

No more bear, just as I thought, but I hang on to the pine club anyway. Sweating heavily in an uprush of hot dry air from the lowlands, I plod onward through oak brush where dead damp leaves are inches thick underfoot. The reddish rock battlement appears just above me, an ancient lava flow with fissured cliffs and shaded overhangs. The trail angles up through a break in the barrier, and I see I'm almost to the top of the mesa. The last switchbacks wind up through pastel boulders and dense Douglas fir forest. Pieces of black obsidian are scattered on the ground all the way up.

All at once I emerge onto a dirt road on the flat top of the nameless mesa, blinking in the breezy dazzling sunlight. I made it—the steepest part of the day's hike is over. According to my map, this is St. Peter's Dome Road and I've reached 8,300 feet. The trail continues on across a narrow neck of mesa before dropping down into Capulin Canyon beyond. And here the mesa-top forest has been logged and burned—dead black snags stand up from brushy young aspen trees fluttering in the wind. Everywhere I look on the ground I find hand-worked pieces of black obsidian—the same "flint" that gave Chicoma (Flint-Covered Mountain) its name. I know I'm at the site of an ancient campground used by Indian hunters and flint gatherers, but decide I'll investigate things more closely after a rest and something to eat.

Four

PERHAPS THE SINGLE most important resource for the Native people of the Southwest, before metal tools were introduced by Europeans, was a material that could be shaped easily into a sharp, durable blade. With it, they could bring down game animals, cut up carcasses, skin and scrape hides, chop wood, and use it in a hundred other ways necessary for a good life out in nature that we can scarcely imagine today. Even at the height of agricultural production, the Pueblo Indian people depended on deer and elk as critical sources of protein and raw material. No other stone quite fit the bill as serviceably as several smooth, glassy kinds of rock known collectively as flint, or *pedernal* in Spanish.

The name "flint" in English originally pertained to only one variety: a very hard, fine-grained quartz that sparked when struck with steel. Over time, it came to designate any similar lithic resource used by Native peoples in the Americas, whether actual flint in various shades of white, gray, and tan; or the translucent milky cherts and chalcedonies; or, most well-known in the Southwest, obsidian.

All were used to make arrowheads, spear points, knives, choppers, and scrapers, but high-grade obsidian was the best. Found in deposits of nonexplosive viscous lava that oozed across the land, obsidian is rapidly cooled, silica-rich, volcanic glass that has formed large glossy boulders in the Jemez Mountains, many of which can be seen in highway cuts. When fractured, say by a heavy chunk of basalt (with eyes covered by safety glasses—I once just squinted trying this and got a splinter embedded in my eyelashes a millimeter from my eyeball), it shatters into curved shards with lustrous shiny surfaces. These shards are the raw material of ancient tool kits. Usually jet black in color, workable obsidian also can be banded, brown, smoky, amber, dark red, and in rare cases, even green. Flint knapping, an arduous process using the tip of an antler to scour along the face of the stone, removing thin flakes to shape and sharpen a piece into a useful tool, is actually most easily and productively accomplished with obsidian.

So prized was this rock it was traded vast distances and came to be a valuable commodity for those who lived near the deposits (like the Tewa) long before similar trade developed for turquoise, coral, and shell. At various sites in the Jemez Mountains are the remains of prime locations where excellent black obsidian was acquired and worked in huge quantities. I had arrived at one of them—here on the old hunting trail above Los Utes Spring in Capulin Canyon and on nearby Obsidian Ridge, beyond the canyon, the ground is littered for miles with chips of black glass.

After lunch and a nap I wander around looking at everything. Emerging from aspen woods onto the road, I see a young fearless coyote staring at me from the trees on the other side. Without betraying any surprise, the critter peers around at other things as if indifferent to my sudden appearance, and then slowly trots off to the right in plain sight up the road. The lack of concern it shows in my presence seems odd. But coyotes are tricky, so I stay alert.

Up on a high mesa now, I can see for miles in every direction. The world of ancient flint knappers is high, wide, and handsome. I walk out a ways on the Los Utes Spring Trail, munching trail mix and sipping a bottle of water. Despite the stumps and fire-blackened snags, the young aspens and wild flowers and tall green grass make the place seem lush. And on one short section of trail I find ten pieces of worked flint, each with sharpened edges, but nicked and dulled in spots like cast-off skin scrapers. I decide to keep one the size of my little finger. Toying with the idea of hiking down for a water fill-up, I go as far as the rim of Capulin Canyon, but one look down at how deep and entirely burned out it is makes me turn back. I'm sure I have enough water to make it to Alamo Spring anyway, only another four miles up the mesa. As if in confirmation of my decision, on the way back to my pack I find a beautiful, black obsidian arrowhead, a long, slender, delicately worked piece with a perfect sharp tip. I keep that, too. When I look up, I find myself gazing into the yellow, slanting, predatory eyes of the same coyote behind a nearby stump. Before I can react, it melts away into the aspens. No other animal in the wilds is as unpredictable as a coyote.

Lifting my pack, I head north up St. Peter's Dome Road, which is much easier than a narrow foot trail, and just like the road up Cochiti Canyon, nobody is up here but me. As the road climbs more steeply around broad lava-rock hills, there is nothing but wind and silence and awesome views. I look back and see St. Peter's Dome itself, a dark and rounded extinct volcano floating out beyond the ends of mesas.

From here on up I'm following a long narrow mesa between two deep canyons (Cochiti on the left and Capulin on the right) until it meets other long parallel mesas of the Pajarito Plateau in a vast forested apron at the base of the Sierra de los Valles, a row of rounded conical peaks ahead that form the rim of Valles Caldera. Looking toward the eastern or western horizon is the same—long sloping mesa tops alternating with dark steep-walled canyons. Westward, beyond Cochiti Canyon, I see Medio Dia, Bland, and Colle canyons. Eastward beyond Capulin are the deep chasms of Alamo and Frijoles canyons, the main attractions of Bandelier National Monument, today probably swarming with hundreds of tourists and hikers.

The road levels off and goes only slightly uphill for miles. I march along at a fast clip. Except for a few turns and dips, the roadway is an endless dusty straightaway, the hike a boring unchanging chug along to the tune of various melodies that float through my mind. I'm still amazed and pleased how that morning's hike had been like a tour through a secret wild-animal park, the encounters with a foraging bear, a goshawk attacking a squirrel, a herd of tame deer, and a curious coyote like a zoological showcase of what is normally going on in nature only behind our backs. It makes it all worth what I see along the road, a ponderosa pine and Douglas fir forest essentially destroyed by logging and wildfires. Small wooded areas remain, mainly second-growth jack pine, but the mesa is mostly clearcut stumplands and vast burned areas that are coming back to life with low thickets of aspen and locust. Logging skid roads take off in all directions. In damp spots, white fir grows thick and the roadside is covered with raspberry bushes. Unfortunately, the new berries are pink, not quite ripe at this higher elevation. A big, gray tassel-eared squirrel with a white bushy tail runs across the road ahead of me. I see others perched on stumps, dining on pinecones, each with oversized, tufted rodent ears, intently watching me pass by. The forested mountains loom closer.

In record time I cover almost four miles and the road dips down toward the meadows of Graduation Flat. The hike has been a satisfying waste of an afternoon, and I quickly find myself in something like civilization. Dozens of parked cars line the road ahead, tents and campers fill the woods, and people mill around everywhere, talking. I've arrived at a group-permit camping site, a park-like area of tall conifers and lush green grasslands dotted with wild flowers at about 9,000 feet. As I plod by, I notice everyone is dressed in costumes—either medieval or Renaissance garb—even the children. I've stumbled upon the annual Lonely Mountain campout of the Society for Creative Anachronism on the day before a weekend of competitive events and exhibits and socializing. I actually knew about this and planned to be here.

I see someone I know and greet a tall, husky, bearded young man with red-blond Viking hair curling down his back. He wears a chain mail garment over his torso, leather shorts (it's very hot), and carries a hefty steel broadsword. I apologize, confessing I can't remember his Society name.

"All hail Cyrin of Erlinstar!" his two friends shout in unison. Beer slops from the aluminum cans held high in their hands. They introduce their little pug dog, Reggie, as well, who stands bug-eyed in the shade, panting.

Cyrin is also my son, Cameron, so we hug and stand chatting about our recent adventures. I show him the sharp worked pieces of black obsidian I found. He holds the skin scraper up to the light.

"Hmm, not razor sharp, but we could still use it to skin Reggie," he says with a droll wink. "Poor doggie's so hot—maybe he'd feel cooler that way!"

Reggie's master draws his own sword, but before he can call out a challenge, Cameron (oops—I mean Cyrin) says, "No, no. Reggie's too cute to mess with."

Later I head down a spur road almost impassable to vehicles in my search for Alamo Spring. The track follows a damp, sloping meadow surrounded by a heavy forest of spruce, fir, pine, and aspen. At the locked gate where the trail to Obsidian Ridge continues on across Sawyer Mesa, I hunt around for the spring. The map I'm using is no help. There are beautiful empty campsites and a broad swampy area with tall spruce trees around it, but no more than a few puddles of milky-looking water. Not a good sign.

I had purposely inquired about this spring so I know it has to be here somewhere. It sits in the very headwaters of Alamo Canyon, a deep twelve-mile-long gorge through Bandelier that opens up only at White Rock Canyon on the Rio Grande. Studying the landscape, I see that the soggy vega becomes narrow as it curves around a point and drops down a ravine. Following it downhill in brilliant afternoon sunshine, I realize it is the very beginning of Alamo Canyon. Yellow butterflies flutter around tall golden coneflowers. A vulture circles overhead, rocking on a breath of hot wind in a blue sky with white puffball clouds. I make my way over smooth, rounded lava boulders to a little drop-off, and voilà! The vulture's hope is foiled, for immediately below is a deep pool and tiny tinkling waterfall. Hidden in giant rocks, the spring pours forth fully formed, and from the pool a stream races noisily down into a dark forested chasm.

Despite the concentrated mosquito larvae and other miscellaneous organics, the water is good and cold and tastes delicious after being pumped through my filter into bottles. Refreshed and at ease after a long day's hike, I sit among the dense wild flowers crowding around the spring, which are crawling with bees and insects. Securing and drinking my own water while journeying on foot over the land has become an ever-present preoccupation. Having it on hand, thinking about it—how much is left, when it will run out, where I might find more—all these work out to a moment like this when swallowing gulps of fresh new water is a wondrous peak experience.

In the evening, after a meal, I stroll up the track for a visit at the group camp. Along the way I meet my Indian friend, Scott Thomas, walking down. He's been up in the mountains gathering sweat-lodge rocks and decided to stop in and look for me. He parked his car at the group campground and has been walking out various spur roads, certain he could find me. We laugh at our sudden meeting, and continue on.

Just over a rise in cool, still spruce forest, we sniff campfire smoke wafting from the campground ahead. It carries the scent of cooking food.

"Wow, that smell really takes you back, doesn't it?" Scott says.

I nod in agreement. "Yeah, there's just something about it."

"That smell is probably in our DNA, don't you think?"

"Huh, you're probably right."

We decide that a hundred thousand years of humans cooking food over open fires has rendered differences of race and ethnicity relatively inconsequential in comparison. Ten thousand years ago we all lived in the Stone Age. We all have the gene marker that wakes up and says, "Hey! Food being cooked ahead!"

Even though we can't find my son's camp, we cover a lot of ground, talking and laughing about various subjects. Scott, a famously effective psychotherapist with a private practice in Santa Fe, has a devastating sense of humor that keeps me laughing. We find other campers in the area who are not in costume, or at least not in anachronistic garb. We walk behind a teenage boy with baggy jeans slung so low, we see daylight showing between them and the crotch of his underwear. He walks as bowlegged as an old cowboy to keep his jeans from falling down. We laugh so hard we have to stop and catch our breath.

Since I'd brought along a bag of marshmallows to surprise the children where my son camps, we stop in and offer them to another camping family. The parents approve, but unfortunately the marshmallows, congealed by heat in my backpack, have been compressed into a single hard foam ball that has to be sawed into pieces with a knife. The boy and girl toasting these over the campfire decide to call this new treat "foam squares on a stick."

After so much laughter—the magic bullet of long life—I wave good-bye to Scott heading back in his car to Santa Fe, and walk back in the dark to my camp by the spring. The sky is empty of clouds. Stars glitter with a high-altitude brilliance above the black, velvety spires of conifers. I make out the major northern constellations easily—the Big Dipper, Cassiopeia, Draco, Boötes. At my tent, an owl hoots a few times, and then a dark form flies across the stars overhead. In the silence of night in the mountains, I turn in and sleep soundly.

Five

DAY THREE IN the Jemez Mountains dawns clear, breezy, and warm. My wife Theresa joins me for the day's hike, a short four-mile route to the top of Cerro Grande, located at 10,200 feet on the high edge of the caldera. But first she surprises me with a breakfast of bacon and eggs, buttered toast, and fresh white peaches from a roadside vendor.

Our first destination is an overlook on the rim of Frijoles Canyon, and it's a pleasure to hike with someone else again, sharing the discovery of a new country with someone special. The trail is easy to follow as it loops through logged forest over rolling flatlands, the birds singing cheerfully in the morning sun. Theresa, a busy, talented social worker with a heavy case load, seems delighted to be off in the hills with me. Her long dark hair in a French braid under a white baseball cap, she wears a black Arizona Jean Company tee shirt, cargo pants, and trail runners.

At our first rest stop, I show her a mock orange bush in full, white, delicate blossom and tell her the flowers smell particularly good. She sniffs them.

"Oh, my goodness!" she says. "It smells awesome!"

She sees me writing in my journal and asks what I just wrote. I say, as if reading aloud, "Her ample behind was squeezed into cargo pants."

Squealing in sudden fury, she slugs my arm. "You scratch that out, right now!"

Laughing, I show her I didn't really write that.

The air carries a sweet high-mountain forest scent after yesterday's rain. Our hike is like a stroll in a lovely wooded national park—except for the rotting stumps everywhere. We're inside Bandelier National Monument now, the part purchased in 1977 from the Baca Land and Cattle Company, owners of the Valles Caldera before it was turned into a national preserve. Dry, open, second-growth pine forest and green carpets of kinnikinnick line the path out to the overlook.

We arrive at a volcanic rock rim at the edge of a deep wooded gorge. Theresa takes photos as we make our way out atop a narrow peninsula of bedrock and gaze down into the green depths of upper Frijoles Canyon. The wind blows, singing through the twisted branches of tough old limber pines along the edge. In the distance, southward, I can just make out the faint blue outline of the Sandias beyond the long sloping line of mesas I came up. About a mile off to the east is the road cut of New Mexico 4, the only paved highway through the Jemez Mountains. We can see but not hear the cars going by. We'll get to it and cross it in another mile or so.

Back on the trail, close to noon, the sun glowering down on us, we cross more flats and pass day hikers heading down to the overlook. In logged clearings we find low, spreading thickets of common juniper, a cedar-scented circumpolar species also found in the mountains of Europe and Russia. Tiny sky-blue berries, which are used to flavor gin, cluster thickly on the prickly twigs. The pale trunks of aspen trees have been recently clawed by a bear, and old punky stumps have been torn apart. I tell Theresa about the bear I bumped into twice yesterday, and she looks around excitedly, hoping to spot this one. We find huge yellow fungi growing in the earth—not a mushroom but some kind of foliose growth—and it, too, has been clawed up and tossed around by the bear. I sniff a broken chunk of it, a piece a foot thick, and it smells like raw fish!

Chipmunks run about everywhere. Mountain chickadees, flocks of tiny seed-eating birds that remain in the mountains all winter, cry out urgently from high in the trees. We watch another flock arrive, brilliant yellow birds flitting through aspen branches, and wonder what they are. I finally see one closer up, eating bugs, smaller than a robin, a butter-yellow bird with a scarlet head and black-and-white barring on the wings. I realize it is a male western tanager, one of the most colorful of the neotropicals—forest birds from tropical America that visit the Southwest mountains only in high summer.

We cross grassy green meadows with nodding lavender harebells. In view of the busy highway with cars zooming past there are giant, solitary white firs and other old-growth trees. It's the same scam used by logging companies (and the national forests) all over the West—they leave a row of big trees uncut on both sides of a well-used highway so travelers don't notice the miles of logged forest beyond.

At the trailhead we read a billboard sign the National Park Service has put up facing the highway. It announces that this is "Bandelier's Backcountry" and quotes the 1964 Wilderness Act, the part that defines wilderness as "untrammelled by man, where man himself is a visitor." We've been following trails through that same backcountry routed along overgrown logging skid roads through second-growth forest and thousands of giant sawed stumps. The message on the billboard makes me laugh in scorn.

"I think it's been a little trammelled by man," I say to Theresa.

After crossing the highway, we sit in the shade and have lunch near the parking area for day hikes to the top of Cerro Grande, our next destination. Two middle-aged men in shorts and fanny packs return down the trail, talking loudly. One unlocks a new blue Subaru while politely assuring the other, "There are very user-friendly training programs available—there's no reason you can't go online to pay your bills and buy the things you need." I don't know if they're hard of hearing or what, but their voices boom across to where we sit eating.

Over the roof of the hot car with doors open, the other guy responds: "It's not that I can't figure out how to use the computer. It's that it's *boring*!"

"Boring? How could it be boring?"

The guy shrugs. "It just doesn't interest me." He waves his hand around at the surrounding forest. "*This* is what holds my interest. The *real* world."

"Well, computers are a part of the real world, now."

"Yeah, like staring all day at your TV screen is being in the real world!"

The doors slam shut and the Subaru zooms away toward Los Alamos.

"Yes, what's wrong with us, Theresa?" I say with an anxious look. "What are we doing up here? Sniffing flowers, for God's sake! Why aren't we living in the real world?"

Theresa laughs and throws food at me.

Cerro Grande means "Big Mountain" in Spanish, and of all the peaks in the Sierra de los Valles, it looks the most like its name. Nearby Pajarito Mountain, for example, comes from Pajarito Canyon, which comes from a common local Tewa Indian surname meaning "little bird." Rabbit Mountain does not look like a rabbit, but does have two side-by-side summits that could, conceivably, be visualized as chopped-off rabbit's ears. Scooter Peak was probably named after somebody named Scott.

From the highway, Cerro Grande is just a big mountain off to the north with a bald summit, a hike of a mile and a half up a relatively new trail neither of us has hiked before. I once bushwhacked through this area like a greenhorn twenty years ago, but nothing looks familiar. And although the afternoon is hot, a cool wind blows and clouds form overhead for a possible monsoon shower later.

We take off across undulating green meadows broken by groves of trees where the tracks and scats of elk are everywhere. The first signs of the devastating Cerro Grande Fire appear—burned-out areas of bare mineral earth scattered with bits of charcoal. In the distance are vast acreages of missing forest, nothing but barren hillsides dotted with black snags, some covered in young green aspens and locust that have sprung up in the ten years since. The upper slopes of the mountain are untouched by the fire. I presume they named it for Cerro Grande because it started here on May 10, 2000. When old slash piles from the logging days were being burned under the supervision of crews from Bandelier National Monument, unexpectedly high winds drove the flames out of control. It became a "running crown fire" that swept north and east, burning through the upper parts of the National Laboratory and the city of Los Alamos. Blazing onward across the entire east face of the Jemez Mountains until it ran out of forest thirty miles from its start, it destroyed 235 homes and forced the evacuation of 18,000 residents. My wife and I saw the giant smoke cloud from the fire while driving home from a trip to Colorado.

Today, groups of noisy hikers come down the trail, having reached the summit before noon, and pass by, warning us the route is very steep. It appears to be a popular and convivial trail. Then it turns and abruptly shoots up a hill through ponderosa pine forest. Every tree trunk is burned black at the bottom, but all the trees are still living. We pass through more burned slopes and see charred black snags with ragged holes burned through like windows. The only green things here are dense stands of bracken fern, waist high, which we wade through.

Once over the top of a boulder-strewn ridge, the trail turns up an old logging road through a mosaic of alternating vegetation microzones left after they cut down all the big spruces and firs. Open grassy areas are thick with nodding wild flowers. Young aspen saplings flutter in the wind. Shaded groves of young spruce and corkbark fir close in with mossy silence. At an open ledge we look up and see the bald, grassy summit of the mountain still alarmingly high above us.

Then the trail simply heads straight up the mountain. Our steps slow to a mindless plod, both of us wheezing in the ninety-degree heat and thin air of 9,000 feet. The clouds have disappeared. Maybe it won't rain after all. We stop in the shade of trees to pant and recover. At least we're only carrying day packs—and the heavy gurgling weight of liquid is going down our throats fast. Nearing the saddle between Cerro Grande and a smaller summit, we pass through a hissing grassland of shoulder-high mountain fescue. I emerge with hundreds of flaxseed-shaped hulls stuck to my bare sweaty arms.

Panting, dazed, in view of the open sunny meadow at the saddle, I lean one arm against a fir tree, head hanging. Theresa passes by with a smirk.

"You holding that tree up, hombre?"

She rushes out onto the flat, passing her hands over tall flower blossoms. When I don't emerge from the shade, she starts to come back with a look of concern. I wave her off, and do my best to totter after her. When I catch up, she stops to rest and have another drink.

"This is what I get for choosing an older man," she says wryly. A decade younger, she is usually left in the dust by my mountain-man pace. This is her way of gently taunting me when the tables are turned.

Quoting a New Mexico dicho, I reply: "*Mejor adorada de viejo que esclava de joven* (Better an old man's beloved than a young man's slave)."

She lets out a quick laugh. "That means nothing if I have to carry you back down this mountain over my shoulder!"

We banter to keep our spirits up. We can see the trail now turns right and yet again goes straight up the bare mountainside another five hundred feet. It was not designed to contour up the mountain like actually constructed trails but is only a route marked by reflectors nailed to trees and posts. The foot trail we follow has developed from the heavy use of hikers. If we had known beforehand, I would have sought out a more gently ascending route that bushwhacked around the easier eastern slope. Too late now.

A wall of dark timber blocks the view into the caldera ahead. Starting up the last killer ascent, step by panting step, we soon see out across it. It resembles the giant basin of Crater Lake in Oregon, but instead of water (the lake drained out millennia ago) we see a seemingly endless bowl-like prairie. This is the Valle Grande, or "Big Valley"—the most celebrated portion of the caldera floor from which dark, forested sugar-loaf mountains stand up like islands in a sea of grass. There are other *valles* (valleys) but none are even close to being as large as this one beside Big Mountain. We drink in the vastness and go on.

Halfway up we meet an older couple descending from the summit, each wearing brand-new hiking boots. The white-haired gentleman announces to nobody in particular that they are exactly eleven minutes down from the top.

"What's that going up?" I call out to him in exasperation. "Half an hour?"

He and his wife laugh and stop to talk. The slope is so steep we all stand with one knee cocked, propped precariously on a hot mountainside on the rim of Valles Caldera. They are voluble and eccentric retirees from Colorado who interrupt each other with familiar ease, telling us anecdotes about their recent travels in New Mexico.

We forge on. The heat is stupefying. A peregrine falcon shoots off the mountain above and banks sharply over our heads, the sudden stress on its wings producing a startling booming sound. Nearing the top, the tall grass is mixed with blooming blue lupine and white seafoam, a shrub named for sprays of tiny flowers that look like cresting surf. At each solitary Douglas fir tree, we rest in the circle of shade. We agree we're lucky there's no lightning this afternoon, exposed as we are on a grassy bedrock height with only stunted trees around the fringes.

At last we make it to the rounded peak. At a small flat area ahead is a tall cairn of lava rocks where two men are taking photos. We hang back, looking at the view from the top of the world. To the east, blocked until now, we can see far across the Rio Grande Valley to the long marching wall of mountains behind Santa Fe. To the west, beyond the airliner view of the caldera, we see the high plateau wilderness called San Pedro Parks, and beyond that, the Navajo desert lands on the horizon. Tall trees on the north block any view of Chicoma Mountain. We talk to the two men as they leave, the younger recently hired at the Lab in Los Alamos, the older his father from Illinois who has never been to New Mexico before. This is their first hike in New Mexico and they are delighted at our willingness to identify the landmarks in the distance. When they head down, we have the summit of Cerro Grande to ourselves.

It is still unbearably, gaspingly hot, even at 10,200 feet. (We learned later that the high temperature recorded that day in Santa Fe, ninety-seven degrees, was a new record.) The sun blazes down on us without any wind. We start jiving back and forth at each other like light-headed idiots:

"This ain't *that* bad!"

"*This* ain't that *bad*!"

"This *ain't* that bad!"

We find some shade, slump down in grass and wild flowers, guzzle down liquid. After energy bars, apples, oranges, and trail mix, we laze about like stunned livestock. It's too hot to even think clearly. We hear the shrill cry of a hawk hidden in spruce trees, repeated every minute or so. Ravens float over, cawing.

I begin to recover and amble around in the cooling shade of a single cloud blocking the sun. As Theresa naps, I grab binoculars and study the floor of the Valle Grande—where I will be going next on my pilgrim trek, across the bottom of the caldera to the north rim dimly visible to the northwest. I see herds of cattle and meandering creeks. I examine the round wooded mountains, which are the remains of "resurgent domes" that built up in the floor of the giant crater after the volcano blew and sank millions of years ago. All of them, including the largest, Redondo Peak, are spiraled with old logging roads.

Clouds form over the caldera, turning black. Shafts of sunlight dapple the grass-green floor of the Valle Grande with spots of cadmium-yellow brilliance. Theresa joins me on a ramble northward, a side trip along the ridge toward Valle Pass to see if we can get a view of Chicoma, but it turns out to be a fruitless quest. Solid, dark spruce forest closes in completely. We follow elk trails with fresh tracks and droppings to a little glade, a small, open grazing area. A spruce sapling has been mangled by a bull elk rubbing velvet off its antlers. We hear the rhythmic, sharp, lonely whistle of a solitaire, a tiny bird hidden in the conifers.

Turning back, we cut east around the base of the summit and find a great open bald, a moist grassland with a scattering of delicate mariposa lilies. Each flower cup is a brilliant magenta hue with a greenish-yellow center inside. Theresa, ecstatic to find a rare and amazing flower she's never seen before, takes dozens of closeup shots with her camera. Working around the shoulder of mountain toward the trail down, we discover a few more mariposas, after which they simply disappear. We hear what sounds like the same hawk whistling from the top of a lone sentinel spruce tree out in the open, but it turns out to be a Stellar jay—quite the skilled mimic!

At the trail, I sit and sketch the panorama southward into my journal—a very unusual view of the Jemez looking down the spine of the Sierra de los Valles. The great cauldron to the right boils with dark clouds, and to the left, long fingerlike mesas stretch down to the Rio Grande in brilliant sunshine. As clouds thicken overhead, I realize it's getting late. Theresa is far below, taking pictures of the caldera floor where gorgeous golden glow spots shine under a black lid. I head downhill and almost immediately bump into a mama grouse and her flock of flightless, pigeon-sized young, scratching for seeds and bugs in the grass. She flies up to a nearby aspen, clucking and cooing to her scattered brood. By her heavy gallinaceous body, dark mottled brown plumage, and black tail with a terminal gray band, I identify her as a blue grouse, *Dendrogapus obscurus*, the *gallina* (or mountain chicken) in local Spanish. I'm fascinated to see her call her family back together, fly down, and resume foraging as if I'm not even there.

Theresa shouts for me to catch up. It's 6:30 and the light is fading.

On the steep wooded trail down from the saddle, she finds a perfect black raven feather and attaches it straight up at the back of her head, in her French braid, a simple act that pleases her even amid clouds of whining mosquitoes. I find a fir branch to carry like a club. Mountain lions start their evening prowl when the light gets dim like this. Theresa raises her eyebrows.

"It's a lion beater," I say. "You never know."

Pure bravado, of course, but she stays close to me as we cut through deep timber. We've discussed the recent lion attacks on people in the West—how the smallest person in a group is usually the one who gets attacked. Theresa is a head shorter than me, and as we approach a dark tunnel of oak brush, I stop and suggest she go through first, ahead of me, as lion bait. She is not amused.

Descending into the silent gloom of lowland woods, I bang the club on dead trees. We come upon long, green, pitchy pinecones strewn on the trail—some a half foot long, two inches thick, and weighing a pound. Examining the stems, we see a squirrel has gnawed through them and dropped them from the branches of a limber pine since we hiked up.

We barely arrive back at the trailhead at dusk when it starts to rain. There is no lightning, no thunder, just a steady refreshing shower that makes all our sweaty effort worth it. Right at the gate of the rail fence at the highway, with a thin mist falling, we come upon three young male tourists in stylish city clothes—visitors from Mumbai, India—doing a rain dance. They haven't hiked the trail, merely jumped out of their car to take photos of each other with arms draped around the trail sign as if they had. Their shrieking impudence somehow pisses me off, but when they politely ask me to take their camera and shoot a picture of them all together, I meekly submit.

(What has been lost: One year later, while I was still writing this book, the Las Conchas Fire, the largest wildfire in northern New Mexico history, devastated large parts of the Jemez Mountains. The country I passed through from Dixon's Apple Orchard to the top of Cerro Grande no longer exists as I described it. Hardly a tree has survived.)

Six

WHEN I FIRST studied maps to plan my trail across Valles Caldera, I assumed I'd simply hike from one end to the other, rim to rim. It didn't turn out that way.

Valles Caldera National Preserve is not a unit of the national parks (as the name would imply) and yet not exactly a huge private ranch (which it was previously). A hybrid of both, the 88,000-acre preserve was purchased from the Dunigan family of Texas by Congress in 2000, and created as a new experiment in the management of public lands. Governed by a board of trustees that includes federal employees and private citizens, ranchers and environmentalists, it can't quite capture the public's mind, accustomed in New Mexico, at least, to either huge land-grant private ranches or classic federally operated "preserves" like adjacent Bandelier National Monument. Caught in limbo—with cattle grazing and elk hunting permitted alongside hiking and guided scenic tours in shuttle vans—the place is still something of an enigma ten years later.

The situation is not helped by big, garish yellow signs at the main entrance on Highway 4 that announce, "COME ON IN, FOLKS! WE'RE OPEN FROM 8:30 TO 5:30!!" and list the attractions and activities that can be found by going inside—just like a private roadside tourist trap. Cave of Mystery! Black Hills Gold! Wall Drug! Royal Gorge! Valles Caldera!

Adding to the confusion—for my purposes, anyway—was how the preserve's online website was designed, and how the employed staff had been trained to deal with the public. Both provided only the information that the management wanted to make public, which was precious little and left me with a false impression. Yes, I could hike in the preserve, the lady on the phone said, but only by taking a shuttle van to be dropped off and picked up from designated day-hike locations. Each hike was described on their website, she said, and each was about seven miles round trip. No, there was no provision for getting permission or paying a special use fee to hike across the preserve from one side to the other. And no, there was no overnight camping allowed.

None of this was strictly true, but I didn't find out until later, when it was too late. I didn't have time to dig deeper, question more people up the chain of command. I was on a quest to Chicoma Mountain—which stood tall just outside the preserve to the northeast—and I had to keep moving. So, I got online confirmation for a 10:30 a.m. shuttle on July 23. It would take me from the "staging area" at the south end of the caldera all the way across to the north end, where for ten dollars I would be permitted to hike four miles up to the boundary—and then have to go all the way back! Later, I would have to pick up the trail from the north rim and continue on national forest land to Chicoma.

The morning drive to Valles Caldera passes by the Santa Fe Opera House on a four-lane highway with heavy traffic going seventy miles per hour. Along the shoulder I spot two deer, a two-point buck and a doe, both young, walking close together like teenage lovers, oblivious to the rushing cars. Theresa calls my cell phone to inform me a bear got into her chicken coop again and smashed open the grain cans. I tell her about the deer along the shoulder.

She says, "Hmm, it seems to be a very noticeably wildlife-in-your-face kind of summer. So be careful."

"Roger that."

The day is cooler than usual, with great freighters of cloud cruising the sky. Near Otowi Bridge over the Rio Grande, I look across the wide valley of San Ildefonso Pueblo and see Chicoma Mountain at the far end of the Jemez range, high up, remote, and dark under a ceiling of overcast. Zipping through Los Alamos and up Highway 4 into the Bandelier Backcountry, the roadsides are wet from heavy rain overnight. The crisp mountain air is humid and scented with pine. Over the pass and into the Valle Grande—the largest bowl-like prairie in the caldera and all that people see from the paved road—the sea of grass is lush and green. At the very height of what is turning out to be an unusually wet summer, the Big Valley is emerging from snakelike dissipating mists.

I'm late. At the shocking yellow entrance signs, I swerve in and head across the flats on a gravel road that crosses the East Fork of the Jemez River—here a swampy creek. The "staging area" is a muddy parking lot with portable outhouses and a prefab building on skids, which turns out to be the visitor center, gift shop, and office for the employees. Leaping out with my loaded daypack, I discover the shuttle isn't going to leave on time anyway. This is New Mexico, after all, not someplace businesslike and anal like Colorado.

I go inside to check in. When I see all the people who work there are wearing smart, long-sleeve, quasi-official-looking green shirts, which are not quite ranger uniforms, it suddenly hits me: *They themselves don't quite know what they are, either!*

Brash and cheery, the woman in charge of getting me to read and sign a release form doesn't actually stop her manic rap, so I don't get past the first sentence of a useless legal document. (Such releases are bullshit and don't prevent liability lawsuits. They only make it look like you're getting your money's worth from the attorney you retained. Ask a lawyer you're not paying.) She also could not answer a single question I asked without deflecting it with a jokey platitude—"Oh, it's so if you get eaten by a bear, we're not responsible, ha-ha!"

The situation these good people face is not of their own making. The unfortunate management style they labor under is perhaps best illustrated by the fact that every shuttle van into or out of the preserve from the staging area has to be let through the barrier gate by a stern and authoritative woman named Bernadette, who must physically walk out of the office with her walkie-talkie and raise and lower it by hand. The effect is like a border guard waving each vehicle through with a grim, "Welcome to Bulgaria!" It's so hokey, I'm embarrassed for them all.

It is always the little people, the ordinary folks, who have to bear the responsibility and deal with the consequences of often incomprehensible decisions made by higher-ups. Like enlisted foot soldiers carrying out the misguided orders of their commanding officers, they make do, usually with resigned aplomb, but sometimes with heroic calm. I once met an old Hispanic man who, as an army sergeant during World War II, was put in sole charge of the first atomic bomb for a few hours. The military convoy transporting the device to be tested in the desert of southern New Mexico passed through Santa Fe after midnight, and was parked in Burro Alley beside the Lensic Theater while all the officers walked uptown and drank booze at the La Fonda. New Mexicans are used to making do.

Outside, a church camp bus drives up and disgorges about thirty screaming kids under the age of eight. They beat me to the portable pissoirs, so I get in line, hopping in anxious need after several cups of coffee. When I finally get inside, it's clean and nice, but the little boys before me have piddled all over everything.

As the only hiker arriving for the 10:30 North Rim Shuttle, I jump in shotgun beside the driver and introduce myself to the full vanload of people who are going along only for the scenic drive through the caldera. Immediately behind me are a raucous and beefy bunch of guys from Tuscaloosa, Alabama, on a university field trip, who laugh at everything like giddy kids. Their teacher asks the driver intelligent and unexpected questions, such as, "Y'all have any invasive species of plants that cause problems?" At 11:05, the driver, Todd Bernardy, an older guy from Oklahoma, waves to Bernadette as she holds the gate open for the van to pass through, and we're off. Todd introduces us to the preserve with a slow, quiet, folksy spiel that reveals him as a scientific type more interested in geological processes and theoretical debates than your average tour guide. He and the University of Alabama professor are well matched, and their interests dominate the conversations. Unfortunately, Todd does not know the names of flowers or trees along the roadside, and as a result the ladies asking questions from the far back of the van are eventually silenced.

Formerly known as the Baca Ranch, the area of the preserve is mainly the bottom of a collapsed volcano's giant caldera, about fifteen air miles from rim to rim, which a vast lake once filled in with sediment about three thousand feet thick. This fine sediment has produced incredibly rich grasslands with the capacity to feed thousands of cattle and elk in the summer. Like islands in a sea of grass, round forested mountains, the previously noted "resurgent domes," stand up from the caldera floor. We head off to a gap between two of them, Todd driving at a leisurely pace over well-tended gravel roads. He says it will take about an hour to cover the fourteen miles to my drop-off point.

I'd always wanted to go deep into the heart of the Valles Caldera, the central feature of the Jemez Mountains, and here I was, at last, doing it with a guide who knew the place intimately. Swinging up through old log and tin-roof buildings—the Baca Ranch headquarters and now the preserve administrative center—we pass numerous red-backed sparrow hawks, kestrels, hovering over the waving prairie grass with wings beating like hummingbirds, watching for a mouse breakfast to appear. Passing an oddly swooping stone mansion that looks as if it was made from two A-frame kit buildings, Todd says the last owners, the Dunigans, had it built, and called it the Witch's Hat. Skirting the upper side of the largest, grandest valle, we drive through History Grove, a gorgeously scenic stand of giant trees, mainly ponderosa pine, which were saved from the saw as a pathetic reminder of what the forest used to be like all over the caldera before logging came to the Baca Ranch.

We cruise by old board buildings used in B westerns like *Buffalo Girls* and cross a series of smaller bowl-like prairies. Cattle of many different colors and breeds graze everywhere. The Valle Jaramillo and the high Cerro del Abrigo are to the right, Todd announces. The road turns wet and muddy. Springs and wet vegas abound. Wild flowers bloom by the millions. And all the conifers are small—the typical second-growth forest growing up around giant stumps you see all over the West.

Todd claims that here in the caldera is the only place on earth where two major fault zones cross each other—he uses his forearms to make an X and almost veers off the road—or at least on land, he says. The other places are all deep under the ocean. And because of this unique crossing of fault zones, scientists studying here have finally proven the theory of plate tectonics, of continental drift.

"It was just a theory before," he says. "That the earth's continents drifted around and collided with each other and broke apart. But right here it was proven as fact."

He hasn't given us enough information to understand how they proved it, so I'm not convinced. He sees me scribbling down what he said in my notebook.

"You writing a book?"

"Something like that," I say.

"Well, tell 'em Todd says he's not handsome, but he is faithful!" The crew from Alabama roars with laughter.

We drop down into the northernmost valle, running east-west, the drainage of San Antonio Creek. Todd says there are hot springs, sulfur vents, lethal bubbling mud ponds farther downstream to the west, just like in Yellowstone National Park. Valles Caldera is still hot and considered an active volcano, he adds. We turn east, passing under the ramparts of Cerro de la Garita ("Sentry-Box Mountain") and through a gap in the hills to the Valle Toledo beyond. He stops the van at a side road and tells me this is where I get out. Just like that, I'm alone on the shoulder in hot sunshine, waving at everybody in the van, which turns around and heads back.

Seven

IT LOOKS LIKE I've been dropped off somewhere in the wilds of Montana. Forested hills hem in a wide prairie where San Antonio Creek meanders across marshy flats. Thick spruce tops the Cerros de Trasquilar ("Sheep-Shear Mountains"), and everything looks utterly pristine, despite the fact that thousands of sheep used to be sheared here every summer in the old days before cattle ranching. I can see for miles. I spot only one other person, a fly-fisherman working the creek. According to Todd, the trout fishing in the preserve is some of the best in the West.

Two-track road VC13 heads north, my route up the valley of the Rito de los Indios, which according to the map follows the stream up around forested Indian Point and then eastward into the headwaters behind Chicoma Mountain. Checking my timepiece (Todd, dropping me off with a vigorous handshake, reminded me the last shuttle will stop here at six o'clock, don't miss it), I head off at a clip up the road, my pack gurgling with a single jug of water. After a jouncing hour-long ride in a crowded modern stagecoach, I'm alone at about noon on a beautiful warm day at 8,600 feet, crossing a vast, high, wide-open prairie with towering mountains in every direction. I never get tired of heading off on foot like this into a wide new world I've never seen before.

The road winds along beside a looping cutbank creek a few feet wide, running clear and cold and deep. Tiny German brown trout dart away from my approaching shadow. For the first mile a long banco runs along the east side, not a tree on it, and to the west a few ponderosa pines stand alone on low hills. La Garita looms high to the left and Indian Point to the right. They are not rugged, not gouged and incised by the elements, but instead are smooth and sculpted, steep in places, yet rounded like giant gumdrops covered in dark forest.

In the grassy center between damp-dirt tire tracks, white daisies bloom in profusion. Miniature grasshoppers leap away ahead of my steps in a continuous cloud of dozens. Biting deer flies swarm my face. Perched atop a dead pine snag at the side of the road, a hawk whistles, then tracks me passing underneath, head cocked with sharp hooked beak and one livid watchful eye.

As the grade gets steeper and I begin to pant, the valley closes in with almost perpendicular hillsides shaded by spruce and fir. The road stays high to one side of wet meadows and a rushing creek. I find flakes of black obsidian in the roadside soil, then a broken arrowhead, only the rear notches intact. In muddy spots I see fresh tracks of cattle, elk, coyote, and turkey. This would always have been a rich area for game animals, for meat hunting.

Clouds build higher and darker overhead. Rain is likely this afternoon, but so far only a cool breeze has sprung up. From far uphill come the grating cries of Clark's nutcrackers, crow-like jays of high altitudes. I come upon a flock of red-shafted flickers, maybe fifteen of the large woodpecker-like birds, inexplicably fluttering around on the ground under a shady spruce. Then I remember their fondness for feasting on ants. They scatter suddenly as I march past, each a flash of salmon red shooting away, crying out in familiar trills of alarm.

About two miles up, the creek valley curves to the right in a wide bend. Thunder rolls off Indian Point; dark clouds are massing. Then more thunder sounds far off in the mountains behind it. A storm is definitely coming, but slowly. The creek roars down a steep, narrow defile, cutting a channel through a series of old rotten beaver dams. Above shady riparian woodlands of alder and willow, at a grassy flat, I find more worked pieces of flint.

I'm not surprised. Nearby are the ancient flint quarries of Obsidian Valley, and I'm following the route of the "Old Indian Trail" that appears on 19th-century maps of the Jemez. Going up Rito de los Indios, the ancient pathway passes through a gap in the caldera rim and descends Santa Clara Canyon. For a thousand years, this was the footpath between the Tewa pueblos on the Rio Grande and the Jemez pueblos to the west. The Jemez people were the preeminent mountaineers of the pre-Spanish era, living in communities scattered all over the Jemez Mountains and tending summer gardens even inside the high caldera.

Farther up the roiling *rito*, past a talus slope of dark, volcanic boulders, a nameless noisy side creek comes rushing from a ravine on the left. I'm in rough rocky high country with old barbwire fences strung through heavy moss-draped timber. Back to the south rain is falling, but overhead is deep blue sky. Up the side creek I find a one-room plank cabin with a tin roof, the door wide open. Inside is a wood cookstove, a table and chairs, and a small bunk bed. The floor and every flat surface is littered with fecal pellets—the droppings of pack rats (or, as they are known to hair-splitting wildlife biologists, bushy-tailed woodrats). Unwilling to enter the Hantavirus Hilton, I look around outside. Split firewood is still stacked under the roofed porch, elk skulls dangle from nails, and up the hill in the outhouse I find a dry roll of toilet paper.

The place seems to be one of those "bare minimum" line cabins that lonely cowboys live in when they ride herd on cattle in remote areas. But what's this? A foot-square mirror is securely fastened to the wall next to the front door—and there's another one just inside. Was this who the cowboy talked to, goldurn it, looking at his own reflection, so's not to be just talking to himself?

Turns out nothing of the sort. This place isn't what it looks like. Todd told me on the ride over that after the last owner, Mrs. Dunigan, was widowed and remarried, she had this remote cabin built as a place to get away by herself. A rich Texas oilfield socialite with a private wilderness fiefdom of nearly 150 square miles chose this isolated spot to be alone and commune with nature. And the mirrors beside the front door? I guess even out in a lonely hideaway in the bush, a woman wants to look her best.

Thunder booms and rumbles from a storm growing over the mountains. Time to get a move on.

Hiking up what is now a steep-walled forest canyon, the creek is no more than a sluggishly flowing ciénaga. The road narrows to a stock driveway. The north rim of the caldera closes in high on the left. Spruce gives way to groves of aspen, soughing softly in the breeze. Signs of cattle disappear—only the fresh tracks of deer and elk show in the mud. The silent solitude of wilderness deepens. Hundreds of orange butterflies flutter about in the damp air, and dozens gather on the ground around a pile of bear droppings, wings opening and closing slowly.

In an area of great, rounded house-size boulders thickly mantled in skins of lichen and moss, I find hard red elderberries, green gooseberries, pink raspberries—nothing ripe enough to eat until I discover a few wild strawberries hidden close to the ground. Each is so tiny and difficult to pry off, the effort is hardly worth it. But then a handful in my mouth is shockingly delicious, infinitely better than the giant farmed varieties.

A vast wide valle opens up and I see the road winding northwestward for half a mile across sloping grassland above wet meadows. A spring bubbles out beside an old corral made of poles. A rusty flatbed truck from the 1930s is sunk in the black mud. A raven caws loudly, and it echoes. It feels like a warning, but of what? The grassy park opens wider and extends another half mile. I realize the raven has been cawing as I walked on, but then stops, the silence somehow foreboding. A sudden boom of thunder makes me look up. Dark churning clouds spill over the forested summit of Cerro Toledo to my right. Sudden jagged bolts of lightning dance and twirl in the black above it, followed by a battering roar of more thunder rolling toward me. Billowing rain clouds close in, blocking the sun overhead.

Suddenly aware I'm in the open and exposed (quoth the raven, "Here comes the storm!"), I duck into a grassy draw and cut uphill into the small trees at the edge of timber. Bushwhacking along under protective thickets of aspen and Douglas fir, I notice every moist draw coming down from the north rim has a well-beaten elk trail leading to prime summer pasture in the open below. Fresh elk droppings are everywhere. Through the trees uphill I glimpse a meadow where a small herd of elk bulls graze, one with bloody streamers of velvet hanging off an enormous rack of antlers. But I can't linger. Even at a rapid pace, the deer flies are homing in on me and biting so fiercely, I'm slapping at myself continuously. My bare arms and neck are favored targets, but they also bite my belly and shoulders through my tee shirt. I sometimes kill a dozen with a single slap of the hand. By the time I reach the road again, where timber closes in, I've killed literally hundreds of the bloodthirsty little buggers. Half crazed, I break into a trot up the road and leave most of the swarming cloud behind.

There's no creek anymore, just a road climbing up a shaded draw with overgrown logging trails taking off to left and right. I slow to a fast walk. After a long ascent up a dry rocky slope, the deer flies at last left behind, I come to a locked gate and a barbwire fence that marks the boundary between the preserve and the national forest. The sky is black and the air is still and humid. Rain feels imminent. I hop the fence and hurry on through aspen woods until the canyon bottom levels off. An easy walk brings me to the base of an open bald to the left going all the way up to the north rim, only a few hundred feet above. Ahead, the canyon drops downhill to the east, starting the long torturous descent of Santa Clara Canyon.

Brilliant stabs of lightning and pounding thunder keep me from climbing up to the rim. The Highline Trail is up there, my next leg of the journey, and I can see the summit of Chicoma Mountain, enormous this close up, swathed in misty rain. But I must turn back. I've pushed hard to get here, and eaten almost nothing since early morning. I'm famished, but gauzy clouds hang ominously low, and thunder grows louder. Better hurry back to the cabin first, I decide.

Lightning strikes lower down the mountain, thunder crashes, and I break into a run downhill, a cold wind at my back. Retracing my path through brushy woods above the open valley, I see down the V of canyon out across the caldera where showers fall in slanting curtains. So far not a drop has fallen on me. Then as I enter the aspen groves and giant boulders, a refreshing sprinkle starts hitting my sweaty face. I get a whiff of moldy mattress and realize I'm trotting through a mucky stand of bedstraw, the white flowers giving off a fetid scent. Wind whips in gusts through thrashing branches. The rain comes harder. Lighting glares and thunder booms much closer. I pull on my poncho and shelter under a clump of thick young spruce trees, waiting to see if it gets any worse. It does.

The thunder is hair-raising, like giant boulders rushing down the mountain toward me. I drop on all fours, terrified, feeling the ground quiver. Rain pours down as if I'm crouched under a waterfall. Another boom, and another, the crashing so close, I hug the ground. But then the worst sweeps past. When the rain slows a little and the thunder seems far away along the north rim, I get up and go on. Splashing down the muddy road in a daze, I notice the gloomy downpour increasing again.

Then out of the blue, a bolt of lightning blinds me. An almost instantaneous crash of thunder knocks me aside. Stunned for a few seconds against a mossy bank, the nearmiss echoing in my ringing ears, I suddenly crawl like a madman uphill under the spreading branches of a spruce tree and burrow into wet duff. This time I wait it out. Although I did not literally have the shit scared out of me, a quick search in my pack for toilet paper leaves little time to spare. When only faraway thunder mutters, I dash down the road to the cabin and dart in under the protection of the porch roof.

It leaks like a sieve. There is only one dry spot a few feet wide on a wooden bench, and there I perch and have a picnic. It leaks inside the cabin, too, and the moistened stench of what could be considered a public health menace wafts out the front door. I kick it shut. Behind the cabin a little creek rushes by through a raspberry thicket with tall flower spikes of purple monkshood standing up through prickly canes. They nod at the hit of raindrops like dancing friars delighted by water, water everywhere.

More pounding rain falls and more thunder booms. It pours in the forest clearing like a biblical deluge, but I'm protected from it, barely, waiting it out, dozing off after a big meal. Finally, the rain slackens to a light and filmy shower. I am at peace again in the limpid aftermath of a battle of the mountain powers. Not wanting to miss the last shuttle, willing to risk another soaking if I have to, I pack up and take off. Fortunately the worst is over, and eventually there is just a misty sprinkle that continues into the evening.

Back on the wide-open prairie, steam-like swirls of cloud rise from the wet timber, and far-off blue holes appear in the clouds. Placid and gleaming, the Valle Toledo drifts in and out of view through pale ground fog. Named for the Toledo clan—Jemez Pueblo Indian people who previously inhabited this area and raised livestock here until ranch owners fenced them out—the great valle seems to emerge fresh and new from the primeval mists of time.

The five o'clock shuttle, which I thought I'd missed, is waiting at the fork in the road, ten minutes after. I jump in, the only passenger, and ride back with a different driver, a husky young local guy named Joseph. He reports by walkie-talkie to Bernadette at the staging area that he's bringing in the last hiker "as we speak." He tells me he's from the nearby village of Ponderosa and is grateful for a job so close to home, in the mountains he loves.

We pass seemingly endless herds of grazing elk, mostly antlerless cows. There are few calves. Joseph says only about 15 percent survive their first year—the winter is that harsh. The roadsides we drove past this morning, empty of anything but cattle, are now teeming with elk in the hundreds. He says they come out like this every morning and evening, and are so tame, sometimes they block the road and won't get out of the way until he honks the horn.

At the staging area (yes, Bernadette comes out in the rain wearing a smart red jacket and raises the gate bar), frogs croak loudly and it feels cold. Wet to my knees and squishing around in soggy boots (I fogged up the windows of Joseph's van on the way back), I listen for a while to Jim Trout, a flint knapper and wildlife expert, as he warms up a group of visitors prior to taking them out on an evening wildlife tour in another van. He tells them about the seasonal elk migrations in and out of the caldera. Joseph, also listening, tells me Jim's favorite hike in the preserve is the one I took up Rito de los Indios.

"I can see why," I say. "There's obsidian all over up there, and lots of elk."

"You're just in time to jump in with him, if you want to," Joseph says helpfully. "Your ten dollars you paid covers anything you do today."

I'm tempted. But it's six o'clock, and the moon, a few days from full, rises like a dim yellow saucer through thin clouds over Cerro Grande. I'm exhausted and face a long drive home.

"Next time," I tell him.

Eight

ON A RADIANT and beautiful morning a few days later, I stand at the very top of the north rim and look out across Valles Caldera. I'm at the edge of a flat green meadow, a saddle where it drops off a steep slope to the bottom of a canyon. I can see the spot, down below, where I turned back. From here there's no question it would have been an easy climb up the open slope along angling dirt trails trod by elk and cattle. That is, had the threat of lightning not changed my mind.

At 10,400 feet I have a bird's-eye view of the route I walked up Rito de los Indios. The sunlight is brilliant, illuminating the dark spruce summits of Cerro Toledo and Indian Point, which seem about even in elevation to where I stand. Of all the views into the caldera, this is the most expansive and complete yet, a breathtaking panorama of mountains and valleys from the north that few see. And turning to my left, there it is—the object of all my effort, the sacred mountain of the west, Chicoma at last. Maybe four miles away as the crow flies, at the end of a long rolling ridge, the peak stands high above all others, a great rounded cone all by itself, solitary and aloof. One single round puff of cloud floats above it, the only cloud in the entire deep blue sky, hovering like an omen.

Fully prepared with everything I'll need for the next few days, I'm ready to start off on the third and last phase of my excursion through the Jemez Mountains. I've stashed all but my Scooby-Doo daypack under the resinous brush of a big fir tree freshly blown apart by lightning. Carrying only the essentials for a day's hike, I plan to ascend the peak and return here before going west and north the rest of the way down and out of the Jemez country.

Thumbing a ride along the forest road to the flank of Chicoma, I jump into a battered Chevy pickup with Freddie Coriz, a stout young woodcutter from Española, and his ten-year-old nephew, who he introduces as "Juanito

Moco" (Johnny Snotnose). Juanito fits the part, filthy with mud and sawdust and a runny nose. The pickup is heavily weighed down with a full load of chainsawed spruce rounds, already this early in the day, and they're heading home, creeping along low to the ground, eating a box of Little Debbie powdered donuts, which they share with me. Young Mister Moco studies the daypack on my lap, the goofy look on Scooby-Doo's hound-dog face looking at butterflies flying all around him, and asks in a serious, thoughtful tone, "Are you a hippie?" His uncle roars with laughter.

Freddie, who says he is half Spanish and half Tewa Indian, does not know the name of the mountaintop I point out ahead (Chicoma) but thinks the lower one off to the left is called Polvadera. The closer we get, other rounded summits intrude and make Chicoma less prominent. The road winds around through spruce forest and we pass more local people cutting firewood and loading pickups. One has wood stacked fifteen feet high inside a truck bed enclosure made of steel pipes. Turning off, we bump along on an overgrown track through puddles of rainwater into a wide-open clearcut. Cattle line the road, tearing aggressively at the grass with their teeth. Blue columbines and purple harebells nod in the sunlight. It looks like British Columbia, the coastal part, incredibly green and wet, but logged bare for miles, a sloping sea of stumps with young aspen coming up.

Several wild pigeons fly up ahead of us and land on the ground, walking about cooing and bobbing their heads as they hunt seeds and bugs. Common in the Jemez, these band-tailed pigeons, or "palomas" as Freddie calls them, are delicious to eat—squab *del monte.* With their dove-gray look altered by a green sheen, bluish wings, and red eye-rings, they look like exotic wayward migrants from the tropics, which is exactly what they are.

Halfway up a logged mountainside on a road covered in enormous fly-swarmed cow pies, I spot the unassuming forested summit of Chicoma just six hundred feet above us and about a mile away. Freddie doesn't believe me when I point at the very top of the mountain he has looked up at all his life. A prominent and commanding peak when viewed from the Rio Grande Valley, the highest peak in the Jemez Mountains, it mysteriously looks no different here than any of the other rounded forested summits nearby. No forest service signs guide the way. Only because I am zealously studying a topographic map of the area am I able to direct Freddie to my jump-off place, a flat spot on a saddle northwest of the summit.

Freddie loops around to head back down and drops me off under the shade of a lone tree left standing. He drives away with his nephew hanging out the window solemnly watching me left alone in the middle of nowhere. But I know exactly where I am. I'm just under 11,000 feet at the upper edge of the clearcut on the north side of Chicoma Mountain. I see a flock of grouse moving away out in the open, another hen and her almost full-grown young. While I sit on a log studying my map, a huge cow grazes right up to within a few feet of me and suddenly stops still, staring. A brown-and-white Hereford with a numbered plastic tag hanging from one ear, she has a brand on her ass I can't decipher. People here are apparently a curiosity—the cow turns aside and grazes around me, as if shrugging off an apparition.

Despite what the map shows, there's no trail up the mountain—the old Highline Trail, unused for decades, is gone without a trace. In a meadow there's a ring of rocks, an old campsite with paintball splotches on the trunks of huge tall spruces. Gray jays, the famed "whiskey jacks" or "camp robbers" of the northern forests, glide down silently to lower branches and watch me. Nobody but a determined pilgrim would come this way. I'm told the Tewa come up the grassy south face on the other side, from pueblo land in Santa Clara Canyon, coming and going without non-Indians aware of it. Above the clearcut is old-growth, spruce-alpine fir forest, and many of the enormous trees have been blown down into piles like windrows. I pick my way around and over the obstacles, working my way up a timbered slope.

Once away from all the disturbances—the sign of cattle replaced by fresh elk droppings—I stop in airy pristine forest where crisp high-altitude sunlight illuminates thick wet duff underfoot. As a precaution, I light a sprig of dried sage and smudge myself off with the mint-scented smoke. John Pesendo, the Tewa elder, spoke with great emotion about Chicoma, without question the most beloved and prayed-to mountain of the four Tewa directional peaks. It is also sacred to the Jemez Pueblo Indian people, who call it *Pashun* ("Flower Mountain"). I'd be a fool not to acknowledge something special about where I am and what I'm doing.

Plodding on uphill, I see the ominous single cloud ball is still there, but it is diffusing into many vaporous clumps and swirls. The forest floor is rich with mushrooms: white fairy rings, yellow crinklies, tall shaggy manes, and bright-red panther amanitas, some of which are huge. Not only is there nobody else up here, but there's no sign of anybody having been up here in many years.

Only elk, in great numbers. I see and hear a few birds—gray jays, woodpeckers, chickadees, kinglets—where not a breath of wind stirs the majestic columns of spruce, but there is little sign of terrestrial animal life except elk. Their trails crisscross my route, dug deep by many passing hooves that leave the familiar "split heart" impressions clearly visible in moist dirt. I hear them moving off in small family groups to my right, in forest so littered with fallen logs their hooves clunk on dry hollow wood. I glimpse them watching me labor past uphill, huge cow-sized deer with thick necks and dark manes and red-brown summer coats, flashing a white rump when they trot away, like shy wraiths of the high timber.

I find faint traces of the old trail to the top, but no signs of recent use. Many trees have been blown to pieces by lightning strikes; ragged splinters twenty feet long and too heavy to lift, oozing pitch, are scattered far out from exploded tree trunks. Gooseberry and elderberry grow in thickets, their fruit red and sour to the taste.

It gets steeper. Panting and slowing at well over 11,000 feet, I come to a long narrow flat with impenetrable windrows of dead timber and then start up another steep slope of pure spruce forest. The bones of the mountain show through in smooth gray outcrops of rock covered with wet lichens. Potholes in the rocks are full of rainwater. Breezes swish through swaying trees. More elk move off invisibly to the right, hooves clunking. A huge amanita appears in the shade, almost flat-topped and a foot in diameter—a deadly poisonous fungus like a polka-dot stop sign heralding the wide-open mountainside I see above.

Stepping out into the open, I'm at the base of a grassy bald that leads another hundred feet up to the timbered summit itself. The altitude starves my lungs of oxygen and empties my mind of thought. I barely keep on with a slow, ox-like plod up the slope, only vaguely aware of wild flowers tossing in the breeze, wet grass, flies, fresh elk tracks, boulders dotting a sunlit green hillside. Flattened spots show in the grass where elk rested last night. Old burned snags are worn to a silvery smoothness. Several partially disarticulated elk skeletons lie about.

Then a pause to breathe, and I turn, startled by my first look at the horizon so far away from so high up. South over the wide maw of the caldera to faraway mesas, I make out the hazy outline of Mount Taylor. West are the San Pedro Peaks, and northwest the open red-rock country beyond the Pedernal—a high black butte that looks puny and low from here. North over a fringe of spruce is the high flat prominence of Canjilon Mountain, with higher peaks—the San Juans—dimly visible beyond. Clearly I'm on the highest peak in the vicinity, and there's so much to see, I can't take it all in.

Slowly, step by step, I struggle upward toward the last trees and angle to the left, onto the north face where it looks less steep. The soil turns to gravel, and bare rocks show, all a grayish pale-maroon color with tiny white flecks. Rounding a grassy point, the whole wide world seems to open up in every direction like a spread-out map of the globe, a circular disk of planet Earth with Chicoma Mountain standing high in the center.

Panting and elated, I stop at a cairn of rocks piled up around a worn stick. The noonday sun hammers down and icy wind blasts in gusts. Beyond the wide tawny valley of the Rio Grande, a far-off line of jagged mountains, the Sangre de Cristos—Truchas Peak among them, due east—stand like a wall blocking the way to the vague flat expanse of Great Plains beyond. Far below I see the forest road Freddie drove down to Española, looping back and forth to the lowlands. Farther north I see the burned-over country from the fire that kept me from coming this way a few weeks ago—fingers of blackened forest lapping up the green slope of Polvadera Peak. Beyond are the oval valles of hidden Spanish American settlements, old and almost forgotten: El Alto and Rechuelos and Joya de Tio Gregorio. The promontories of Window Rock and La Utah. The timbered gorge of the Rio del Oso. Lobato and Polvadera and Gallina mesas. A whole new country seen for the first time.

Turning away, I climb the last easy way up to where the mountain levels off. I'm surprised to see the top is more or less flat. The summit appears timbered when viewed from afar, but the spruce trees are mainly just a border around an open *mesita* running north–south. As I wander around, thoughtlessly marveling at the view of my homeland far below, I find numerous shrines erected and maintained by the Tewa people. One is ten feet long, a rock-lined enclosure in the shape of a gourd rattle on a stick, the stick end pointing north. It is carefully kept up, and the hole dug in the rounded end is freshly weeded and packed smooth. I was told this honors where the Tewa came from in the north, and receives the blessing from their lake of origin in that direction.

The reality of the living shrine on the summit stops me in my tracks. I haven't even begun to explore the place and yet I am inexplicably reluctant to go on. I sit down and examine my feelings.

Something has changed. Maybe because I'm alone on this mountain, with no trail to the top, and no sign until now of anybody having been up here. It's nothing like arriving atop Sandia Peak distracted by other noisy hikers. Nobody comes here but unseen pilgrims who obviously tend this shrine with love and reverence. I detect something uneasy under the awe and wonder I feel. Not like I'm trespassing, exactly, because this is national forest land, and besides, I'm convinced something would've happened to warn me away from making it this far if I wasn't meant to be here. No, it's more like a feeling that I've entered a place where others fear to tread, and for good reason. The shrines here acknowledge a great indifferent power present behind the visible surface of summit rock and windblown trees and empty vault of sky. Not something overtly threatening, but beyond my ability to fathom, and therefore dangerous if I am not careful and respectful and certain about what I'm doing here.

I decide to proceed with circumspect caution. It proves to be an important decision in light of the strange events that follow, that day and the next.

Nine

JOHN PESENDO HAD referred to the summit area of Chicoma Mountain as "the governor's rooftop." The name is apt. No other sharp high peak I've ever been on is like walking across the interconnected flat roofs of a large pueblo house block. The "governor" or chief of the Yellow Kachinas—godlike beings who come from the west bringing rain and who were once impersonated in masked dances in Tewa towns—is said to live here, inside the top of the mountain. At first, my every step across it makes me feel self-conscious, as if making my presence known to some underground awareness.

But such thoughts fade away easily at 11,561 feet. Flowers bloom in profusion—more drooping purple harebells, rose-yellow potentillas, wands of white yarrow. Flower Mountain indeed! On closer inspection I'm on a rolling volcanic cap rock consisting of higher and lower flat grassy areas unevenly joined together by rounded stony outcrops. To one side, where a shallow pond once stood, a basin of deep soil lies at a slight tilt to the east.

Here I see excavations that at first seem like the desecration of trenches dug with pick and shovel. It looks like a halted construction project, perhaps to lay concrete footings. Then I see how carefully smoothed and rock-lined the trenches are, and how they radiate eastward from a large circular pit, which itself is lined by a double row of concentric rock walls like a giant horseshoe. The ditches run thirty feet or more to the edge of a steep drop-off overlooking the Rio Grande Valley. It dawns on me that this large elaborate earthwork is the Tewa shrine that connects their village homes below to the top of this mountain.

The two main channels are large and regularly dug out, weeded, and smoothed to bare gravel soil. Two others are older and less deep, less cared for, hard to trace if not for rocks lining the pathways. One is very old and overgrown—untouched for a very long time. As I sit and contemplate this amazing ancient place of prayer and offering, it occurs to me that the ditches run out in the specific directions of the various Tewa pueblos below. They are like irrigation ditches channeling to each community the precious blessing of rain and snow that falls up here. The widest and deepest and most well-tended ditch (a yard wide and a foot deep) runs off the edge in the direction of Santa Clara Pueblo, and the next prominent one heads toward San Ildefonso. Both pueblos are clearly visible from here on the summit. The drop-off falls almost vertically for hundreds of feet into spruce forest with blue columbines flowering in the cracks of rocks.

Touched by the simplicity and purposefulness of such an important shrine, I notice orange ladybugs swarming all over tall clumps of grass around the horseshoe part of the pit structure—and nowhere else. They cluster in the dozens, in the hundreds, on the swaying tips, mating, just like on Sandia Peak where the girl let them crawl on her.

Between the two main ditches is a flat boulder that has a four-pointed star shape and natural pothole depressions in the right positions for two eyes and a mouth. This "face rock," I'm told, has a secret name and is considered a person who lives here. It resembles a cartoon-like star that fell to earth and now lies gazing up at the sky. The expression on the stony face is startling and otherworldly. When I examine it more closely, the eyes and mouth are filled to the brim with rainwater alive with twitching mosquito larvae.

Clouds have built up thickly overhead. The shade is cold as I make my way to the far end of the governor's rooftop to eat lunch and look down the giant bald on the south face of the peak. The abyss takes my breath away. Curving downward thousands of feet in a grassy swath surrounded by dark forest, the descent into Santa Clara Canyon goes down so far—so terrifyingly far—only with binoculars can I make out the forest service fence that runs across it partway down, marking the beginning of pueblo land. Even on the steepest pitches all is waving green grass.

The pressing serious business of eating and drinking holds my attention; then I return to the view. The horizon reaches from Truchas Peak to Mount Taylor, and between the breaks in the mountain ranges are vast level plains. The cities of the north—Albuquerque, Santa Fe, Española, Los Alamos—are spread out below, too. The Rio Grande, seen as if from an airplane five thousand feet above, flows through green woodlands at the foot of the Jemez, sweltering in ninety-degree sunshine. I sit under the darkness of a storm moving northward over the Sierra de los Valles toward me. The wind is cold. A few raindrops fall, then nothing. Underneath the mass of clouds, the front range behind Los Alamos rises to timbered heights, powerful rain magnets themselves. I can see the scar lines of ski runs on Pajarito Mountain, and on nearby Shell Mountain are strange, tall white hoodoos standing up like giant industrial chimneys from deep woods.

Back on the summit I discover that the very highest point is perfectly flat, picked bare of loose rocks that have been piled in a cairn to one side. The sparse vegetation has been packed down recently by many feet, as if a group of people gathered here for some purpose. I find other packed-down spots like resting places in the lee of low, bushy spruce trees. I don't disturb anything, nor do I presume to add my own offering to what are clearly well-used shrines belonging to another people. Making my way to an empty area behind a screen of spruce, I find a place on bare rock to make my own personal connection with the mountaintop. Here I linger, feeling the same ineffable yet familiar sensation I've felt on other summits—an urge to give thanks. Which I do, softly, from the heart—for my own existence, however brief it may be, and for the joy of being alive in such a world of beauty. My concentration is so complete that the rest of the world practically vanishes for me.

A mutter of thunder intrudes from overhead, the first I've heard. It rolls along and then thumps down in frightening waves of louder booms, clobbering the mountain. Shocked back into conscious sober thought, I realize I need to get off this high peak.

Going back down the way I came up, I'm startled by a falcon that flies up to the very top of a lonely spruce out in the open bald. I feel somehow reassured. When it flies off, leading the way down, I follow after at a trot. Once in the relative safety of thick mossy forest, thunder crashes and booms on the summit, high above. I stop, panting. Scribbling a few notes so I won't forget what happened on the summit, I dash on. Later, I read in my notebook: "Feels like I was allowed up there for a brief look and then warned to leave. Now my heart pounds in the fear of danger."

Downhill at a clip, much faster than going up, I pass through tall trees, feeling the air grow colder. A fisher, a dark weasel of the high forest, races away ahead of me. Slowing up in tangled gooseberry brush, I "jump" a group of resting cow elk, which is what hunters say when wild animals bolt up and lumber away after being surprised so badly their hearts jump out of their chests. It grows darker and a light rain starts to fall. At a wide clearing, I'm stopped in my tracks by the fact that thick moss covers the ground in an area thirty feet in diameter. Nothing else grows there. What could cause that?

I walk the rest of the way down in drifting showers of light rain. Along the upper edge of the clearcut I find plenty of flint—worked pieces of conchoidal, shiny black obsidian, some with pressure-flaked flutings. Many have the dull damaged edges of cast-off skin scrapers. All are less translucent than the obsidian I've seen in other localities, and have white flecks, impurities, embedded in the glass. Some large chunks are as opaque as charcoal, hard to see on the gray soil.

Back at the saddle where Freddie dropped me off, the rain stops, and thunder only mutters from far off. There is a weird and deceptive calm under black skies. Breathing easier, I strike off to the west along the undulating ridge where, again, there is no certain evidence of the historic Highline Trail, once an important pack route along the north rim of the caldera. Instead, I follow heavily used cow paths that soon fork and fork again without regard to my intended direction of travel. I've been warned the trail has "fallen into disuse," a forest service euphemism for what happened when they built a road to replace it (the road Freddie drove down below) and then obliterated it with clearcuts and a maze of logging skid trails.

To get back to where I stashed my backpack this morning, I have about five miles to hike along the mountainous ridgeline as it descends another five hundred feet in elevation. Right off the bat, I pick my way over a logged summit through stumps, thickets, and blowdowns along stretches of game trail or overgrown skid tracks that lead to nowhere. Dropping down into another saddle, another open meadow, I see out to the south where the dark thunderstorm is still growing and expanding toward me. There is an ominous heaviness in the air, a lingering dullness despite the distance I've put between myself and Chicoma Mountain. I trudge on through thickets of young spruce and aspen like a man dragging himself through a strange dream. I assume my oppressive mood has to do with the wanton destruction of the forest I pass through. The north rim, I find, has been logged to within an inch of its life—few large trees exist around the edges of extensive cutover areas.

Working my way around the wooded south face of the next long hill, following elk tracks that cross each other like the strands of a braid, I give myself wholly to the task at hand. Without a trail to follow I have to focus far more on the lay of the land and where I'm going moment to moment. Bushwhacking consumes your attention but ultimately draws out the best in a person—if you don't get lost. At each open bald slope, enormous spruce trees line the lower, uncut margins. Grasshoppers fly up ahead of me in waist-high wet grass. Without elk and cow trails to follow, the steep angle of the hillside, almost 45 degrees, would be too slippery to manage. Looking back, I see the summit of Chicoma high up under dark clouds about two miles away. Out across Santa Clara Canyon at my feet, a violent thunderstorm rages over the Sierra de los Valles and the city of Los Alamos perched on the Pajarito Plateau. Inside a blurry curtain of falling rain, lightning strikes light up like glowworms on the summits, and continuous distant thunder rolls on the wind. There is only pale-blue sky above me. Then a shockingly brilliant stab of lightning hits Shell Mountain above the white hoodoos across from me. Big rain is coming.

Hurrying on, I come to a lone cow, mooing. It stands, watching me pass by, still mooing in a long forlorn bellow that echoes across the canyon. Then I come to a pair of cowboy boots just lying out in the open. Nicely tooled, yellow and mahogany facings, nothing wrong with them. Weird.

For a mile, I cross another steep bald slope along now heavily used cow paths, passing through lines of timber that run up in fingers from the forest below. An old two-track, four-wheel-drive road leads through whooshing aspen forest, but then turns aside. I leave it and descend an open slope to the next saddle. There are so many chipmunks and ground squirrels and cows and, up above, vultures soaring overhead, I don't even notice them anymore.

Crossing the grassy flat, I come upon an old campsite with a cast-off chaise lounge still in position for me to take a breather. It creaks under my weight but holds up sturdily. The sag between two mountains where I recline has no name on the map, so I try out some possibilities: Lazy Boy Saddle. La Silla de la Barcalounger. Siesta Gap.

Amused and relaxed for a moment, I notice the forest road swings close, about fifty yards away. It's too windy and cold in the shade, so I heave up and look for a sunny spot to have a snack. Out on a grassy slope the sun is shining under spreading overcast, so I plunk down and dig into some trail mix, drink up the last of a bottle of Gatorade. From there I can see down to long flat meadows along the bottom of Santa Clara Canyon—which, because I've been descending the ridge at the same rate as it has been coming up, doesn't look that deep anymore. With binoculars I make out a rectangular corral at the upper end. The storm appears to be bypassing me, but Chicoma is now shrouded in falling rain.

While I sit there in the grass, about to pack up and move on, I hear a noise. A white SUV roars out onto the grassy flat and cuts toward me. It has the official markings of U.S. Forest Service Law Enforcement on the sides, and a panel of lights on the roof. Before I can react, the lumbering vehicle comes to a halt thirty feet away, and two uniformed officers climb out and walk toward me.

Ten

ALONE SINCE EARLY morning, resting in a solitary meditative state, the last thing I expect is two cops driving up and coming over to talk to me. As they cautiously approach where I'm sitting on the grass, one calls out a greeting.

"Excuse us, sir. We're just on patrol, just checking to make sure everybody's all right."

"Everybody?" I look around to see if I missed somebody. "Nobody here but me and Scooby-Doo!"

They flash wan smiles but their eyes are alert to everything about me. This is not a routine check. They stand over me in crisp dressy uniforms, their radios and sunglasses glinting, their belts heavy with handguns, handcuffs, ammo clips. I read their name tags: The speaker is older, an Anglo named Olson. The younger is Hispanic, named Valles. I tell them everything's fine, it's a beautiful day to be out and about.

"Were you just out glassing?" Valles asks. He means scouting for game with my binoculars, which I have left out on the grass. If I'm a hunter, I'll know what he means.

I tell them, "I'm hiking the old Highline Trail, but there's hardly any trace of it left anymore. And by the way—is that trail down Cañones Creek any better?"

They shake their heads. Have no idea. Never get out on trails, only patrol in vehicles. As we talk, I realize they know nothing about the landscape or landmarks, either. Olson says he envies me out roaming the country like this, but it sounds fake-friendly. In fact, everything they say is designed to elicit information about what I'm up to.

"You guys aren't from around here, are you?"

Olson admits they're from another forest unit, patrolling up here for the first time, but is noncommittal about why. They shift from foot to foot, leather belts creaking. They are casual but guarded, looking at me with cop eyes, which convey an implied threat of force and an air of entitlement being nosy about other people's business. Valles bluntly leans close, peering inside my daypack.

"Were you just out glassing?" he repeats, absently, as if he hadn't already asked me. Pushing a little to see how I react.

"No," I say with a shrug. "But there's plenty of elk around here."

Valles loses interest, but Olson pursues the topic of elk hunting until he, too, seems satisfied.

"Well, you have yourself a fine day of it, sir," he says, touching the brim of his hat. They saunter back to their patrol vehicle, climb in, and drive off.

Alone again, I pack up and move off. The encounter adds to the unease I've felt ever since coming down from Chicoma. I try to shrug it off and let go into the wonder of my wild surroundings. Soon I notice the trail I'm following descends into the very head of Santa Clara Canyon at a point where it levels off and starts going down the other way—where it turns into Rito de los Indios and drops into the caldera beyond.

I have to halt, backtrack, and angle upward. Climbing steeply in the tall grass, now almost dry in the ceaseless wind, I approach the timber along the top of the ridge. Panting, I reach the rim again and continue along toward distant Cerro de la Garita to the west. In between, I see where the rim curves around to the last bald slope, the last saddle—my destination about a mile away. At a steep pitch facing north, my first view in that direction since the top of Chicoma, I see down the whole vast stretch of forested mountain to the red-rock desert spread out below—another world, far away. The sun shines on the hot lowlands where the milk-blue waters of Abiquiu Reservoir sit on a pale plain surrounded by pink and yellow tablelands. Shimmering heat waves make me squint against the glare. To one side is the Pedernal, a sharply truncated butte of black flint standing alone over the foothills, my last destination before leaving the Jemez Mountains.

Between where I stand on the rim of the caldera and the open country about three thousand feet and fifteen miles below is the north slope of the Jemez—a wetly forested volcanic flank falling away in a series of dark plateaus cut by numerous cliff-walled canyons. A virtual terra incognita to all but a few loggers, cowmen, forest rangers, and hunters, this rugged remote highland might as well be on the North Slope of Alaska for all anybody else in New Mexico knows about it. I plan to find out what secrets it holds in the next few days.

Moving on, I keep to the edge of the south-facing rim, picking my way carefully along to avoid the dense, brushy logged areas whenever possible. Route-finding—blazing my own trail across country—is nothing like hiking along an established trail and worlds away from trudging mindlessly along popular throughways like the Pacific Crest or Appalachian trails, which are essentially the interstates of mountain paths. Bushwhacking by myself, I have no camaraderie or conflict with other hikers, and no trail guide to prepare myself for what's to come. There is nobody else going my way. I have only my USGS Polvadera Peak topo map—last updated in 1977, thirty-three years ago—which I study and compare with what I see, constantly, to stay on track. Maybe someday someone will develop a real trail along the "high line" between Chicoma and La Garita once again, but for now it's only me out here. The trailblazer.

Alert only to the lay of the land and my own progress over the last hill before dropping down to the last saddle, I hear an unnatural clunking sound that makes me stop and listen. The thunderstorm seems to have stalled and spread out in low overcast, making the world feel vague and gloomy. I'm low enough that pines and firs line the rim, the spruce and aspen standing farther back in the dappled light of dark timber. And back among them, off to my right, I hear faint human voices.

Without thinking, I head toward the sound of what I take to be people camping in the woods. Eventually, beyond a screen of young trees and brush, I see what looks like a long-term camp in a forest clearing. Amid a great quantity of gear I make out a tent, a campfire with a thread of smoke drifting up, a man with his back to me sitting before it, cooking, and another man getting something out of a black pickup. I'm about to push through the underbrush and say hello when I stop cold at the sight of military-style camouflage netting all around and over their campsite.

My heart skips a beat and I suddenly drop down under cover. The two men and everything, including the pickup and all the gear strewn about—which I now realize are assorted items of military weaponry and field equipment—are fully enclosed in a huge, interlocking, elaborate structure of canopies that blend in completely with the forest around them. Except for the small opening in my direction, the wild drop-off side of the hilltop, the camp is as invisibly hidden as a Serbian gun emplacement in the mountains of Bosnia.

Yet the men are dressed in civilian clothing. My eyes hone in on the holstered handguns at each man's hip and the automatic weapons—assault rifles—sitting on plywood crates. The men bark back and forth at each other about something the one at the pickup can't find. They are decidedly not happy campers. They are, I suddenly realize, who the forest service cops were looking for when they found me—either militia-movement extremists, paramilitary types plotting the downfall of the federal government, or pot growers, armed freelance *drogueros*, who are spreading all over the Southwest, funded by Mexican cartels. And they have concealed themselves so well I almost stumbled into their secret hideout.

Heart thumping, I melt to the ground. So much for glorying in being the lonesome trailblazer. I've unfortunately forgotten that the most serious threat to personal safety in the wilds is still our fellow man. I've stumbled upon pot plantations before while bushwhacking across country, and the fear of some paranoid dude invisibly drawing a bead on me is not pleasant. As quietly as I can, I crawl back the way I came. Terrified they might hear me, I place each hand and each knee slowly down to avoid snapping a twig or rustling a leaf.

Agonizing minutes pass in slow motion. An unbearable tension builds. I force myself to breathe slowly and silently. Eventually I succeed in easing myself over the rim and down the slope into tall grass. Below their line of sight, I steal away, bent over, listening to every sound. Cows moo, ravens caw, and tufts of grass whip in the wind around me. My fright fading with each step farther away, I enter a sheltering grove of limber pine and straighten up to my full height. Under the cover of fiercely blowing wind, I hustle my tail out of there. In a few minutes I reach the bottom, the edge of timber at the open meadow where I left my backpack that morning.

But when I see the clump of fir brush where I hid it, I freeze again. I'm less than a half mile downhill from the armed camp. Stories my brother, a former ranger for the U.S. Forest Service, told me about the hidden snares and gunfire of pot growers on his district in California run through my mind. What if they saw me stash the pack this morning? I'm paralyzed by indecision. Wild thoughts run through my mind. Is it a trap? Are there more than just the two I saw? Is some guy armed and waiting nearby for me to try to retrieve my pack?

Then I feel foolish. Don't think all paranoid like they do, I tell myself. Sure, you're vulnerable, but don't give in to fear. Trust your instincts. You made it this far safely. Calm down and read the sign.

Inching stealthily forward, I see everything is as I left it: only one way in and out, and only my footprints. Trusting the gut feeling I get that all is well, I ease forward and pull the brush away. My pack is undisturbed. Hoisting it up, I retreat back into thick woods and stay under cover as I circle around the meadow.

Every step farther away lets me breathe easier. Any thought of camping nearby is now utterly out of the question. I concentrate only on how to regain my route and push on. Relieved when I come out on the forest road, I decide to hike along it as the quickest method of getting far away. Feeling like a lone commando in enemy territory, I trot along under the heavy weight of my backpack. At first, the fear-induced flood of epinephrine in my blood carries me along swiftly on high alert, listening for the sound of a vehicle coming along or anything that might warrant a sudden dash back into the woods. But after a mile or so, I'm whipped. I cut up into the safety of silent spruce forest and find a place to rest. It finally starts to rain—desultory showers that seal me into the protection of the wilderness.

As heavier and heavier waves of rain pour down, I cover up in rain gear and take stock of my situation. My previous plan was to camp the night and go on in the morning—follow the road west as it loops around behind La Garita and crosses the headwaters of several canyons to reach the La Grulla Plateau, where the trail down Cañones Creek takes off. Now I'm not so sure. With armed weirdos maybe out and about in the morning in their pickup, I'm reluctant to walk the seven miles in broad daylight as I planned. The only alternative short of abandoning the route I've chosen—pushing on right now under cover of rain and oncoming darkness—seems beyond me. It's been one hell of a long day at high altitude and I'm not just starving, I'm exhausted. I need to cook food over my primus stove and set up my tent.

Then faintly in the distance I hear gunshots. I strain to listen over the hissing patter of raindrops, and hear it again, from the direction of the hill-top hideout—shots fired in rapid succession. Unnerved by the sound, I decide there's no way I'm spending the night here. Suddenly resolved, I lift my pack, cover it under my poncho, and head down the road in a ceaseless downpour.

Eleven

THE RAIN IS my friend, I keep telling myself.

Under dark watercolor skies, a midsummer evening light gleams on the muddy road winding through ranks of dripping spruce. Impossible to lose my way, I slop along at a steady pace, ears cocked to every sound, eyes scanning ahead.

Resolved and on my way to somewhere else, I pour it on. The gunshots fresh in my mind, I imagine the two men arguing over a missing can of peaches or bottle of whiskey, a rapid escalation of displaced rage under the camouflage dome, a wild gunfight that leaves neither alive to bother anybody else. I snort grimly, but don't let down my guard. The dim rainy daylight and wet scented forest are my friends, too.

It's the easiest hiking under a heavy backpack I've had yet. Even wet, the road is firm underfoot and the grade is not even challenging to fully loaded logging trucks, for which it was primarily built. The logged-off, burned-over look of the country has a northern feel, the dog-hair thickets of young trees shooting up in the same way as those growing along hundreds of miles of the Alaska Highway. Here the slope of the ancient Jemez stratovolcano faces north, the dark wet spruce are stringy with hanging moss, and tall stands of fireweed in pink bloom add to the boreal impression.

The road drops, then climbs, then drops again, then runs flat and straight behind La Garita, just outside the fence along the Preserve. I pass cattle in great numbers standing on the road. Another long gradual descent winds down to a valley and climbs back up. There's no more rim, no views, just endless low thick spruce-fir-aspen forest, burned or logged. The rain falls in brief earnest showers and in sprinkly mists. A grouse, a fool hen, invisible until it moved, flies up to a low tree branch.

The road rises and falls, rises and falls, all at around 10,000 feet. The long climb out of Chihuahueños Canyon tops out on an open sloping ridge where a herd of elk—maybe sixty strung out on the road and surrounding meadows—stare at my approach. In one surging wave they all leap away downhill in graceful bounding strides. The southwestern equivalent of caribou, elk run with their dark heads up, their reddish summer-smooth coats rippling with big bunching muscles. Even the spotted calves, maybe twenty of them, look like huge African veldt creatures running off. Then a startled cow and calf run across after them, bolting to catch up only ten feet in front of me, the young one racing right along behind the all-out strides of its mama.

After four or five punishing miles from where I started, I notice the road narrows to a rocky double tire track. I get glimpses to the right through mist-shrouded timber of many-fingered forested canyons, the headwater tributaries of Cañones Creek. Elated to be closing in on the end of a marathon day, I feel a second wind climbing the last uphill stretch. On a bare hill where the road forks, I stop and admire the view while tanking up on water and several Snickers bars for the last push. A sunset I can't see glows orange on distant wet mountains. Nearer to the north I see down La Grulla Plateau (*grulla* is Spanish for sandhill crane) and make out the huge prairie called Valle de la Grulla, dotted with shiny ponds and marshy lakes—prime habitat for the whopping big birds that still migrate in reduced flocks across North America. Beyond, last light glimmers atop Mesa Pinabetosa, Cuesta Navajo, and Mesa Alta.

Suddenly aware I've gone for some time without remembering the possibility of danger, I look back and listen. Nothing. Nobody else is out, and night is falling. The last two miles are all downhill, more or less, so I plug on. The rain pours down harder and harder. It roars like a waterfall, plastering my poncho to my head and body, drumming on the backpack high behind my head like hailstones. I hear no thunder, but there is a wild, unholy rushing underfoot as brown creeks flood down the ruts ahead of me.

More cattle stand on the road. But they are too miserable in the deluge to move out of my way until I flick my poncho. One is so startled it goes down onto the mud with a thousand-pound thrashing of hooves. Their eyes glare at me in numb fear.

I can no longer see the topography around me. Relying only on the curve and dip of the road, I forge on. This is no shower, I realize. It means business, continuing like a tropical monsoon, unabated for more than a mile into the serious dark of night. When the road curves around on itself, I switch on my flashlight. Full night is upon me and I'm approaching a low saddle where the trail forks off. Forest opens up to flats and meadows. The rain slackens. I am exhausted beyond belief but keep searching the roadside on the right for sign of a trail. It is listed in guidebooks and on national forest and geological survey maps as "Cañones National Recreation Trail" so I expect some clear evidence of a trailhead, a sign, something.

When the road starts uphill into forest again, I stop, confused. Deciding I must have gone past it, I backtrack, searching more carefully with the flashlight beam. There is nothing but a logging road heading off into fresh stumpland. I give up. It's too dark and rainy. I head downhill in the direction where the trail should be, and once far enough away from the road in a grove of young spruce trees, I drop my pack and start setting up my tent.

Mercifully, the rain fades to a light sprinkle. In ten minutes I'm inside the tent, giddy at the pleasant prospect of shelter and rest, but struggling to get myself inside the damp down sleeping bag. Everything is wet, even my underwear, and the air in the tent is like a foggy night in a half-full dumpster. Yet in a few more minutes, mission accomplished, I drift off into the sleep of the innocent.

A beautiful day arrives on planet Earth. Very moist. Quite fragrant. A wet world of subalpine conifers waits outside my tent flap, the sun not quite over the mountain, aglow on the underbelly of low clouds. The only birds are brilliant golden tanagers flitting about. The creamy speckled bark of smooth alpine firs shines wetly.

After blessed sleep and the dawn of a new day, the threat that seemed so real last night has evaporated. Stiff and sore from yesterday's climb of Chicoma, followed by a five-mile bushwhack and an eight-mile forced march in the rain, I crawl out and heat water for coffee. Tallying up the miles, about fourteen, I figure it's the farthest I've hiked in a day, so far. Nothing like the twenty or thirty miles that distance hikers crank out on a daily basis, of course, but all the same, I'm impressed with what I can do when I push myself.

A new sense of assurance pervades my thoughts. A review of my actions the night before—how I kept my fear in check and took evasive action to avoid the threat from armed crazies in the lawless wilderness—makes me feel confident facing a new day. Morning coffee never tasted better. Bring it on! But with one trial behind me, another looms—the sun does not clear the top of the mountain and shine down on me, drying things out as I'd hoped. Instead, it disappears behind dark, threatening storm clouds coming my way from the direction of Chicoma Mountain. Oh well.

I decide to eat first and then pack up and search for the trail. I cook up what I had on last night's aborted menu, freeze-dried chicken teriyaki with rice, two helpings, plus a special course of granola and dried fruit stirred in hot water. Wolfed down with the appetite and gusto of an escaped prisoner, it tastes memorable in the way mess hall food does when you're starving and there's no other alternative.

Backpack ready and leaned against a tree trunk, I head back up to the forest road. Distant thunder mutters; a light sprinkle falls. Pulling on my rain poncho, I examine, by the light of day, the half mile of road across a meadow where the trail should take off. I find nothing, not a sign or post or track leading off. Only the eroded ruts of a logging road fork off into a recent clearcut. Following it, I come to a pink spiral of plastic hanging from a spruce limb at a hunting camp. A pole is tied between two trees to hang elk carcasses during the fall hunting season, and a ring of blackened rocks is filled with aluminum beer cans. A cow path heads downhill from it.

According to my map, this could be it. It winds along deeper into spruce forest, only cattle and elk prints visible in the mud. It stays along the left side of a drainage dropping off into the canyon where the map says it should be. Yet well-trod trails soon fork off one after another, in every direction—it's like a maze in thick rainy forest, until I notice that all the trees along one route have the trailside branches sawed off. Blown-down trees block the way, slowing me down, but soon there's no doubt. No more than a route chain-sawed through the forest, the "national recreation trail" is in bad shape and could be a dreadful trek if the rain keeps up. On the way back uphill for my pack, thunder booms louder and fresh hissing rain pours down.

But I don't care. I'm dropping off into a wilderness canyon with everything I could possibly need on my back, and I'm up for it. Once beyond the last signs of logging, the trail drops steeper and steeper into a primeval forested abyss, a side gorge leading to the bottom of the main canyon six hundred feet below. In the diffuse daylight of endless rain, there are no shadows. I pause when necessary to reposition the weight of my backpack or plan a route around deadfall trees or shelter beneath great dripping conifers for a reprieve from the slanting rain. Also, I admit, for communion: to admire the mossy splendor of the spruce bark, the scent of the mountain air, the perfection of the silence.

A sloping valle awaits me—broad slick grasslands above Cañones Creek, the trail slimy with mud, gradually descending northward. Here the clouds lie vaguely on canyon walls, and I make good time cruising along above a rushing stream for a mile or so. Huge miasmas of fresh cow droppings are the only obstacles. Then the canyon narrows. A herd of cattle barely parts for me to pass through. A creek comes in from the right, from Mesa del Medio, roaring and tumbling, adding more volume to the brownish-clear water of an already flooding stream.

After about two miles and a thousand-foot drop in elevation, I shelter from a stinging fall of hail under a gargantuan leaning spruce. A barrage of lightning and thunder for ten minutes finally fades into sporadic flashes of intense light and sound. The electrical storm moves on. Once it does, I drop my pack and get out from under my poncho. Except for the white noise of rain, an immaculate stillness pervades the world. Details emerge: An oriole. Ravens. More tanagers. The splash of some big animal crossing downstream. The canyon creatures busy even in the endless summer storm.

Slog on. The canyon narrows even more, descends even steeper through fog-shrouded timber. More downed trees block the trail. Passing around the upended roots of a giant fir, I slip and fall into a wet clay hole and come down on my right foot wrong. It hurts bad. Limping to the relative shelter of a grove of aspen, I rest and doctor a nasty gash on my lower leg, have something to eat and drink. Will this rain never end? Wet to the knees, I change my socks. Only one pair of dry ones left. The rain almost stops—nothing but mist drifting for a few minutes—but then starts coming down hard again. I get up and go on.

Then creek crossings—what was I thinking changing my socks? Icy water swamps the alder banks, and there's nothing I can do but wade across, slosh through, go on. Opening to meadows as the canyon curves to the northeast, the trail crosses back and forth, the current rushing over slippery boulders under overhanging willows. No use trying to stay dry, I tell myself—just keep plodding onward in squishy boots, get through this tunnel of rain.

The canyon walls become dramatically steep on both sides, disappearing into low clouds. I can see the steam of my own breath. Spruce forest dwindles in the transition to pine and Douglas fir. More stream crossings. It all becomes a blur. I've come maybe six miles and the trail stays on the left bank again for a long stretch. Trout dart away as I cross the swollen stream yet again.

Then clouds thin overhead and I see a patch of blue sky. A Stellar jay flies past, calling out in alarm. Startled, I stop and look around. I'm in the deepest gorge imaginable, under tall dripping alders and cottonwoods, the stream thundering by over boulders. Across it, I see a series of pumice slopes descending to the left bank and what looks like a trail that goes up. It dawns on me that this unlikely spot is the trail fork I should have been looking for—where I hike up out of the canyon.

Grateful to the blue jay for keeping me from continuing down the canyon in a daze—there's no signboard or rock cairn or anything to mark the turnoff—I pick my way over mossy logs and boulders to the far bank, my first dry crossing, and start uphill along a wide, well-traveled path. Long steep switchbacks slow me to a panting plod. But here it feels and smells drier, despite the misty rain. I stop and change into my last dry socks. Then onward and upward like a pack mule climbing out of the Grand Canyon. Not much more than a washed-out horse trail cut into white ash and brown boulders, the way climbs through thick oak brush and thickets of aspen. Up from 8,000 feet at the creek to a windy open world hundreds of feet above it, I top out on a flat overlook, dazzled by sunshine suddenly showing through parting clouds. Here at a primitive dirt parking lot enclosed by a rail fence is a trailhead under swaying ponderosa pines, and a trail signpost with no sign. The locals emphatically don't want outsiders using this national forest trail into their secluded wilderness retreat.

And here I throw off my poncho at last, hang things up in the sun and wind to dry, even my soggy jeans and skivvies. There's nobody around, no parked cars. I haven't seen another human since yesterday and it seems perfectly fitting for me to lounge about like a naked savage in the hot sunshine.

Twelve

WHEN I GET everything dry and packed away, I'm amazed it's only a little past noon. The bad dream—the slog down Cañones Creek—actually took only about five hours. After lunch, I'm on my way again, following a sandy washboard road as it climbs up and out of the canyon of canyons.

My plan is to make it as far as the base of the Pedernal, about five miles away, where I'll camp for the night. In the morning I can scramble to the top, stand on the summit of the lone flint butte that towers over Abiquiu (and figures so prominently in the paintings of Georgia O'Keefe), and then hike down and out of the Jemez Mountains at last.

The roadway—even steeper and more eroded than I expected—is a piece of cake. Looping upward around smooth pumice hills to avoid reddish volcanic cliffs, it passes through a beautiful, park-like open forest of pine and fir typical at middle elevations in the Jemez. The trees toss and creak in the warm wind. The sun is bright, incandescent, unbelievable overhead—all I need to keep going under a heavy pack.

After climbing back and forth in long switchbacks between unimaginably deep chasms (known locally as Los Barrancones) the road threads a convoluted way through a bizarre landscape of pinnacles, drop-offs, and slender mesas. One last push and I top out at a sandy saddle, one mile from the trailhead, at a junction with the main forest road that drops down Rito Encino toward Youngsville, at the foot of the mountains.

Puddles of rainwater stand in the sun. The wet pine smell is intoxicating. I head down the steep grade through fluttering aspen, obsidian boulders gleaming in the road cuts. Loaded wood trucks drone along downhill in low gear. Nobody waves back at the lone Anglo backpacker on the shoulder. The animosity the locals on the north side of the Jemez have toward outsiders is legendary (and a perfect cover for paramilitary nuts with assault rifles and illegal immigrants from Mexico tending marijuana gardens).

Below Mesa Escoba the broad winding forest road drops into green pastures yellowing with wet clover and tall groves of Gambel oak. Just past an old weedy corral, I turn up a side road that ascends Temolime Canyon to the Pedernal. Oak brush closes in tightly around a rough, narrow double track with a high grass-grown center. As soon as I reach pine trees again, things don't feel quite right. It's not that steep or difficult, just a steady plod along an old logging road through dark, hot, muggy thickets swarming with flies and gnats and moths, but I press on with growing unease.

About a mile up, right when I see the Pedernal looming like a square black butte through dry jackpine on the left, a stab of lightning strikes the very top. Thunder batters the air around me. I can't believe it—a towering black thunderhead has appeared and spread over the summit. No wonder I felt something impending. I wait and watch. More lightning strikes the mesas around the Pedernal, and booms of thunder crash violently through the pines. Clouds churn and grow higher overhead. The shadow of the storm sweeps over me with sudden cold wind. Beyond the dark roof that closes in over the butte, blue sky and vivid sunshine frame the red-rock desert below.

Fat drops of rain fall from the sky. It's too much. I abruptly turn around and head back down the way I came. It rains lightly along the road, hissing in oak brush, but roars over the Pedernal. Something has snapped inside me and I just want to get this thing over with—get away from the rain that sweeps over in ever more drenching showers. Thoughts of hot sunny desert dance in my head.

Back on the main road in gloomy rain, down and down and down I go. Oak and pine give way to piñon and juniper and sagebrush. Yucca and prickly pear cactus glisten wetly on muddy hillsides. The rain stops and the sun pops out at about 7,600 feet, raising my spirits again. I look back, and the Pedernal stands off to the east in dramatic splendor, about two miles away and two thousand feet above, still draped in curtains of rain. I don't regret at all my impulsive decision to skip climbing it.

The road curves and switchbacks down an amazing side canyon of eroded volcanic badlands with deeply incised ravines of pure-white ash. Desert heat and aridity flow up the canyon over me. I'm delighted. Just as I see the mouth of the canyon and the houses of Youngsville out on a vast yellow plain, a rainbow appears to my right. With one end glimmering over the still-dark Pedernal, colored bands of light curve over and down to a shiny red bluff near Abiquiu Lake. Underneath, silvery air hovers above unbelievably radiant hills dotted with junipers. It looks like a portal to another world.

The fresh sweet smell of rain on dry sagebrush blows me away. The Pedernal finally emerges into sunlight and the storm fades away, only now, when I'm almost out of the mountains. And as it does—as I trudge along the shoulder of the road, leaving the storm and the mountains behind—I have a sudden realization: I've been running away from something vaguely threatening and dangerous ever since I started down from the summit of Chicoma Mountain. First the lightning and thunder on top. Then the maze-like bushwhack and the disturbing encounter with the forest service policemen. Then almost stumbling into the hideout of armed outlaws, and trying to avoid detection by a forced march in a cosmic rainstorm. Then descending Cañones Creek in a relentless downpour and deciding to bypass the Pedernal because of yet more lightning. And having it all fade away as soon as I allow myself to be chased out of the mountains.

Reviewing what has happened to me, I am reminded of a dramatic Tewa myth that John Pesendo told me the last time I saw him. It was the story of a man who climbed to the top of Chicoma Mountain long ago and was chased back down by a terrific storm, too.

A version of the tale appears in somewhat different form in a book called *American Indian Myths and Legends*, selected and edited by Richard Erdoes and Alfonso Ortiz. A Tewa from Ohkay Owinge Pueblo, Ortiz was a professor of anthropology who recorded and translated the story from the Tewa language as he heard it in the 1960s, under the title "The Stolen Wife."

Briefly, a Tewa man's wife is stolen from him by the governor of the Yellow Kachina people, whose home is on top of Chicoma Mountain. The man climbs the peak to retrieve his wife. The powerful governor, who provides rain to the Tewa, engages the husband in magical ordeals and tests to see who has the most power to keep the woman. The husband, aided by Grandmother Spider, wins and temporarily destroys the governor. Husband and wife run down the mountain. In the distance, a small white cloud forms over the peak, signifying that the governor is coming back to life—is beginning to breathe again. He unleashes all the forces at his disposal upon the fleeing couple. The sky darkens, thunder and lightning strike at them, and rain falls on them, harder and harder. Hail pounds down violently, and only because birds gather protectively above them are the husband and wife able to survive and make it home.

In John Pesendo's version, it was more obvious that the events in the story were metaphors for what happens when people come in contact with the supernatural power on top of Chicoma Mountain.

"When somebody goes up there, on the governor's rooftop, something always happens," he said after telling me the story. He clearly made the point that trials will ensue and that a person will not come down unscathed. I could now vouch for the fact that what he predicted had come true—for me, at least.

And just like in the story, after the danger and hardship have been left behind, the world is refreshed and renewed by the blessing of moisture in an arid land. A shimmering rainbow, so delicate and ephemeral that it already fades before my eyes, has welcomed me back to the ordinary world of the desert lowlands.

PART FOUR

Antler

He must be a witch to seek knowledge in such a place, in such miserable weather.

—John Muir's Tlingit Indian companion, after they climbed an Alaskan mountain in a blinding snowstorm

One

A WEEK OR two later my injured right foot seems healed and sound. On the very hot morning of August 12, I resume my walk around the horizon at Poshu Owinge, a Tewa pueblo ruin on the Chama River near Abiquiu. It sits baking on a high flat bench above green irrigated farmland. I'm not alone—joining me for the day is my wife and a friend, Cody Burch, who both lead the way up a rocky hillside on a trail through Apache plume brush, cactus, and juniper. The Pedernal stands aloof nearby, a dark glaring butte above wooded volcanic mesas.

The top of the bench is wide open and bare of anything resembling the once-busy Indian town, just mounds of earth and rock covered in weeds. It has been empty and silent like this for almost five hundred years. From a high vantage point we make out the rectangular outlines of room blocks and walls, the circular kivas, the greater and lesser plazas. Otherwise, all is wind-swept desolation.

Closer up, we see broken shards of pottery and fragments of worked flint everywhere. The two women wander off under a burning sun talking about what life must have been like here in the 1400s and 1500s, the heyday of Poshu Owinge, the Tewa name for this place, which means "Village Above the Muddy River." And today, living up to its name, the Rio Chama runs high and muddy between tall fluttering cottonwoods, the water a creamy, silty, reddish color from summer rains.

I skirt around heaped masses of ashy-white adobe dirt and lava rocks, avoiding weed thickets and thorn brush, marveling at how little of the native plant life has grown back after so long a passage of time. In the center of a huge plaza area I come to a mounded circle of dark boulders about sixty feet across, a "great kiva" all by itself.

According to Tewa oral history, this town and the one in ruins at Ojo Caliente, fifteen miles northeast, are the places where the two migrating divisions of ancestral Tewa paused before joining together (as winter and summer clans) in the eventual founding of the Rio Grande Valley pueblos we know today. My pilgrimage to the top of Canjilon Mountain, their sacred peak of the north, starts here and will end at the ruin near Ojo Caliente.

At a lookout structure on the rim of the bench, I rejoin the women.

"This place is amazing," Cody says.

"But a little sad," Theresa adds.

Even with mountain breezes blowing, the morning grows uncomfortably hot on the dry flat. We retreat to the shade of a scrubby piñon and finish off the water we brought. We are surrounded by cane cholla, prickly pear, and broom snakeweed. Wild flowers only a few inches tall have tiny blue blossoms. Underfoot, most of the pottery pieces we see are dull gray or brown, undecorated "utility ware" of everyday use. A few are painted—black dots and lines on pale buff or shiny red surfaces. And most of the flint is milky white, rare in this area.

Sweating profusely, we troop back down to Cody's Honda Civic parked at a highway pullout, and go on. After lunch at an upscale tourist trap in Abiquiu called Bode's, we shoot up out of the canyon where Abiquiu Dam sits and emerge onto a wide plain. Across the reservoir to the south, I see where I came out at Youngsville after crossing the Jemez Mountains. The dark volcanic landscape recedes to a distance as the brilliant reds and yellows of sandstone cliffs appear. In a flash, it's as if we've been transported to the red-rock country of Utah's canyonlands. An isolated remnant of that same geology, a bit of the Four Corners and the Colorado Plateau exposed around the Piedra Lumbre Plain, this is the same bright-colored countryside that Georgia O'Keefe celebrated in her famous paintings.

Highway 84 crosses the lowest of the sedimentary rock layers, the purple and gray shale of the Chinle Formation, and at rounded eroded hills thick with dinosaur bones we turn off on a road leading up to Ghost Ranch, our immediate destination. Spectacular areas of maroon, lavender, and yellow earth appear, the shale interlayered with pastel shades of sandstone and conglomerate. Upper layers are harder, forming brick-red headlands and slickrock palisades that grade into the vertical cliffs of yellow Entrada sandstone visible from far away—I saw them from the top of Chicoma Mountain.

The bare cliffs of the Entrada Formation stand like yellow walls for miles around the basin and form long deep side canyons. A hard rock formed of windblown sand, it hollows out in scalloped overhangs and grand amphitheaters, arches and windows, pinnacles and slot canyons. On top, the cliffs are capped by even harder white gypsum and limestone of the Todilto Formation. Above that are receding ledges and slopes of the Morrison, pastel layers of softer shale and sandstone that lead up to the skyline mesas above, great plateaus of resistant Dakota sandstone. Our hike today will be a closeup look at these formations carved by the Arroyo del Yeso into a once-secret place now known by the prosaic name Box Canyon.

The reason for what at first glance might seem like a side trip is that unlike the connecting links between other mountain ranges, the only wild unroaded area on the way up to Canjilon Mountain is right here between the Chama Valley and the midlevel mesas south of the irrigated Canjilon Plain. Day-trippers to an ancient place of power, we follow the road to where Ghost Ranch sits in the mouth of the canyon like a small town. A pair of glossy black ravens squabble and caw at each other in a moist wash lined with juniper and box elder. Once a cattle ranch known locally as *Rancho de los Brujos* because of the Indian sorcerers who still frequented the hidden water canyon after Hispanic settlement in the 1800s, the spread was purchased from the Archuleta family in the 1930s and converted into a retreat and conference center. Told by previous residents that evil spirits still inhabited the narrow Box Canyon, the new Anglo occupants came to call the place Ghost Ranch. It was donated to the Presbyterian Church, a powerful presence in northern New Mexico, in 1955.

The stylish adobe buildings and irrigated hayfields obscure the remains of older Indian settlement. We sign in at the office where sprinklers ratchet lazily around on a wide wet lawn, then park in the shade of giant cottonwoods near the cafeteria. The place has a decidedly offbeat resort feel as two young women in bikinis and flip-flops saunter in and out of the laundromat. A bus pulls up and disgorges a Christian youth group. The noonday somnolence between shimmering cliffs of golden sandstone is shattered by the screams and laughter of teenagers.

We gear up and head off with daypacks under the blazing sun. Thunderheads grow tall over Kitchen Mesa to the right, and a nice breeze blows from behind, from the faraway Pedernal to the south. We pass hidden casitas, overnight cottages lining a draw to the left, and a large conference building full of people with handwritten name labels stuck to their shirts and blouses. The road degenerates into a wide track that climbs up onto a sagebrush benchland beside a deep arroyo watered by a small creek.

Theresa and Cody stop and lather up with sunscreen. The sage bushes are tall, minty-smelling, peeping with flitting tiny birds. Shiny black Pinacate beetles (armored stink bugs) almost an inch long crawl everywhere on the reddish dirt. When my shadow passes over them, they raise their tail ends in the air and give off a foul odor (to warn off predators, I presume). Disturbing them or messing with them intentionally can cause thunderstorms, I was once told by a Paiute Indian friend.

We pass two six-sided log hogans, the traditional houses of Navajo people, constructed decades ago by hired local Diné men. Instead of dirt roofs, they are covered with concrete painted brown to look like dirt. They are cool and empty inside, the dirt floors littered with trash.

A single floating cloud gives us our first shade at the base of sandstone-cliffs—red and yellow and creamy-white banded layers of glittering rock glaring down from on high. Recent heavy rains have washed out the trail in places. Wet soil around an irrigation ditch pond grows sage and chamisa bushes tall enough to hang over our heads. The damp desert smells are rich and heady. Lone chimneys of rock stand out from high walls. Some have fallen into piles of angular, flat-faced boulders the trail skirts around. One is carved with hundreds of initials and graffiti.

At the edge of a shady riparian woodland, we leave the main route up the mesa and drop down into the arroyo itself. Cool and damp among cottonwood and willow, surrounded by junipers thick with frosty purple berries and oaks heavy with pale-green acorns, the way up Box Canyon winds back and forth between steep rock walls. The earth of the bare trail changes color with each different rock layer exposed. Our brisk gallivant slows to a crawl as we gawk at the amazing transformation around us. The stream is clear and cool, lined with brown birch trees and tall Douglas firs dwarfed by brooding shadowy cliffs high overhead.

Dark clouds appear in the slot of blue sky above, and we hear distant thunder. A few stray raindrops fall—great icy plops of water hit my bare neck. The creek bed has been scoured out to bedrock at one place, exposing alternating layers of maroon and turquoise shale so brilliant in the limpid air the colors seem unreal, artificial. The canyon becomes a winding gorge.

Dense birch and willow drape over tunnel-like passages. Great aged fir trees lean out into moist air filled with darting swallows. A side canyon comes in from the left with deep pools of milky water (from the gypsum, or *yeso*, washed down from above) caught in a wedge of orange sandstone boulders. One is a perfect swimming hole, we decide, now that the sun glares down again, but we'll take a dip later—first we want to reach the end, the box in the canyon, not far ahead.

Soon the walls close in and we follow the only route possible—the bedrock floor of a classic red-rock slot canyon. We splash up the rushing creek, the air redolent of mud and sandbar and moss. Hanging hillsides of luminescent birch, skunkbrush sumac, and poison ivy give a subtropical feel despite the massive boles of Douglas fir and ponderosa pine reaching high overhead. Yellow flowers of goldenrod show in open spots, and pollen floats thickly in shafts of sunlight. Cody, suffering from pollen allergies, has been taking Chinese herbal capsules. I ask her if she's okay.

"So far, so good," she says cheerfully.

The bare bedrock channel passes under a mossy log four feet thick spanning the gloomy narrows over our heads. There are hanging curtains of wild grape and wet clay banks with a million green stalks of horsetail. It grows cooler. Water bugs skitter across every pool, and songbirds twitter happily in the vaporous twilight. We become silent and wide-eyed in the natural cathedral. No wonder brujos came here: the underworld is revealed.

The two cliffs on either side then come together in a vast hollow amphitheater, the box, the end of the trail. The vault of moist air is cut by endlessly swooping swallows. The solid rock of the stream is blocked by a jumble of fallen boulders we have to scramble over. We are shushed by how the chamber echoes with our voices, as if some hidden people were muttering in the eaves above us. Even our panting breaths echo. I can't imagine how forbidding this place would be in the dark of night when nothing would be familiar (and when witches are abroad).

We halt in the center under a dry pour-off a hundred feet up, a horseshoe of rock framing blue sky and puffy white clouds. The pointed tips of fir trees poke up into the light. Partway down the curving wall there's a horizontal mossy layer, and below that everything glistens with dripping water—a spring oozing from porous bedrock in an arc sixty feet around us, the source of the stream. The shade is deep. Virginia creeper vines cover all the bushes. A flash flood would kill all three of us—the pour-off impact zone is bare and muddy and scattered with shattered boulders that came down with the last flood.

After gazing in wonder, inspecting the flowing cliff wall (and tasting the water—earthy with an odor of portland cement), we retreat to a higher safe spot to one side. We marvel at the deep silence of an ancient grotto carved deep into the red-rock plateau. The muffling of the walls is so complete we can hear amplified echoes of faraway wind from the outside world. One fir tree is immense, the trunk six feet in diameter, the black furrows of bark a half foot deep. It would have been alive a thousand years ago—a living witness to all those other visitors, sorcerers or not, who have come here before us.

Two

ON THE SUNNY side of the canyon box, up a bank from the tinkling stream, I discover a large thicket of berry bushes. Mixed together are red wax currants and tart black gooseberries. I call Cody and Theresa to feast with me. The spiny gooseberry canes draw our blood. It seems fair—extracting a price for gorging on such delicious wild fruit.

Eventually we head back the way we came. (There is no alternative short of bouldering up a terrifying narrow chute behind the giant fir tree.) On the way back we find that the youth group has taken possession of the swimming hole—about fifteen teenagers, each with a plastic bottle of Arrowhead spring water—wading, splashing, shouting, climbing boulders, taking photos. Their blonde female counselor, hardly older than they are, smiles and waves at us with weary resignation. The pool is stirred-up soupy mud. Boys fling heavy flat rocks to splash the screaming girls and then chase each other across logs and up slimy banks. It's a scene from Orwell's *Animal Farm*, but probably not as destructive as the periodic flash floods that sweep through here.

Back at the car, Cody discovers she has lost her keys. As she and Theresa wait for a friend to bring her spare set from Santa Fe, I hike back and climb up the mesa beyond the hidden box. The way is littered with empty Arrowhead water bottles and screw caps, even along the stream bed. The kids just threw them away.

Beyond the box, the canyon continues northward and the trail climbs the left side onto Mesa Montosa through open piñon-juniper woodland. The clifftop views are breathtaking glimpses down into the convoluted maze of gorges and mesa tops, a surreal sandstone wilderness where only truly hardy sorcerers of nature seek for knowledge. About two miles up, deep in dense piñon and oak brush, I climb a rock-pile summit, panting, and see off to the north, about fifteen miles away, the pointed edge of Canjilon Mountain. In between are roads and fences and rolling grassland—the national forest and private ranchlands given over to hayfields and cattle grazing that I will bypass when I drive directly up to the base of the peak.

An enormous swallowtail butterfly lands on a purple thistle flower and delicately probes for nectar. The plant is untouchable, a variety called "prickly lettuce," and the butterfly is incredible to see close up—an incandescent yellow, a velvety black, and little spots of periwinkle and pumpkin on the "swallowed" tail parts. Then I notice the other wild flowers blooming around the rock pile. Yellow clover. A pinkish-violet variety of verbena called *dormilón*. And with a start I see rare blossoms of *cachana*, or gayfeather, a weedy-looking, grayish low herb with purplish-red flowers that look like individual tiny tufts of wispy threads. The roots of this plant, *Liatris punctata*, are used as a remedy for sore throat, but more important, they are still carried to ward off the "evil eye" and to protect from the malign activities of witches and sorcerers—brujos. The underground corms are also edible as survival food in an emergency. I dig one up. The long tapering taproot is brown and pearly with many threadlike rootlets.

I put it in my pocket. You never know.

Circling around the wooded mesa top, I cross a dirt road and hear the whine of a distant chainsaw. Working my way down a rocky drainage that I believe will lead me back to the trail I hiked up, I suddenly see a fox or something running uphill toward me, chased by a big white dog. I stand still and watch. Storm clouds block the sun and a stiff warm wind blows from the south into my face. Neither animal is aware of me. The dog slows, panting, and the fox, which I quickly realize is actually a small coyote, stops only thirty feet away and turns to look back at the dog.

Another coyote I can't see breaks out in a weird warbling yapping call from just behind a low hill below. The dog, a scruffy ranch critter, a huge dirty white mutt, turns back toward the other howling coyote. And then so does the small coyote. It slowly follows the dog back down and out of sight in the brush. Fascinated, I run down to the hilltop to see what happens next. The wind is strong, steady, and coming from a perfect direction for the animals not to hear me or catch my scent.

The dog has almost reached the other coyote, which I see standing on a long flat sandstone boulder in plain view, yipping and quavering in full song.

The small coyote yaps sharply in response, and the dog, caught between them, stops and seems confused by the fearless noisy outbursts of both coyotes. As the formerly chased coyote closes in on the dog, the dog retreats, cutting away to the left. I watch it trot off in the direction where I heard the chainsaw.

The coyote on the rock paces back and forth, stopping repeatedly to tilt its head back sharply and open its muzzle wide in the piercing, barking, howling cries that give the animal its nickname, "song dog." Even though I've heard coyotes sing like this, I've never actually seen one doing it in the wild. I'm mesmerized. The coyote keeps it up for five minutes as the other one slowly drifts down and nonchalantly leaps up onto the boulder beside it. Then the second coyote sings out—*awooooo!*—taking over from the first one, which jumps down from the rock and noses idly around in the brush.

All this time only my head is above the line of hill as I watch in rapt, total concentration. Then as they go silent and move off to the left together, one of them finally seems to make out my shape and comes to a halt, staring directly at me with those deep, unnerving yellow eyes. The other one does the same. I don't move, don't twitch, don't blink, but I know the game is over. In a flash of ratty gray fur they both melt away into the brush and disappear.

I run around the hill in the direction the coyotes are heading and wait, panting. I realize I am looking down where the hidden box canyon appears like a dark serpentine slit in the earth far below. A sudden thought occurs to me—according to Navajo Indian friends, there are Navajo witches called Skinwalkers who take the shape of coyotes and roam around at night. I dig in my pocket for the cachana root, then feel foolish. It's broad daylight, anyway.

Sure enough, the two coyotes appear, trotting across country at a leisurely pace, a splendid pair of wild creatures on the move in the open world. As a sort of experiment, I make a wet kissing, squeaking sound with my lips, which I've done before to draw the attention of coyotes. It mimics the sound of, say, a wounded rodent. One coyote stops and stares back at the sound, listening, ears twitching in curiosity. It reassures me that these are real flesh-and-blood coyotes, hunting for a meal, at least. When they disappear over the far ridge, I head back, still giddy from the stirring experience.

John Pesendo once casually mentioned that Tewa pilgrims on the way to somewhere powerful try to pay attention to what the world is showing them. He said that sometimes in the flight of birds, the passage of water, the sound of wind, the configuration of clouds, or the appearance of wild animals, the pilgrims can glean some secret shared with those who seek life out in the open air. After witnessing the secret behavior of coyotes, I could definitely relate.

Back at Ghost Ranch headquarters, at dinnertime, Theresa and Cody sit on wooden easy chairs under the shade of cottonwood trees, still waiting for a friend to arrive with a spare key to Cody's car. I plunk down into an empty chair, exhausted. People stream by to the cafeteria for supper, more people than I ever imagined were there—easily seventy or eighty—coming in golf carts and on foot from every direction.

Cody tells me about a disagreeable encounter with the front desk lady in the main office where she went to ask if there was somebody at Ghost Ranch who could unlock cars. Cody Burch is a Doctor of Oriental Medicine and a case manager for developmentally disabled people receiving government services—one of my wife's coworkers. A fit, happy, and ambitious woman who is famously professional and competent, she has little use or patience for puffed-up, self-important people.

"So there I am," she says, "explaining how I locked myself out of my car, asking her a simple question, and she goes all witchy and says, 'Hmm, well, *you* should have a car like *I* do, with *OnStar*, and a simple phone call unlocks your car!' And I'm like, 'Well, I don't. Is there anyone here who can help me?' And she's all, 'Nope. How could you do that? Not keep a spare key?' And I'm like, forget this person. She is so rude, so impossible. So I ask, 'Since there's no cell phone reception here, can I use your phone to call for help?' and she says, 'No, sorry. There's only one public phone, a pay phone around the corner.' But there's somebody using it, deep in a long conversation, so I go back and there's the phone on her desk not being used. But do you think she'll let me use it? No way!"

Eventually Cody reached the office in Santa Fe where another coworker, Teresa Maestas, a case manager who lives near Abiquiu, agreed to bring Cody's spare key out to her on the way home. As we sit in the shade talking, I see Teresa's car pull up on the other side of the cafeteria. We jump up and go look for her in the throngs of people. We find her talking to the rude front desk lady, a tall, florid Anglo woman with stringy gray hair who seems surprised and disturbed by Cody and my wife so happily and thankfully greeting Teresa. As my wife hugs Teresa, the old lady snarls, "I've known her longer than *you*!"

All three younger women are taken aback. How someone so emotionally immature could be left in charge of the front desk at Ghost Ranch is a mystery. But nobody snaps back at her, perhaps wary of a nasty bruja's malevolent power. Our friend Teresa blushes and, once away from the woman, explains that she herself once worked at Ghost Ranch before she was married, teaching traditional weaving, and that she knew the old lady from that time.

Teresa, who has a small farm on the Rio Chama at Medanales, is from a long line of strong women—she's the daughter and granddaughter of the famous weavers Cordelia Coronado and Agueda Martinez, respectively. (Agueda has a beautiful piece on display in the Smithsonian Institution in Washington, D.C.) At Cody's car, she hands over the key, and we're back in business. Cody digs out snack food and warm drink and we stand around talking. Teresa says when she worked here at the ranch she spent nights in one of those Navajo hogans we saw up the canyon.

"Because nobody would stay in them, they were free," she says. "So I stayed there instead of one of the casitas, which would've been deducted from my pay. And, believe me, they didn't pay much here, not for locals anyway."

A storm is finally closing in on us as we say our goodbyes and drive off, following Teresa's car out to the highway. I ride in back. We plan to stop in Española for dinner at a restaurant. Lightning strikes all around us and thunder booms. Cody and Theresa squeal at each closer stab of brilliant light. Black clouds lower overhead and rain comes in blinding curtains, pounding the desert in a roaring deluge. Cody slows to a crawl, the Honda's wipers at top speed barely enough to see ten feet ahead.

"It's like we're going through a car wash!" Cody shouts over the din. "The power rinse cycle!"

Once on the highway and down Trujillo Hill into the Chama Valley below the dam, the rain slackens and thunder rolls farther away. But then two crazed horses come clopping down the pavement through sheets of flooding brown water. They finally veer off and we pick up speed. It rains and thunders all the way to Española.

Just as we get to Angelina's Restaurant, the power goes off. They say they can't seat us—the place is dark and hushed, full of people eating. We get back on the road and cross the Rio Grande. We pull in at Joann's Ranch-O-Casados Restaurant on the Taos Highway. The lights are on inside. We're starving and thankful.

Cody says, "Angelina's was packed. Look at this—hardly anybody is eating here. That probably means the food is not as good."

"I will overlook that," my wife announces, climbing out into the rain.

Cody laughs. "You'd eat your tennis shoe right now!"

Three

BACK THE NEXT day to continue my journey alone, I pass Ghost Ranch in a speeding pickup and continue up the Chama Highway toward the canyon of Canjilon Creek. Out in the middle of nowhere is the Piedra Lumbre Educational Center, which used to be called Ghost Ranch Living Museum, a much better title—but both are euphemisms. The place is a zoo, plain and simple, that houses the wild animals of northern New Mexico in cages. That said, it is also the best and most effective place to become familiar with the wild fauna of El Norte.

The highway curves north into an opening of sensational red-rock cliffs, a mouth of canyon that divides Mesa Montosa on the right from Mesa de los Viejos on the left. As a historical route to the Hispanic settlements in the Tierra Amarilla country to the north, it avoids what is now called Chama River Canyon Wilderness farther west. That remote gorge through a rugged plateau is still an empty corner of New Mexico, a land of unfamiliar names like White Place, Spring Canyon, and Wolf Draw. Cañada Simon, Cañada Jose, and Cañada Tanques Lleguas. Horse Heaven Canyon, Boot Jack Canyon, and Daggett Canyon. Mesa Golondrina, Mesa Laguna, and Mesa de los Indios. Pollywog Pond, Dead Man Peak, and Dead Deer Tank. Places left for another time; a different expedition than this one.

I pull in at Echo Amphitheater, an enormous natural recess and overhang in the sandstone wall of Mesa de los Viejos, a rare and special spot I've visited since I was a little boy. In brush and woodland at 6,600 feet, the trail from the parking lot heads up a short canyon under the towering face of cliff. A national forest trail guide says, "As clear as crystal, your echo comes bouncing back at you at this delightful scenic area set amid the giant red rocks." The interpretive nature trail, which takes you to various viewpoints and shouting spots, is best walked when there are no crowds of visitors, like today.

The only person I meet is a little old lady coming slowly back in mall-walkers and a crumpled yellow bonnet. She has an amazed look in her eyes and carries a handful of picked flowers.

"I've been here since the sun rose," she tells me. "This place is like a tiny national park!"

Already blistering hot in the scalding sun of the desert, but cool and damp in the shade of the amphitheater, the red-earth banks are still wet from yesterday's rainstorm and covered in nodding wild flowers. Unlike other visitors who shout and scream, I wait until I'm at an elevated promontory overlooking the bare bowl-like basin and then simply say "Hello" in a normal voice.

"*Hello*," I hear myself say back. The echo is perfect and uncanny and makes my hackles stand up.

"Wow."

"*Wow.*"

Then before I can say anything else, I hear an eerie muttering of faint voices from the wall. Startled, I listen until I realize more people have arrived and are hiking up. The echo of them talking to each other is what I'm hearing.

The highway climbs up out of the oak and pine of Canjilon Canyon onto open sagebrush plains at Las Jollas, where yellow clay dirt shows through. The Tewa, Navajo, and Spanish names for this higher tableland all mean "yellow earth." Here I get my first unrestricted view of Canjilon Mountain about ten miles away due northeast, looking just as the Tewa name says—*Tse Shu Pin*, "Hazy or Shimmering Mountain." The summit is a few curved points like an indistinct antler lying on the highest promontory of broad mesa. Hazy Mountain is the least known of the four directional peaks on my pilgrim path, despite the fact that it is possible to drive to the very top in a four-wheel-drive vehicle. I choose to climb it on foot, of course, but first I have to get close enough.

The intervening country is all cattle-grazing lands crisscrossed by dirt roads and barbwire fences and no real hiking trails per se. Four miles up, I turn right on a two-lane highway that cuts back east over pine-wooded hills to a wide, sloping irrigated plain where the village of Canjilon sits. At the ranger station I get the last word on the latest conditions in the high country from a lovely, dark-haired Hispanic cowgirl who plies me with maps and brochures and assurances that I'll have a wonderful time on my journey. Then she admits I'm the first person she's ever met who plans to walk up instead of ride a horse or drive an ATV!

A paved county road heads north uphill, then east, past rural homesteads and alfalfa fields. There are many abandoned adobe buildings and new mobile homes. Horses and cattle roam green pastures. At 8,000 feet the rolling grasslands are dotted with isolated dense clumps of trees, called *mogotes*. Here they are pure stands of Gambel oak, but higher up they consist of aspen trees. There is very little relief to the land—just a steady, steep uphill trend toward the high mesa-points of Canjilon. Sunflowers line the road and dusty chokecherry thickets hang with ripe black fruit.

At the turnoff to Canjilon Lakes, cowboys riding horseback and driving ATVs herd a hundred cattle up a long grassy valley on the Martinez Ranch. The road northward is newly paved and smooth, winding and looping up rolling prairies and through *mogotes de alamillo*—isolated aspen groves. I quickly arrive at the south-facing balds of Canjilon Mountain, itself in dense spruce forest at 9,900 feet.

From where I pull in at Lower Canjilon Lake, the summit looks like a gentle grassy bluff with timber dark on top. A deceptive impression, I fear, caused by the fact that there's nothing else standing up high for dozens of miles in any direction. The map says it goes up a thousand feet above me, to just under 11,000 feet. The country here is obviously the result of intense glaciation. Thick sheets of ice flowing south from the San Juan range as recently as fifteen thousand years ago smoothed and rounded the landscape, as well as deposited all the rocks and boulders. Granite, quartzite, schist, marble, gneiss, limestone, and other hard rocks are all spherical or globular and sanded to a smooth polished surface from being rolled along for eons under thousands of feet of ice.

The Canjilon lakes—Lower, Middle, and Upper, as well as scores of others, most unnamed—are spring-fed pothole trout lakes. They fill the basins left by moraine deposits surrounding the last lobes and chunks of Pleistocene glaciers. Some are ponds or just wet vegas—meadows with thick stands of corn lily. The Englemann spruce and subalpine fir and quaking aspen that form irregular patches of dark northern forest around the lakes make the scene as picturesque as somewhere in the Canadian Rockies.

A few people are fishing but this is a remote and little-known corner of highland New Mexico. The silence is deep, the air thin, the view of the faraway south incredible. I ask one fisherman if he's had any luck.

"Not even a bite," he says, shaking his head sadly.

Up the road, at Middle Canjilon Lake, solid stands of aspen glimmer in the breeze, then give way to unmoving, deep dark spruce forest, then abruptly to open undulating hills of grass swept by ceaseless gusts. At the end of the road is what appears to be the largest of the lakes (Upper) and where most of the few people present are gathered, fishing. (The largest lake is probably

Laguna Honda, hidden away from the main swath of lakes, as long as three football fields and one wide.) The water is low, there's an algae bloom, and weeds choke the narrow coves and bays.

Near the forest service outhouses are concrete benches and cook stoves along a trail, an old livestock drive route into higher country. Here the creamy white bark of tall old aspens is carved with names and dates going back fifty years. Mosquitoes are thick from all the standing water. Mixed in with lush grasses are dark-blue gentians, white yarrow, pale-purple asters. Orange paintbrush flowers cover entire hillsides. (They have to be the most ubiquitous wild flowers in El Norte—I've seen them everywhere, at all elevations along my trail.)

I make a quick reconnaissance to figure out the lay of the land and decide which way to climb to the top of the mountain. My hike out the trail skirts marshy ponds, crosses breezy meadows, wends through shaded conifer forest. At a bare rocky moraine I find springs flowing, rivulets of icy water tumbling down among nodding blue columbines to Canjilon Creek in the valley below. Boulders are piled up in conical cairns—the trail becomes less a path and more a vague route.

A hawk circles above a high white rock bluff. Routes fork and horse hoofprints take off in two directions. I startle a flock of grouse—the full-sized mother does the usual thing of flying up to a tree and clucking to her young, which foolishly act like I can't see them tiptoeing through the grass twenty feet away. I cross a mucky-smelling peat bog that wobbles under my feet, and spot a mama turkey and seven young in single file melting away quickly over a hill.

Eventually I decide to set up camp at Lower Lake campground, site number four, where nobody else is around. A concrete picnic table and steel fire ring sit on a flat beside a sloping meadow in full view of the summit, perhaps a mile away as the crow flies. Under a lone spruce tree, I set up my green teepee-shaped tent I use for car camping—it's much roomier than my backpacking pup tent; I can stand up in it to change clothes.

As I settle in and prepare for the ascent, a light sprinkle falls from drifting clouds. I've had the feeling all morning that I would be able to climb Canjilon this afternoon without fear of lightning, even though dramatic dark thunderstorms are building to the south, over the Jemez Mountains. Just a gut feeling, no more, but after my bad feeling coming down from Chicoma turned out to be a premonition of things to come, I tend to trust it. And if I'm wrong I can always come back down and start over tomorrow morning.

The sprinkle stops, patches of blue sky show. Strong breezes blow through swaying aspen. Yellowing stands of corn lily on the meadow look bedraggled and autumnal. Clumps of elderberry bush hang with scarlet clusters of tart bitter berries. And overhead, an endless high-pitched cawing of ravens fills the air from where they perch in the tops of swaying spruce trees.

Tent secure, my pickup locked, I lift a heavy daypack and head off. I'm carrying a poncho and heavy flannel shirt, food and water, a strap-on head lamp that replaces my old battered flashlight (in case I come back after dark), and the usual survival stuff I always bring along, including knife, matches, pitchwood kindling, and first aid kit. According to the forest service trail guide and the fisherman I spoke to, I have two options: the long way over the summit and back down Canjilon Creek is about nine miles, the short way maybe five or six. I should be fine either way.

Four

BELOW MY CAMPSITE I cross a bubbling alder-lined creek and follow a two-track 4x4 road uphill. A giant black raven circles high over my head, cawing like crazy. I look back. The view south beyond tall spruce skims over rolling grassy hills, over distant Mogote Ridge and the last wooded mesas, to where the entire world is blotted out by dark storm clouds, rain, and lightning. But perfect here—cool, breezy, a few raindrops, areas of blue sky. Maybe seventy degrees in the sun, when it shows itself.

I go on. The route leads through more wide glacial potholes that used to be lakes but are now marshy meadows ringed by forest. The local ravens keep flying over me, cawing, checking me out, dogging my trail. I presume they think I'm a fisherman and are anticipating the magical appearance of fresh delicious trout guts. In wet woods along the nameless creek are elegant monkshood flowers, deep dark blue and poisonous, tiny monk's cowls swaying at eye level. The route has been freshly blazed on trees with an axe. Thistles as tall as a man have ragged flower spikes that sting. A garter snake whips away over a log, reminding me that I have yet to see a rattlesnake this summer—which is really not all that surprising. Rare at high altitudes, in heavy forest, rattlesnakes are found mainly from 5,000 to 7,000 feet in El Norte, where most people live, and even then are relatively small and shy compared to the big aggressive diamondbacks in the southern deserts of the state.

The grade grows steeper. I stop frequently, panting. The tall-grass prairie looks spent and golden with so much faded corn lily mixed in. I come upon solitary sentinels of the alien, exotic sebadilla, too, some ten feet tall, and all have gone to seed. Spruce gives way to aspen. Waves of wind whoosh through the groves, making millions of individual leaves flutter.

The track goes through a drift fence and inexplicably heads downhill. After a careful search it dawns on me that there is no trail where the forest service has it marked on their handout map. I'm on my own finding a route along a barbwire fence that climbs a ridge to the left of an unnamed creek. It doesn't matter. I'm never out of sight of the summit or the lakes to my right. I couldn't get lost up here if I tried.

With blue sky overhead and wind blowing the flies and mosquitoes away, views open up to the east to the long sawtooth sierra of the Sangre de Cristo far away. I can see all the land like an apron around the mountain now, and although managed by the Carson National Forest, this whole landscape is a giant ranch, fenced and roaded for cattle grazing. I see fresh tire tracks of pickups in every meadow. Obviously the ranchers who hold permits up here check on their cows from the comfort of their trucks, rather than on horseback.

The compass bearing for the summit is due north so I plunge into a dark grove of aspen with confidence. I come upon a well-used elk trail angling up through young spruce and follow it. Spindly aspen trunks have been chewed by elk teeth higher than I can reach—their winter food when deep snow covers the ground. Blue feathers of a Stellar jay appear on the ground, one after another, in the direction I'm going. Even in dense woods the land goes up in a series of levels or terraces, as if going up gigantic stairs.

Another elk trail cuts left over jumbled rocks. It follows what I suppose glaciologists would call an "esker," a sinuous ridge running along above the surrounding land, the uphill side a deep basin, a wetland. Or it's a great slumping of the unconsolidated till, a landslide feature. However it was formed, it looks strange and unusual.

At about 10,500 feet I get an incredible view south from below the summit. The dark storm has spread out over Abiquiu Lake and looks to be coming my way; rain falls in slanting black veils on Mesa Montosa and Mesa de los Viejos. The shadow of storm cloud creeps up the Canjilon Valley, up Mogote Ridge, where the vegetation is a sunlit mosaic of four types of green, like a patchwork quilt: dark conifer forest, light grassland, mint aspen grove, and rich oak woodland.

Climbing a lateral moraine until it levels out, I find myself on the western edge of a wide basin where a glacier sat for thousands of years digging out a bowl, now studded with timberline spruce. A vulture rockets by. I cut across the head of the basin and hear cows moo in the lowlands and thunder rumbling from miles away. Will I make it to the summit before it gets too dangerous? I keep on.

Before long a view opens up to the west. I see out beyond the Tierra Amarilla country to the high mesas of the Jicarilla Apache Nation on the horizon. Way down, far below, I can see the red rock of the Echo Amphitheater area glowing in the sun. A flock of Stellar jays flies over, calling out stridently. The grassy summit area appears ahead. Plodding on at a breathless elevation over rocky grassland scattered with wind-sprawled spruce, I come to the last slope upward. Out to the northwest a storm passes by, circumventing the mountain, spreading out over the milky-blue skyshine of El Vado Lake and Heron Lake. Beyond the wooded country of the upper Chama, high snow-flecked peaks shine on the horizon—the San Juans in Colorado. Where the slope starts to level off are fresh tracks of many ATVs scoring the hillside, as if riders were racing in a wild pack, chasing each other. The ground becomes hard-packed soil with sparse low grass, and with unexpected ease and suddenness, I find myself standing on the highest point.

Canjilon, the great peak of the north, is basically the flat top of a mesa sloping gently to the east for half a mile, where it drops off more steeply. The immediate summit area where three dirt tracks converge, ATV central, is about the extent of two football fields side by side. A plank cabin sits back from the high point, and beyond it to the north and east is a wall of forest.

Where I stand looking idly around is an old, low rock cairn, and nearby a newer, taller one. A pile of rotting logs and poles covered in rusted wires is all that remains of a forest lookout. Fresh elk tracks show in damp soil. I follow them around until I can read the story: An adult elk, probably this morning, came up over the steep western drop-off and ambled along northward toward the dark spruce timber. Looking down the mesa to the west beyond a hundred-foot scree of rock, I see row upon row of what look like the same kind of parallel moraines I climbed up. A fierce west wind pushes at me, and clouds begin to form overhead.

The cabin turns out to be a one-room frame structure painted white on the outside and three shades of national-forest green on the inside. It has a pitched roof and a loft. The inside is completely trashed, the walls carved with initials and obscenities, the windows broken out, the floor covered in elk droppings, human waste, and beer cans. Most of the graffiti is dated since 2000, but one old message says, "Rich T. and Angelica, Sept. 25, 1954."

Over by the edge of the timber is a sign that says, "This restored cabin is the oldest surviving lookout structure in the Southwest. The cabin and now dismantled tower were built around 1910. Being the highest point around at 10,913 feet and very open, lightning strikes frequently up here. In the summer of 1922, Victor Ortega and his family lived in the tiny cabin while he watched for forest fires from the tower. One afternoon, lightning struck the tower twice, killing Victor on the second strike. The tower and cabin were abandoned and dismantled."

The disturbance of modern human activity on the summit has distracted me. I return to the drop-off and follow it back to the tree line, where I find what I'm looking for—a dry basin, what was once a pond with no outlet. This is the sacred "lake" of the Tewa peak of the north, but the nearby remains of rock cairns are not the currently used shrine.

I head back across the summit area. Behind the cabin are two twenty-five-foot spruce trees growing from the former outhouse pits. Giant, white puffball mushrooms look like five-inch-diameter golf balls sitting on the grass. Picnic trash blows everywhere. And based on the dozens of aluminum beer cans I see littering the mountaintop, Coors Light appears to be the beverage of choice for those who drive up here on ATVs. A line of rock cairns heads east, the "short route" back down to the lakes, but I head off another way. Through thickets and groves of timberline spruce, across open gravel flats and copses of snow-flattened juniper with violet harebell flowers poking through, I come to the end of a long bare point where the earth falls away.

Spread out below I see the shiny glimmer of dozens of small lakes. Thunder rolls from black storms over the land to the south and west. Due east in brilliant sunshine I see Taos Mountain and the vast volcanic field cut by the Rio Grande Gorge. The landmark butte called Tres Orejas ("Three Animal Ears") stands in black shadow against the tawny shine of the plain. My eyes follow the Sangre de Cristo range southward where Truchas Peak is visible beneath another fierce dark storm. The long low wall of Black Mesa, closer, disappears into the vortex of yet another storm centered over Ohkay Owinge and Española.

Nearby I find the ancient main shrine of the Tewa. Lichen-encrusted rocks are piled up in a horseshoe curve, and before it sits a platform mound with a kind of dry moat around it, which is squarish and lined up along the four cardinal directions. Upon all the rock features are piled many smooth, white quartz cobbles, brought and placed here by fasting pilgrims. This is where *Nan Sipu*, the guardians of this "earth navel" live, I was told, represented by the stone structures.

I, too, have been fasting. I'm weak and light-headed. After saying some words of thanks and leaving my own offering at a nearby boulder, I work my way back into the timber out of the cold wind. Here I bump into yet another flock of grouse on grassy openings in spruce. Another mother grouse, again, clucks from a high tree. She nervously paces back and forth along a limb and then bursts away with a pounding flap of wings in the direction her young are fleeing on foot.

Sheltered from the wind, I stop and eat. Lunch is green chile *carne seca*, handfuls of piñon nuts picked last year (big ones), dried apricots, a candy bar, an apple, and fresh sweet water from the campground faucet below. Contented, the lazy wayfarer kicks back with his head propped on his pack and idly regards the sky to the west—from which clouds roll swiftly overhead. The sun lowers into cloud banks. I guess the time to be about five or six. (There is, of course, no cell phone reception on any of these mountains.) I've seen nobody up here at all. Shall I take the long loop back, or the short?

Back on the summit I see that all the storms have forked around this high mountain and are working their way north, far to the east or west. Only a few dark clouds pass overhead, but I'm reluctant to take the long way back, not sure if the weather will stay like this. As I stand gazing around at the late afternoon mountaintop scene, pondering my options, a peregrine falcon swoops suddenly over the west rim and shoots past in front of me. I watch it careen upward behind me into the wind, circling in a banking glide, and then head north along the rim, over the timber and out of sight.

I am instantly enthralled. Falcons have mysteriously appeared at odd moments like this all my life. This one flew off in the direction of the long loop, and I automatically set off after it, knowing the six- or seven-mile tramp across country means I will, at the very least, end up hiking the last part after dark. But who cares? I'm willing to face whatever awaits me after such an amazing omen. Choosing to follow what appears to be guidance from above doesn't mean I won't face danger or challenge, or that I'm sure to survive and be safe. It only means that this is who I am at my best and boldest. And trusting that is what this tramp around the horizon is about, after all.

Five

NORTH OF CANJILON Mountain the steep west face continues for miles, an abrupt edge of a tilted, dissected plateau that's still a wilderness high country despite the sandy tire-track crawling along the crest. A sign placed by the forest service closing the old road to motorized traffic is being ignored—plenty of ATV tracks go the same way, along with the first horse tracks I've seen, two shod horses ridden the same direction I'm going.

I hike easily and steadily along the rim, in and out of spruce forest, wondering why I've seen no bedrock up here. Glacial till, an unsorted mix of boulder, rock, gravel, sand, and clay, covers the land everywhere. Even below the rim, where hundreds of feet of overburden have slumped away, there's only more of the same stuff exposed. I've never seen anything like it in New Mexico. The parallel lines of rocky ridge far below look like strip-mine spoils in rows being reclaimed by spruce trees, or like the side of the mountain slid down that way until it bunched up like the folds of an accordion.

Not far ahead, two elk suddenly look up from grazing. They bolt over a rise, both of them young, a cow and a bull with small forked antlers. I go look where they went. Fresh tracks of running hooves go over the rim and down a steep game trail, which is quickly swallowed up in thick woods. No sound of them below. I go on. Off in the distance the land below the rim spreads out in lush meadows surrounded by forest—Canjilon Meadows. Down there somewhere, hidden, is Burns Lake. More elk tracks crisscross on yellowish sandy dirt. One and then another grouse shoot out from trees and fly away. I see the falcon again, way out on the wind over the western emptiness—sometimes hanging still, rocking in the wind, and looking down, and sometimes riding sideways in the slanting blow.

I come to an open saddle between two hills where dune-like blowouts ring a wet seep. Atop the next hill I enter a very old forest of large wind-twisted trees. Snow-bent trunks, either maroon-gray spruce or corky, white subalpine fir, are all a yard thick. On the soft duff floor littered with spruce cones are elk beds—oval depressions with scuffed places where the large hoofed animals knelt down and got back up. Here all is silent but for endless birdsong. The wind can be heard only far away, out on the edge of the drop-off.

In fact, the birds are so noisy here and beyond, where the backside of the hill opens up to aspen and wild flowers, I'm amazed. They cry, hum, sing, twitter, yelp, hiss, rumble, and warble. And of course all the racket is being made by LGBs, "little gray birds," a not-so-tongue-in-cheek category used by ornithologists to encompass all the difficult to identify songbirds that make our world so auditorially beautiful. They all look more or less the same as they flit from branch to branch, but they could—at this altitude, on this mountain—be any of the following: olive-sided flycatcher, golden-crowned kinglet, blue-gray gnatcatcher, American pipit, plumbeous vireo, warbling vireo, orange-crowned warbler, yellow-rumped warbler, black-throated gray warbler, yellow warbler, hermit warbler, MacGillivray's warbler, common yellowthroat, yellow-breasted chat, lazuli bunting, fox sparrow, white-crowned sparrow, dark-eyed junco, red crossbill, or pine siskin.

All are indistinguishable little gray birds with big singing voices. They are also the primary food of peregrine falcons, which hunt them on the wing, and which probably have them all sorted out according to habits and flight patterns and taste. I've seen them take one in the air and land on a branch with dinner hanging from a claw, a practice that has been going on successfully for tens of thousands of years.

The road winds up and down farther back from the rim through mossy woods and across grassy hillsides. A nighthawk comes beeping overhead, soaring on the uplift over the crest, eating insects as it goes. A white stripe across each long, dark rakish wing stands out brightly. Something piled up on the trail catches my eye and I stop to investigate. Fresh paw prints of a big cat show in bare soil. The pile of dirt and debris looks like the scraped-together leavings of a housecat that buried its scat, but much, much larger. Poking the pile with a stick, I uncover a large fresh dropping unmistakably, by its size and shape, left by a mountain lion. One paw print, a forepaw by the shape of the pad, is almost four inches wide.

It's about 7:30 and I'm two miles north of the summit, alone in the wilderness with the sun going down. A lonely time for people who don't cherish such solitude, but as at dawn and sunrise, this is the time when the wild creatures of the earth are most active. Moving along the rim again, I pass through horizontal shafts of orange sunlight. Along the edge of a wet bog, a flock of chickadees perch twittering in a stunted spruce. I see a big panther amanita mushroom, scarlet with white ragged flecks, like an evil, poisonous gnome face grinning at me from between two boulders. I suddenly see a hawk soaring toward me, above the rim, and then realize it is actually a golden eagle. I watch it glide past overhead, silently, effortlessly, majestically, until it disappears over distant treetops.

Turning inland, a whole army of full-grown grouse explodes in every direction. Flapping madly, one flies directly at me through a corridor between young conifers. Perhaps these are the males, all hanging out together. I've never seen so many in one place at one time.

With the sun lingering low behind me, I come to the headwaters divide between the Canjilon drainage and the Rio Nutrias to the north. Crossing damp meadows and strips of timber until the track becomes a faint muddy tracing, I enter deep shadows and spot two elk grazing ahead. I stop still and watch. They don't see me. Both are huge beautiful animals in thin, reddish summer coats, a cow and a bull standing by the trail at a spring. The grass is so thick and tall they can't see when their heads are down. They munch away lazily, languidly, almost sleepily, only occasionally lifting their heads to look around—a placid evening scene in the deep wilds that holds my rapt attention completely.

A squirrel chatters behind me and the bull looks up, staring in my direction for a long time. His antlers are wide, high, with many tines along the main beams. But then he loses interest and kneels down, comes to rest, chewing his cud, facing away. Then the squirrel goes off like an alarm clock. The cow looks up startled and seems to stare at the unmoving shape of me. Damn squirrel, I think. Shut up! Then I realize there's a small calf near the cow, previously hidden in tall grass. Mother and child go back to nibbling grass. The rapt serenity of observing them is deeply satisfying, but the sun is going down and I need to get going.

The cow suddenly lifts her head and barks sharply in alarm. She stares right at me—did I move? The bull and calf stiffen attentively. The cow barks again, then again. The squirrel chatters loudly behind me, and finally I just give up and start walking forward. All three elk leap away into surrounding forest so fast I'm stunned—the bull from a sitting position in such a way that he was actually running before he got all the way up!

Dead silence. I follow the track right through where the elk grazed beside a bubbling bog and then out across the springy turf of a vast meadow sloping away to the east for a mile. Corn lilies stand in golden rows like a field of corn after harvest. Many nighthawks swoop and make their buzzing beeps overhead in the last rays of the sun. Flowers of blue gentian are everywhere. Leaving the old track behind, I take a shortcut directly across the long meadow, hiking on quivery black bog soil, leaping clear rivulets, using the topo map to guide me in the lingering sunset.

Where the wet vega swoops downward to the south, I see Canjilon Creek come in on the other side of a wide grassy bowl, and start looking for sign of the trail that follows it. Lobes and fingers of dark spruce forest extend out from the right. In an opening of clouds in the southeast sky I see a rising half moon. I come to a giant solitary spruce with a six-foot-diameter trunk. Cow beds and cow pies cover the ground around it. The sun is finally down and automatically I start looking for a dead branch or something suitable to use as a lion club. Dusk is the time of the predator, and without any wolves in this country (the natural enemy of the big cats) the solitary cougars are, as the fisherman I met said of them, "thick as flies."

Unlike ancient times when nobody went abroad at dusk or night without weapons, modern American hikers nonchalantly and unwittingly boogie along through perfect ambush spots with nothing to protect them but their bare hands. Not me. A three-foot club may not be much against two hundred pounds of muscled fang and claw, but it keeps me alert and ready for anything. I find a heavy dry spruce limb about the right size and feel its heft. It has a rough knob on one side at the end that makes it look like a shillelagh (pronounced *she-LAY-lee*), an Irish club or cudgel made of oak or blackthorn. In olden times it was all that many poor Celtic warriors carried into battle. I bang it on trees and bushes as I go along. It's highly unlikely I'll ever be attacked by a mountain lion, but I refuse to be easy prey.

My right foot is starting to go lame again. I estimate I have three or four miles more to cover, and all of it more or less downhill, so no worries. There's no road or trail, just plastic route poles planted in the ground about two to three hundred yards apart to show the way. As the light dims, I worry that soon I won't be able to see the poles—I could lose my way. Then I laugh at myself. I've come back bushwhacking through the wilds at night dozens of times in my life. Why now do I worry? Well, a small voice in my head replies, because then I was younger and immortal and stupid . . .

The route stays to the right along Canjilon Creek, but the stream is not running—I see only swampy potholes of still water. The meadow narrows to a grassy valley. Finally I come to a spring and running water, and beyond it, a faint trail. Relieved, I follow it up and down in the dusky dwindling light, aware that solid forest closes in up ahead.

Suddenly, with no warning, something screams in the timber to my right.

My heart is in my mouth. It sounds like a woman shrieking bloody murder but then descends into a purring growl. It can only be a lion. Almost paralyzed by how close it is, I force myself to keep moving and bang my club vigorously on bushes and rocks. Almost instantly I stumble onto a small herd of elk I failed to notice in the gloom, about ten cows and calves standing stock-still and staring in the direction the lion screamed. Startled by the noise I'm making, they all swing their heads to stare at me, and then a split second later, leap away as one, racing off with a clatter of hooves into the trees.

Too much is happening too fast for me to think. I'm so terrified, I make myself stop in the open near some small trees and beat violently on them. I realize I'm not voicing a sound. I should shout, yell—make even more noise to scare off the lion. But when I try, it comes out weak and raspy and thin. Exactly the sound of some terrified prey, which infuriates me. With sudden ferocity I let out a stupendous war cry that booms and echoes across the valley. Then I slam my shillelagh on a dead log and shout, "Come and get me you little fucking pussy cat!" In the utter silence that follows I dissolve into laughter.

Nothing happens. There is not a sound.

Feeling better, I go on. My mind, flooded with epinephrine, coldly assesses and calculates all incoming perceptions, while off to one side a detached part of me idly speculates on various possibilities and scenarios: The lion screamed because I was interrupting its stalk of the elk. I must keep moving to use the remaining light. The lion now knows I'm one mean son of a bitch. But I am fleeing—slow down, take it easy, beat on things as you go by.

While listening to every sound and constantly scanning my surroundings in every direction, I follow the faint trail into thick forest, where I promptly lose it. My mind races: Predators try to minimize risk. Did the lion scream to get all of us to scatter so it could chase whichever lagged behind, which is clearly me? Lions see perfectly in the dark. What is the likelihood that it would follow me, the noisy thrashing two-legged? I flounder through dense brush and over downed logs. Then I get a mental picture of someone finding my corpse, half-eaten by a lion, and noticing my journal.

I abruptly sit down on a log and put my LED head lamp on. The silence is deafening. A moist aspen smell fills the air. I pull out my journal and write: "If I am killed and eaten by the lion out there, it's okay. Don't retaliate against it. I came here on earth a hunter myself. It's good if a great hunter takes me away from this life. So be it. But I will not be stupid or make it easy. Now I go on, lost in this dark forest."

With my headlight shining in the dusk ahead of me, I quickly find the trail again (of course). It's the first time I've ever hiked at night with a headlight, and I realize the guys on Sandia Mountain who urged me to try it were right in saying that it is better—brighter and more effective than a hand-held flashlight. And then, as if to rub my face in my own theatrical overreaction (no lion is going to attack something shining a blinding light into its eyes), I quickly discover the trail is flagged with long, fluorescent, pink plastic streamers every twenty paces or so through the wooded part.

I hike on, humbled, yet still pounding the brush, scanning in a circle all around me with the light beam every few seconds. The creek runs noisily to my left through deep black pools. The country opens up and then closes back in with thickets of young spruce no taller than me. The trail cuts up away from the creek, over a hilltop of boulders, and down a series of quiet forested flats. I feel the tension dissipating. I pass through tall woods where robins sing their little chirping bedtime songs from high treetops. Clouds block the moonlight. In the dark of oncoming night, bugs and moths, drawn to the light on my forehead, land on my face and crawl around. Even with the head lamp I stray often from the trail and have to backtrack and hunt for it. The repeated cheerful phrasings of the robins is at least soothing—it reminds me, as it always does, of the languid summer evenings of my childhood on the wooded residential streets of Omaha and Kansas City.

No more plastic streamers. Going slowly, my right foot killing me, and still scanning behind me and listening intently, I keep losing the way in the brushy parts.

I come to a rough, open, boulder-strewn area, what seems like a steep moraine above the invisible creek rushing by to the left. Ahead on the skyline I see a dark forested bluff. This could be where I hiked on my reconnaissance earlier, but at night nothing really looks familiar. A damp icy flow of air comes down from the mountain. As I stop to pull on a warm flannel shirt, I wonder: Am I the only person on this mountain tonight?

Onward, limping now. A bright star appears above the bluff—a steady unblinking eye. Then I come to a trail junction—yes! The short route comes in from the right, and from there I follow a wide easy footpath the last half mile to the paved road. Through tall, silent, empty aspen forest and around swampy potholes thick with flying bugs, there's no sound but me—my breath, my steps, the gurgle of a nearly empty water bottle in my pack. I feel a wave of incomprehensible gratitude. Life has never felt so precious. Just being out here in the open air like this, I say to myself, following this trail through wild woods and moonbeams and strange night sounds, I am content.

Plodding across a grassy hillside, I hear a noise behind me and swing my head around, scanning for eye shine. That's what I keep watching for, but am relieved I don't see—two glowing cat eyes closing in on me. Gripping the cudgel tightly, I go on.

Then I arrive at the concrete benches, the outhouse, the paved end of road beside Upper Canjilon Lake, which is just a dark void off to the right with a cold wind blowing over it. Nobody is here. I've covered maybe a mile and a half since the lion screamed, and I feel safer. Two more miles down a winding asphalt road, passing spring-fed lakes on both sides, will bring me at last to my campsite. I can see flashes of lightning to the north now, but stars glitter directly overhead. The storms have circled completely around the mountain, but dark clouds are building, blocking out the light of the moon.

As I limp briskly along the blacktop with wind gusting through aspens, I suddenly hear a faint, repeated screaming way back up the mountain the way I came. By the time I stop still and listen, there's nothing. I decide the sound is at least reassuring. Mountain lions hunt alone; another big cat in the same vicinity is highly unlikely. But I've been on high alert so long, I continue as before.

I'm bone weary, my lame foot throbs, and I'm getting desperately hungry. Can't keep this up much longer. Rushing streams and bubbling brooks I can't see pass by on both sides. Open lake shine glimmers to the left. Before long, the hum of an electric generator comes from a motor home, a white hulk off through the trees. A campfire flame flickers beside it. Somebody else up here after all. The scent of hot dogs cooked over a fire makes my guts gnaw in hunger.

One more mile to go. Trudging along, wincing with the pain of my sore foot, I wonder: How can I climb Truchas Peak, lame like this? I'm just about to finish a day hike of nine miles and only a thousand feet of elevation up and down. Truchas will be more like twenty-nine miles with five thousand feet up and down. Oh well.

Not really paying much attention anymore, I hear a stick crack to my left, and then suddenly see the brilliant eye shine of many animals moving on the shoulder of the road. The fright is so unexpected and debilitating, I have to firmly stop myself from backing up and fleeing in blind fear. What are they? Wolves? No, can't be. Coyotes? Bears? I once saw the eye shine of three bears on the side of a highway, but I was in a car. And a lot more than three pairs of eyes are gazing at me.

They don't seem to be advancing on me. Some turn away, and other eyes appear. I can hear them breathing, sniffing my smell. My heart thuds in terror, but I stand fast, gripping my club in both hands, sweeping them with the headlight. Then I realize all the eyes are spaced wide apart, and I ask myself: What animal that's only three or four feet tall has eyes spaced a foot apart?

It suddenly hits me: cows sitting on the ground.

I step closer, and with sudden relief see they are all Black Angus cattle. No wonder I couldn't make them out. They swing their massive heads and blink, their bovine peaceful slumber interrupted by my headlamp shining in their eyes. I laugh, mortified. And because they gave me such a fright, I say, "Hey, cows. McDonald's called and said you're next!"

Six

LATER IN MY tent, bedded down for the night, exhausted beyond belief, I hear the wind come up, roaring and shaking the fabric walls wildly. Eventually the air calms and light rain falls, pattering. At something like three o'clock a wailing serenade of coyotes wakes me. One coyote keeps repeating a call, a sharp yap followed by a quavering shriek, over and over again, keeping me awake. Then I hear one trot close to my tent. I react with a piercing shout—there is utter blessed silence after that.

In the warm sunshine of morning, the memory of the lion scream that froze my blood and kept me on guard against attack during the dark hike down the mountain seems like a bad dream—but I know it has changed me, made me stronger and more sure of myself. As I pack up I hear the same flock of ravens cawing and croaking from the treetops. They are just as noisy as yesterday, but now they sound hoarse.

"You guys really ruin your voices, don't you?" I sing out.

By the time the tent is rolled up and the pickup is loaded and I'm ready to leave, there's a dozen big ravens squabbling and soaring above the spruce trees. This is the most raven-infested place I've ever seen. They no doubt subsist on trout guts and cow placentas and camper garbage, in addition to their usual fare of anything they can swallow.

One last look up Canjilon Mountain in crisp breezy sunlight and I'm out of here, driving my pickup south and east toward Truchas Peak, the last mountain on my pilgrimage, which I can see on the far southeastern horizon. But really, with my foot sore and lame, I'm only heading down to Ojo Caliente, halfway there, to visit the ruins and soak in the hot springs. After that I'll take some time off to heal my foot before attempting the last, most difficult ascent of all.

The drive is slow and winds along a rutted, rocky dirt road that heads over the Tusas Mountains. At the top of Mogote Ridge, where cows and horses graze in numberless herds, I drop down Caño Canyon, heading toward the valley of El Rito. At the Fifteen Springs turnoff, in a grove of aspen, I come upon a retired couple at their camp. They are locking up their Winnebago and firing up two matching green ATVs, about to head out.

Hispanic and local, he has a white beard and a pistol in a holster while she has glossy, dark-dyed hair and a Bowie knife in a sheath at her belt. Not at all friendly (he says he thought I was *la floresta*, a forest ranger, come to harass him), they gun their engines impatiently as I ask questions. All I get out of them is that *caño* is the local Spanish word for "culvert"—the canyon being named for the tube-like steel drains that run under roadways. So much for the romance of the West.

Down, down, down the culvert canyon I go on a better road by far, smoother and wider, until I get up to a mind-boggling twenty-five miles per hour. In roadcuts I finally see bedrock showing through—yellow sandstone and other dull-colored sedimentary rock layers. A huge redtail hawk lifts off from a puddle in the road ahead of me. Near the crossing of El Rito ("The Creek"), a fat yellow prairie dog runs across the road. Called *tusa* in Spanish, this rodent gives its name to the mountains I'm crossing. Interrupting my linguistic musings, the same redtail hawk dives at the critter scrambling down a hole in a bare dirt mound.

Up over the next divide, which is all pine and fir and heavily logged, I follow dusty, rumbling, heavily loaded log trucks into the village of Vallecitos. In the shade of cottonwoods the sleepy community seems empty but for a solitary Chihuahua dog staring calmly at me driving by. South through a narrow granite canyon on a paved state highway, I pass irrigated bottomland fields where farmers on tractors cut swaths of scented hay. At the transition from ponderosa pine forest to piñon and juniper, the valley widens, and above the severe flat horizon of Black Mesa, I see Truchas Peak again, closer, dead ahead.

Two miles down the Rio Ojo Caliente, in hot sun, I turn off into the village of the same name, an old Spanish American settlement that looks somewhat gentrified by its proximity to the world-class resort developed at the hot springs. Crossing a bridge, I park in a crowded gravel lot. At 6,200 feet, the surrounding hills are bare of anything more than a few scrubby trees, which makes the low adobe buildings amid lush landscaped trees seem like an oasis in the desert.

The present town and private spa are only the most recent developments based on the seep of hot mineralized water here. Long before the Tewa arrived about AD 1380, this was a favored campsite for Native people as far back as the Ice Age, when glaciers sat on the high peaks and megafauna were hunted by wandering groups. Later hunting and gathering peoples of the Archaic period left evidence of their time on this land, too, as well as the earliest pit-house farmers. Then according to Tewa oral history, migrating ancestors from the northwest settled on the low mesa above the hot springs and farmed using irrigation techniques for about 150 years before moving on to the Rio Grande Valley downstream. Their pueblo was called Posi Owinge, or "Village at the Green Place," because of the algae that grew in the hot water. The Tewa moved on in the early 1500s but did not consider the land here "abandoned" just because they built towns closer to more dependable water. They continued to farm and hunt and gather and camp here, soaking in the hot springs, and to this day express strong feelings about the place.

The Spanish settled here in the late 1600s but were driven out by 1748 after bloody raids by Ute and Comanche Indians on horseback. Settlers came back later, and in 1807, when U.S. Army explorer Lieutenant Zebulon Pike (for whom Pike's Peak in Colorado was named) was being held prisoner for trespassing on Spanish lands, he estimated five hundred people lived here.

Today the luxurious health spa is a far cry from the muddy pits on the hillside that Pike saw. The place has boomed during the past sixty years along with the influx of moneyed outsiders to the Southwest. The facilities have recently been upgraded, and a new welcome center and gift shop have been built. Walking around, I find wall-to-wall people, with women outnumbering men three to one. The offerings clearly cater to women willing to pay for being pampered—I've never seen so many women in bikinis striding about in the bloom of health and fitness. All are Anglo, of course. The only people of color are workmen doing repairs on the fieldstone-lined drainage channels and women in uniforms doing maintenance tasks and cleaning guest rooms.

At the front desk I opt for the cheapest offering, a soak in the public pool, with access to the smaller arsenic and iron pools. I am tempted by the dazzling smile and exceptional facial complexion of the young brunette taking my money to sample the "life-altering experience" of their "spa packages," but am turned off by the New Age names they give them. There's the Native

American Blue Corn and Prickly Pear Salt Scrub, or the Sacred Journey Aroma Wrap, or a massage followed by the Down-to-Earth Moor Mud Absorption, among many others. The sacred emerald-green algae (which the resort has translated from the Tewa as "greenness," as in calling the nearby ruins "Greenness Pueblo") has been eliminated by chemical treatment, of course, but the mineral scent of the geothermal water is heady and appealing. I prefer remote, undeveloped hot springs, but I'm pleased to sit in the shade and soak for a while.

When I emerge, dressed, about noon, my foot feels much better and I'm ready to hike up to the ruins. A supervisor named John very pleasantly gives me a brochure, map, and directions for how to get there. A lean charming Anglo in his forties with coiffed silvery hair, wearing shorts, colorful Tevas, and a short-sleeve dress shirt of vaguely Indianesque design, he tells me he's been working there for exactly twenty-seven months and in that time he's had "just amazing experiences visiting the ruins."

"Really?" I say. "Like what?"

"Well, you know. Mystical things." He gives me a knowing grin.

"Oh?"

"Oh yes. And a month doesn't go by without someone who previously visited the ruins mailing us a plastic baggie of pottery shards they filched from along the trail—but then had bad experiences and wanted us to put them back."

"Say what?"

"Yes, exactly. It's against the law to take anything from the ruins, but that doesn't stop them. Then later they have bad dreams or bad things happen, so they send them back to us. It's my job to put back whatever they took. So I take them up to the ruins, and I center myself, you know. Get real quiet. And then I follow energy feelings to know where to scatter them. It's just amazing."

"Is that a paid part of your job?" I ask. When he looks startled and doesn't answer, I say, "I mean—I'd like to subcontract if you're tired of it!"

He laughs. He tells me about an Anglo woman who frequently visits the ruins who says the spirits speak to her and tell her things.

"The spirits up there don't actually speak to me," he adds. "Not yet, anyway."

I presume he means the ghosts of the Tewa people buried in the ruins. He says there are literally millions of pieces of pottery scattered on the ground, and that the spirits told this woman they don't mind if visitors pick them up and look at them, but don't like them left on display, clustered on flat rocks, as many visitors do. Apparently the ghosts are fussy about such things. The woman did not report any more serious concerns from her dead and departed Native American communicants, such as the fact that the surface flow of the hot springs has long been depleted by overuse and that wells have been drilled and underground sources are now being tapped to serve the growing clientele. Or the fact that their descendents cannot avail themselves of the sacred ancestral waters without presenting themselves as paying customers. (And what's next? Like other private commercial hot-springs resorts devoted primarily to the bottom line, have they already begun heating the cold water of the river aquifer and mixing it in to keep their business engine growing?)

If the ghosts of Tewa past speak to anybody about important matters, they speak to the Tewa rain priests who still pray to them. As Tewa elders say, their ancestors can be seen by anyone who draws a breath in this land—they are the rain clouds, the *oxúa*, that come floating over the mountains, bringing moisture and new life to all.

Warned how not to handle the pottery shards, and after thanking John for all his help, I head up the trail at noon in ninety-degree muggy heat, swatting at mosquitoes. From the posh flatland resort a trail climbs up a wide sandy cove into juniper-dotted hills. Immediately to my left beyond saltbush and cactus, the hot springs still feebly emerge and trickle down through grassy swales in exceptionally wet years like this. What comes out of the ground on its own now is routed into drainage channels with the rainwater that pours down the arroyo. Near the main pump house drawing from underground are the old broken pipes and debris of frequent repairs.

Higher up, I climb a faulted block of granite, rust brown with wavy veins of pink-and-white quartz, which has eroded into a talus slope of angular rock. Across the cove, beyond a visible fault line (which is no doubt geologically responsible for the upwelling of hot water here) the opposite hill is composed of tilted volcanic ash-flow sediments. I reach the top at a gap where an arroyo pours off, and where the trail continues to an old mica mine. I turn off on a spur trail marked by a sign that says "POSI," with an arrow pointing to the ruins.

The walk is less than a mile to the ruins. The path is helpfully lined by hand-placed rocks as it heads over a hill on sandy volcanic soil and crosses another wash. Juniper and sagebrush scent the hot air. The biting gnats are bad and the midday sun is fierce. A big lizard suddenly runs across the trail ahead of me. It pauses in the shade of a bush and lets me approach for a closer look.

A foot in length and brilliant mustard yellow in color, it has a long brown-striped tail and white spots on its back and head. The definite solid-black double ring around its neck identifies it as a collared lizard, *Crotaphytus collaris*, a member of the Iguana family and the largest lizard in El Norte. The shocking, brilliant yellow color is due to the fact that this male has just shed its old skin—shreds and curls of transparent papery membrane still cling to its shoulders, legs, and thighs. Unmoving a few feet away, it stares at me with one black eye. An orange streak on the side of its head and shades of turquoise down its flanks and legs round out the color scheme and render the lizard unbelievably iridescent and beautiful.

But I can't linger, the gnats are driving me crazy. The lizard simply snaps up and swallows every gnat that comes close. When I move away, it darts out of sight. A little farther on I see another collared lizard just like it, then another, but not so brightly colored. They appear to be having a bug feast right on the trail itself, and when they run away on the hot ground, they rear up over their pumping hind legs. It makes them look like miniature versions of the velociraptors in the movie *Jurassic Park*.

As I make my way out onto a sloping sagebrush mesa, a single white cloud moves in front of the sun, giving cool merciful shade. At a rail fence are signs and a U.S. Bureau of Land Management trail register (the ruins are on public land). Beyond, sagebrush gives way to saltbush, cane cholla, and prickly pear cactus growing on linear ridges of clay and rubble rock—the walls of former adobe room blocks, some three stories high, of the ruined Tewa town. Built with foundations of stone and wood-beam ceilings, there were once more than two thousand rooms in this pueblo, home to many thousands of people.

Viewed from the upper end of Posi Owinge, the ruins are heaped and jumbled in various stages of returning to the earth for hundreds of yards, almost to the end of the low mesa. I can see Truchas Peak to the southeast and Chicoma Mountain to the southwest, but not Sandia Mountain—too far away and below the horizon of Black Mesa. Behind me, to the north, the forested Ortega Mountains block any view of Canjilon.

Old excavations by pot hunters are filled with thickets of wild privet, impassable without a machete. This plant, never quite a tree, has soft, dry, bluish, olive-shaped fruits, and as a distant member of the Olive family is sometimes called New Mexico olive or desert olive. The pale-green leathery leaves do look like those of Mediterranean olive trees, but the bitter raunchy fruits of wild privet, *Forestiera neomexicana*, have no oil to speak of. It is also called ironwood for the superior hardness of its branches, used by the Tewa to make digging sticks and prayer sticks, and *palo blanco* by Hispanic artisans for the pure-white sheen of the polished hardwood.

Across the large rectangular plaza space sits another long mounded ridge of former room blocks. At interpretive guidepost number three, I'm at the highest point on the ruins, a viewpoint situated on what was probably the tallest collapsed building here. And yes, pottery shards are *everywhere.* The decorated ones are black paint on buff slip mainly, just like at the ruins on the Chama River. Dull black flakes of worked obsidian are also common. The remains of large circular kivas are numerous—one right along the trail is about forty feet in diameter.

Out the "front gate" of the old pueblo, a trail drops down to the Rio Ojo Caliente, a clear stream sliding by over rounded cobblestones. I don't go down. There are cottonwood trees, but the extensive river-bottom flats, once farmed, are now covered by thorny groves of Russian olive trees. An invasive alien (not related to privet) that has choked out native trees and created an impenetrable hell along most watercourses in El Norte, this tree is still being planted in home landscaping by unwitting outsiders for the pretty smoke-green color of its foliage.

I return along the trail that goes by the "waffle gardens" outside the former walls. Still a feature of modern pueblos well into the 1900s, these were hand-watered truck gardens surrounded by rectangular low adobe walls. The spa is visible from here. The cloud has moved on. Finishing off every drop of liquid I brought, I stumble back in blistering heat under a blazing sun.

Along the way, in a patch of damp dirt, my eye is drawn to the unmistakable tracks of a large ape-like creature. All five toes show perfectly. The prints were made either by a sasquatch or somebody hiking barefoot (the guy who lost his cowboy boots in the Jemez comes to mind). But who would hike barefoot in this broiling, rocky desert? Then it dawns on me—someone who was wearing the new thin, moccasin-type footwear with each toe individually enveloped like a glove. One brand, the Vibram FiveFingers, is popular for training in the new fad sport of barefoot hiking.

At last I arrive back at the steep part that drops down to the spa, and see Truchas Peak floating in the haze high above Black Mesa. For a moment I forget the heat, the glare, the gnats, the sweat pouring down my face, and even my burning thirst. There on that alpine height, the final peak of my pilgrimage, the last snow has finally melted. The mightiest of mountains in the land of *Nuevo Méjico*—the top of the world—it wears a scarf of cloud flying in the wind thirty miles away.

Technically not the highest (Wheeler Peak, near Taos, is 59 feet taller) the summit is still over 13,000 feet. Bare of timber above 12,000, a soft spring green has spread up along its flanks to the sharp white quartzite tip. Called *Ku Sehn Pin*, "Stone Man Mountain," by the Tewa, it is the farthest, roughest, highest mountain of all their sacred peaks, and is famous for creating its own storms out of nothing.

I can't wait.

PART FIVE

Trout

We are the playthings of the forces that laid out the oceans and chiseled the mountains.

—Alain de Botton, *The Art of Travel*

One

Early this morning I am invited by phone to join John Pesendo to pick medicinal herbs in the mountains. He has been staying at an old Native friend's cabin, located near Taos in the Valle Escondido below Oshá Mountain, a sixty-mile drive from my home. His nephew, in town for groceries, tells me this and gives me directions.

I'm grateful for the chance to see him again. The way it worked out with Truchas Peak being the last mountain on my pilgrimage had seemed perfect—I would be seasoned, tested, in the best physical condition for the most challenging ascent of all. Unfortunately, my lame foot got worse, I couldn't walk on it for days, and after an examination and X ray, my doctor said that although nothing was broken, it was a serious soft-tissue trauma that only time and rest would heal. Weeks passed. It seemed to take forever.

On the drive to Taos, I see several tarantulas, solitary and hairy and brown, crawling along the two-lane blacktop. The fall migration of these giant arachnids is later than usual in northern New Mexico, by a week or two, due no doubt to hot weather persisting into September. On the hillsides above the Rio Grande the prickly pear cactus fruits are ripe. I pull over and sample some that have fallen to the ground. The purplish-red *nopalitos* are spineless and look like small red potatoes, but have to be handled carefully to remove the tiny hairy glochids, which are impossible to remove from human skin. I use leather gloves and handfuls of dry grass. Peeled, the pulp tastes like super-seedy watermelon, delicious but somewhat trying since I have to separate out the seeds with my tongue. After half a dozen, refreshed and invigorated, I just walk away from the mess on the ground, wash in the river, and drive on.

In the afternoon of a crisp, clear September day, I arrive high in the Sangre de Cristo Mountains, park at a washed-out bridge, and hike almost an hour to a log cabin perched on the bank of a creek. My foot feels fine. The directions were easy to follow but nobody is home. The place is ramshackle, little more than a hunting shack, the pitched roof covered in moss. Spruce trees and willow brush scent the mountain air. I sit on a sawed block used to split firewood and wait.

Before long, two men come walking down a logging road and I wave. John Pesendo and his friend, whom he introduces as Virgil Vigil from Taos Pueblo, seem in fine spirits, laughing and telling jokes in some Native American language I don't recognize. Virgil seems more eccentric and non-traditional than John. John's nephew pulls up the rear, carrying a heavy army duffel bag full of plant material. He dumps it out by the creek, sorts out the strong-smelling oshá roots that they've dug in the mountains, and kneels down to wash them in creek water.

Virgil welcomes me to his place (he calls it his "bachelor pad") and goes inside to make coffee. John says he's glad I could make it. We stroll to the edge of the wood yard, talking, and he points up the mountain where a low rounded summit can be seen. He says the Indians call it Earth Goddess Mountain and that all kinds of valuable medicinal plants grow on its slopes. Then he laughs. I can't tell if he's putting me on about the mountain's name or not.

"No, really," he says. "See how the land going up there looks like a woman lying on her side?"

I see what he means. The configuration of forested hills and ridges does resemble a reclining woman. He points out a place where the slopes come together in a deep V-shaped canyon. Right where the V forms, the aspen trees have already turned a pale yellow.

"That's her pubic hair," he says, deadpan. "I guess the Earth Goddess is Swedish, huh?"

When at last I gear up to climb Truchas Peak and finish my grand circle around the horizon, nobody can join me. Later than I ever intended, Theresa drops me off at the Santa Barbara trailhead near Peñasco on the afternoon of October 7—three months after I first started up Sandia Mountain. My foot is not yet 100 percent. When I put pressure on it sideways I can still feel a tiny soreness. But with winter imminent on the high peaks, I can't wait any longer.

Truchas Peak, the most commanding of all the mountains visible from El Norte, has finally brought me to the heart of the Sangre de Cristo Mountains, the long chain of sawtooth peaks always seen previously from far away on my pilgrim path. The two-hundred-mile long range, the southernmost extension of the Rocky Mountains, was named only in the 1800s for the Blood of Christ—nobody knows why for sure. Earlier, to the Spanish along the Rio Grande, it was known simply as *La Sierra*, the cordillera everybody knew because it was the longest, tallest, and most rugged of them all.

My route will pass from north to south along La Sierra for almost thirty miles and will traverse the highest part of the Pecos Wilderness. For this trek I'm carrying thirty-five pounds, which includes six pounds of food for a little over four days. One-and-a-half pounds to eat per day seems like a lot, but I'll need plenty to fuel my ascent to 13,000 feet. I'll be breaking in a brand-new, lighter sleeping bag, and lugging along no more than a single one-liter water bottle since there are numerous streams, lakes, and springs along the way.

Early autumn in the wilderness means hunters. I'm wearing a bright orange ball cap, just in case. It has a picture of deer antlers and the provocative words, "Mount This!" The deer and elk season is open only for bow and muzzle-loader, which means the really trigger-happy hunters with buck fever and booze and high-powered rifles with scopes won't be around. The weather has been cool and dry until today, the perfect travel window finally broken by cloudy skies and light showers. More rain is likely.

At the parking lot at the end of the road, Theresa looks around in wonder while I do a last-minute check. The trailhead is located in the mouth of steep-walled Santa Barbara Canyon, where groves of aspen are turning a brilliant gold among giant Douglas fir trees. Beyond shadowy Indian Canyon to the north stands frowning Bear Mountain. I kiss my pretty girl goodbye, shoulder my pack, and give her my most Determined Explorer look.

"I'll miss you," she says touchingly. "Take care of yourself and come back to me."

"I will."

We turn away smiling.

I've started out later in the day on purpose. Easing gently back into the role of pack animal, I plan to hike up the Rio Santa Barbara for no more than four or five miles before making camp. Break myself in slowly. No need to push it with a foot that's barely healed. Tomorrow the real climb will begin in earnest.

Crossing through the windy, empty national forest campground on a paved loop road, whole mountainsides of bright-yellow aspen appear around me—the climax of autumn beauty in the Rockies. Above, I see the bare rounded summit of Jicarita Peak (12,835) under dark scudding clouds and patches of turquoise blue. An outhouse—new, shiny, ugly, made of concrete—is unlocked, inviting me inside a chemically perfumed stillness for one last whiff of civilization. A government poster on the wall warns about encounters with bears and cougars and rattlesnakes, but also includes alligators and crocodiles: "BE ALERT WHEN HIKING ALONG SHORELINES AS ALLIGATORS LAY IN WAIT FOR PREY." Outside, at 8,800 feet and maybe sixty degrees, I won't even see *lizards* if the sun doesn't come out.

Once through a livestock gate and on the trail, I hear the river rushing off to the left in lush riparian woods. The alder leaves are still green, unlike all the other deciduous trees and shrubs, which are either frost-nipped or fully transformed into various shades of yellow. The trail is trampled by livestock and curves uphill through heavy forest over rough rocky ground. For the first mile nothing can be seen but the dim woodland bottom of a canyon and stream-rounded boulders of brown shale and gray slate.

In no time, the conscious awareness of the weight on my back fades away and I settle into a steady pace, reverting to default mode—a hiker making his way to somewhere new. Once I'm on my way, free from worries, doubts, or distracting thoughts, all I have to face are the immediate real-world decisions of life outdoors. All the crap of modern life is stripped away. Everything is simplified, purified, and pretty much up to me, alone. Life, in other words, is sweet again.

Passing through briar patches, I snatch and taste tart red elderberries and scarlet rose hips. A recent frost has made them sweet, and no doubt rich in vitamin C, but I have to spit out the hairy seeds. Tiny damp meadows appear, dotted with white daisies, lined with bedraggled willows. Chokecherry bushes are turning crimson and Rocky Mountain maple, a faded dishwater-blond color. The foliage of the aspens responds to the slightest breath of wind—I can see a breeze working its way through swaths of trembling gold leaves long before it ever flows over me. Some leaves have already fallen, littering the dark ground with incandescent bright spots under faded bracken and yarrow.

I finally glimpse the river below, rushing in rapids between mossy boulders. Sunny glades open, the late sunlight illuminating knife carvings in the soft white bark of aspens. One says, simply, "AMOR, 1999." Another says, "EL LECHERO," which I believe means "The Milkman," and probably, based on the accompanying carved sketch, refers to an infantile preoccupation with women's breasts. I hear thunder mutter from on high. Raindrops fall briefly. Squirrels chatter excitedly from back in the timber. Buffalo berries, picked from the bush, taste like raisins. At a spring, black mud is churned up by horse hooves. Then a view far up the canyon at last, miles and miles away to a high divide above timberline—the Santa Barbara Divide, to be exact—a glimpse of what I must assault and overcome just to arrive at the alpine basin at the foot of Truchas Peak.

The drainage of the Rio Santa Barbara is unlogged, utterly wild and untouched. The upper reaches are considered some of the best native cutthroat trout fishing in New Mexico. Bear, eagle, deer, elk, mountain lion, and coyote are common. So are cattle, but only stragglers this late in the year. And beyond, nearer to the high peaks, are bighorn sheep. The route up the West Fork, the way I'm going, is twelve miles from the trailhead to the high divide, up a long, straight, breathtaking mountain corridor running north–south. Nothing has essentially changed since the 1830s, when Anglo fur trappers, who called these mountains "The Snowies," passed this way and left a description of what they saw. I can't wait to see for myself.

The mountain pilgrim is happy. The trail is much easier than other first ascents, and the backpack is lighter. I glide along through occasional sprinkles of rain with just a tee shirt on, sweating. As the trail finally comes close to the bank of the rolling *río*, a man on horseback comes down it toward me, leading another saddle horse by a rope.

Trail worn, splashed with mud, he wears an army-drab hunting tee shirt, jeans, and a stained felt cowboy hat. He is obviously an Indian. He halts when he sees me, and then makes a wide berth off the trail as if even though he has the right-of-way he is politely letting me stagger by under a heavy pack because he's only leading another horse. We exchange greetings. The only word I know in Tiwa, the language of Taos and Picuris pueblos (Picuris is only fifteen miles away, downstream) is *mahwán*, or "welcome"—clearly not an appropriate thing for a white guy to call out to a Native man in his ancestral homeland. Did he drop someone off, a hunter perhaps, and is bringing his horse back? He doesn't say. He just gives me a shy smile, spurs his horse, and rides on.

The stream rushes alongside, clear as a bell, twenty feet across and two or three feet deep. The time of wild flowers is past but rank green plants crowd the banks with seed stalks held aloft. I pass an old Anglo couple coming back from a day hike "to see the colors," and then rest on a log on a grassy bank above the river, where I can clearly discern the stream bed beneath the swift current, composed of multicolored rounded boulders. Spruce and fir trees tower over the alders. Rivulets flow in from dank fern gullies. A cold wet wind blows, but then the sun comes out and warms things up. Fickle fall weather.

Up and onward. Hiking closer and closer to a narrowing of gorge ahead, a gap in cliffs the river runs through, my excitement builds. The cliff on the right is higher—a thousand feet of rugged gray granite covered with lichens, shaggy patches of mint green and rust red. At the mouth is a log dam of washed-down tree trunks that channels the river around in a grand loop and then makes it shoot under with a pounding, galumphing roar. Here a sign on a post announces I am entering the Pecos Wilderness. Threading the cold chasm, the trail passes more log dams with deep, clear, glimmering trout pools behind them. There is no sunlight down here—but above, high up the left wall, the rock is lit up in dazzling brightness.

I meet two women in their fifties, Janet and Jane Ann, coming back from a day hike. Very talkative and friendly, they tell me they ditched their husbands in Santa Fe and are on a road trip to Utah's Canyonlands. "Not exactly Thelma and Louise!" Jane Ann cries. Janet says she can't backpack anymore because of a back injury so they do short treks like this to stay fit. I can't help notice they both have the kind of ample bosoms that the mysterious Milkman would no doubt letch after. (Not aware of it at the time, these are the last human beings I will see for three days.)

Then, farther on, a huge Black Angus bull comes down the trail at a narrow spot where the right wall presses against the river. He has no horns and is not aggressive, but he's as big as a rhino—six feet tall, five wide, ten long, with foot-long testicles and an ass splashed with shit. We pass each other warily without incident.

Almost through the awesome gorge, I encounter a brand-new wooden footbridge that has been built across the river. I cross to the left bank over creosote-smelling planks and into the afternoon sunlight again. As the pathway quickly climbs high above the roaring of the mighty Santa Barbara, I see up the west wall where chimneys and chutes of orange granite glitter in light reflected from the east wall. Tiny streams rush in from low bluffs to the left. Red currants hang out over the trail, offering delicious waxy fruit.

The leaves of ninebark brush, which favors damp cliffs and rocky streamsides, are changing dramatically from pastel pink to scarlet maroon. One of the most beautiful shrubs of the mountains, its limbs peeling in papery layers (supposedly nine of them), *Jamesia americana* is also called waxflower, cliffbush, mountain mock orange, or wild hydrangea. It seems to exist simply to please the eye, and thus, as with other rare and striking plants, nobody can agree on a single name for it.

Purple harebells still bloom along the trail, which winds higher and higher above the roaring white water below. The river thunders through an impassable defile of waterfalls and foaming pools, downed trees and sliding screes, a magnificent introduction to the unknown wilderness ahead. I pop out above on a sloping bench of aspen trees swaying in the wind, gold leaves undulating. Ahead, the canyon widens to a U-shaped valley formed by ancient glaciers, with steep, dark, forested walls on both sides, the right or west wall (the slope of Trampas Peak) always steeper and higher. Mind-boggling golden aspen leaves carpet the trail. When the wind gusts, they flutter down by the hundreds.

At the base of a giant Doug fir tree with a six-foot-diameter trunk covered in burn scars, I come to a trail fork. I've gone about three miles and ascended to about 9,500 feet. I stand watching the sun drop behind the shiny white clouds over Trampas Peak and feel the down-canyon wind quickly turn colder. Most of the foot and hoof traffic trampling the trail goes left here, up a forested side valley, but I continue due south on a much-less-traveled route, which heads back down to the river bottom again.

There, coming in from the east over wide-open meadowlands that have been grazed flat like golf greens, the Middle Fork of the Rio Santa Barbara blocks the way just above its juncture with the West Fork. I find a double-log makeshift bridge, sawed and axed flat to walk on, and cross over. The watery scent of chill air carries the promise of coming winter. Baneberry bushes along the wetlands hold up clusters of red shiny fruit, but the shade of red is not inviting—a hue that might be called "witch's lipstick" and could only signify a poisonous flavor if tasted. The trail continues up a long sandy peninsula between the two streams, crosses a dry flat, and climbs high above the West Fork once again. I plod on through still woods under an evening sky turning lavender. Alder marshes fill the bottoms of old glacial potholes, but not a single fly or mosquito is in the air.

Beginning to tire, I start looking for some suitable place to camp, but nothing looks good. Just gravel terraces, clay banks, glacial outwash boulders, and heavy forest on steep slopes. At a high point I look back and see Jicarita Peak again, standing high in evening sunlight. The wooded slopes are covered in aspen, mostly gold but some parts still faded green, with a few dark spruce pointing up out of an amber sea. Going on, I cross a dry pine ridge where the autumn-yellow ground cover of huckleberry gives way to plants with dark-green leathery leaves—stonecrop, boxwood, barberry, kinnikinnick.

At four miles, the pack seems to weigh a ton. A glimpse at the somewhat smaller river running far below reveals white water snaking through dark spruce. An aspen wood becomes a boulder field sloping down from the left. In the gloom, the place feels mysterious and strange. Many aspens are bare, already dormant. The trail crosses a low spot with a hollow sound of water running deep underground. Rocks teeter underfoot. I am relieved when the trail cuts up onto clay banks and solid ground again.

On a long mountainside descent to the river, finally accepting that I may not find a campsite before dark, I stop, rest, and eat a cold supper; take a deep pull on the water jug; then go on in growing dusk. Robins cut loose with evening song. At an open avalanche-impact area, a very cold spot, I see ahead where I might possibly camp on a lateral terrace beside the river. When I get there, I find another grassy flat, another severely cropped golf green thanks to the summer grazing of cattle, close to water among shrubby cinquefoil bushes. Beaver dams slow the stream to a series of wide pools. At a perfectly level spot, relieved, I lower my pack.

As dark comes, the familiar pleasure of making camp out in the bush comes over me. Cleaning the area of rocks and sticks, I set up the tent. Everything on my back is now put to use for a home away from home. Unrolled mattress and sleeping bag get shoved inside the tent and all the smelly stuff is roped up a spruce tree. A coat and a wool toque feel good in air that seems barely above freezing. My headlamp lights the way down a cow path to the river where I pump ice-cold filtered water into the jug. The pallid LED light illuminates a crimson fringe of roots exposed in the wash of the stream bank. Under a tiny mossy overhang is a single ghostlike mushroom with a pointed cap.

Chores done, I take my ease, alone in the wilderness again. Far up the canyon I can still make out Chimayosos Peak, like a bare rounded cone on the skyline. Beside it is a pass, my way over the Santa Barbara Divide. Truchas Peak stands beyond, to the right. The sky is still bright with a few drifting clouds, a few stars beginning to show.

I gather wood by the light of my headlamp—dead dry spruce branches broken from living tree trunks—and build a fire in a rock ring nearby. The flames feel good and hot, and pop with green sparks. The air flows coldly down the canyon, then switches and blows back up. Then it falls to nothing. Spruce-scented smoke wafts over me as the fire burns down to glowing coals. In the long silent vigil, I hear faint crashing noises in the timber uphill—big animals moving around. The elk in rut (mating) at twilight.

A veil of cloud passes and I see stars bright and clear overhead. The long line of the Milky Way streams across the canyon at a 45-degree angle from Jicarita to Truchas. A bright star glimmers beside it, directly overhead. A planet rises slowly and steadily through the trees to the southeast—Jupiter, I think. I recognize the constellations of Cassiopeia, Perseus, and the Pleiades. Down the canyon, in the V of mountains to the north, I see stars outlining Ursa Major, the Great Bear, more commonly known as the Big Dipper.

When the fire dies and the temperature plummets, I climb in the tent and write in my journal, the dull steady murmur of the stream the only sound besides the continuous rustle of aspen in the wind. Later, I climb out to use the bushes and I'm shocked by billions of stars crowding the sky—so many I can't make out any of the constellations! All else is utter blackness. Without the head lamp I barely find my way back to the tent. Sleep comes swiftly.

Two

MORNING ARRIVES ON gusts of wind that lash the tent with brief rain showers. When the rain stops I climb out and survey the world. The sun is already up. Inky rain clouds flow from the west over the steep wall of mountain, very low, moving fast. Chimayosos Peak, the lone sentinel to the south, treeless from halfway up, is lit in yellow morning sunlight, beckoning to me. Beside it is the pass I must get over to reach Truchas Peak, which is lost in clouds.

A study of the Pecos Wilderness topo map before I got up revealed the reason why most traffic goes up the Middle Fork Trail instead of the one I'm on. The Middle Fork Trail is more of a steady, gradual climb to the top of the Santa Barbara Divide, while this West Fork route stays low and then ascends steeply from 10,500 to 12,000 feet in the very last few miles. Funny I didn't notice that before now. Not that it matters—I'd go this way in any event. Going the other way would add many more miles to my hike. And this way, I've been told, is vastly more scenic, besides being the route that hugs most closely alongside the highest peaks.

Breakfast is fresh coffee and boiling water stirred into two cups of oat-almond granola with added dried cranberries and pine nuts. The sky becomes very dark and spits raindrops as I draw more water from the stream. Taking down my tent and packing up, it feels cold, maybe forty degrees. But then the sun appears, a warming glow rising through golden aspens. Looking off at the head of the canyon, the way up into craggy alpine heights looks formidable. Down the canyon, a big patch of blue opens up in the clouds. I'm struck by the silent beauty of wet wilderness spruce surrounding the meadow. After thanking this particular spot of Mother Earth for letting me camp here safely, and saying a few words to the mountains ahead, I hoist my burden and head up the trail.

At first hugging the bank of the stream, a broad bubbling brook with looping bends and deep pools, the trail tunnels under a deep dappled shade of alders where lush leaves turn the dim light greenish, and tiny cutthroat trout dart away. Out in the open, the sun glares from under racing clouds for just a few seconds at a time, then solid overcast returns. I make good time across a wide-open meadow with spectacular scenery, the right wall of the canyon formed of vertical, resistant white quartzite and the left of softer, more rounded sedimentary rocks.

Then much longer and wider meadows open up along the east side of immense beaver ponds, the splendor of the wilderness valley for miles ahead looking just as described by early fur trappers. (That is, of course, before they trapped and skinned every single beaver and moved on. But now, a century and a half later, the beavers are back in full force.) Avalanche chutes—steep ravines carved in the west wall by snow slides—appear every quarter mile or so. Snow roaring down in late winter has shaved off trees and left piles of bleached trunks at the foot of each one. Hundreds of tiny trees have sprung up in the barren pathways.

The clouds abruptly disappear. A cosmic Southwest sun bears down on me from a sky so blue it hurts. Suddenly sweating in summer-like heat among steaming meadow grass, I strip down to a tee shirt and jeans and pack my coat and gloves away. As the trail climbs a rocky moraine of glittering white boulders, the shift in weather is heralded by birds breaking out in joyous song. I hear chickadees, warblers, ravens, Stellar jays. A red-shafted flicker flies up from yellowing huckleberry to a moss-draped spruce. Beyond, the meadow widens to a half mile, exposing me to rapturous views of rocky peaks in every direction. Plodding along across the moist grassland, I begin to see fresh bear droppings right on the trail. One pile is composed of giant black segments in a connected string of undigested elk hair and vegetation. *And could that be a button?* It turns out to be a bone fragment, but now I'm super alert. This is some great wild bear's private banquet meadow.

The grassy open country goes on and on. Because the wind is in my face, stumbling upon unaware wildlife is very possible. The stream to my right is a series of silent lake-sized beaver ponds connected by looping marshy channels. Hummocky hills and dales rise and fall. Emerging from willow brush, I spot a pair of coyotes walking along slowly ahead. For a while, despite the sound of a 220-pound pack animal (me, still plodding along under my pack), they don't notice my presence. They are big and furry like wolves, nothing like the skinny, ratty desert coyotes. And they glide effortlessly forward, predators in their prime, moving right to left across the vast breezy landscape, ears erect, sniffing, nosing into things.

First one, then the other, catches sight of me, and they both lope out of sight. I make a different squeaking-rodent distress call with wet lips on the back of my hand, which is usually irresistible to coyotes, and spot them both watching me from thick brush by a beaver pond.

A little farther on I hear the shrill cry of a redtail hawk and see it high up in a tall spruce next to an old skeletonized beaver dam. It calls out repeatedly in a single piercing whistle as I pass by. I find a well-used streamside campground at the upper end of the giant meadow and am surprised to see a stack of rough, dry twenty-foot-long aspen poles leaned into a tree. It's the way Indian people store teepee poles, even today.

Two more bear scats—this bruin prefers to make a mess on the trail itself. Both are of the same elk/salad combo previously on the menu. I speculate there's a dead elk being fed upon somewhere nearby. (I never do see this bear.)

At a shallow ford in the creek, in complete solitude, I rest and eat. On the west side the trail continues south, climbing higher and higher above the valley bottom through many avalanche chutes. The white of dead spruce and gold of young aspen mark each downward swath. Some have bristly thickets of young blue spruce shooting up among the wreckage. The grade grows steeper along slopes of mossy spruce forest tossing in the wind. Golden aspen leaves look like Spanish doubloons strewn along the path, each with gemlike droplets of rainwater.

Ahead are cliffs and crags the trail will soon pass under—one looks like a monumental hook curved backward. Beyond them the map shows the trail switchbacking upward toward the glacial basin of No Fish Lake. The rocks of the massive hooklike outcrop are gray-banded gneiss with pink-quartz veins, a dark resistant island surrounded by the same translucent white quartzite. This high up the mountainside and approaching closer to Chimayosos Peak, I discover the bare slopes above timberline are covered in yellow autumnal tundra.

Panting in the thin air above 10,000 feet, I halt at a downed tree across the trail, lean my pack, and rest. The pack feels heavier than yesterday, a much more crushing burden for some reason. I've seen nobody up here, and there's no sign of recent foot or horse traffic. Plus, all cow signs ended back at the stream crossing. There's little grass up here for them anyway, just moss and huckleberries, and in damp spots, lush wetland herbs called marsh marigolds. When I glimpse the saddle of the Santa Barbara Divide through an opening in the forest—my goal for today—I'm stunned. It looks to be only a mile or two away but thousands of feet above! I'm not even on the killer steep part yet and I'm already wiped out.

Oh well. Smack that thar pack animal on the arse and git him on up the trail! One step at a time, one breath at a time, I go on. Taking it very slowly, I stop frequently to rest, elevating my increasingly sore right foot.

In every open avalanche chute I pass through, I notice thickets of some kind of spindly deciduous tree I don't recognize. Each treelet has dramatic flat-topped clusters of orange-scarlet berries. I stop and study one carefully: the shiny, smooth, bronze-looking bark, the sticky twigs, the ash-tree foliage of shiny leaflets, pointed and toothed, which are turning reddish like sumac. I taste a berry, really a pome or tiny apple-like fruit with bluish flesh, and discover a lemonade flavor laced with cyanic acids—and spit it out. The taste does it—or the smell of the seedy pulp—and I remember suddenly. This is western mountain ash, *Sorbus scopulina*, called *serbo* in Spanish, a rare understory tree of wet, shady, coniferous forests in the Rockies. I've never seen mountain ash growing out in the open like this. Here the pygmy trees seem to thrive on exposed, gravelly avalanche slides. And the birds love the berries—I watch grosbeaks and robins gobble up several at a time and fly away. Boiled in water to eliminate the cyanide, they aren't bad actually—like citrusy apricot.

Almost under the granite cliffs of The Hook (which I hereby formally name), I hear a bull elk "bugle" twice. Really more of a prolonged nasal honk, a sound a moose should make (but doesn't), the resonant blare of the male elk in rut sounds like some kid blowing a whistle through a plastic PVC pipe. The calls echo across the mountainsides and are answered by others, fainter, farther away. The wind in the aspens makes it hard to determine which direction they come from. Then I hear a whole herd of elk moving along the slope above me, unseen behind dense alpine fir forest, hooves and antlers clearly banging on logs and branches. For a while, the excitement distracts me from the load I'm toting up the mountain.

Beyond a mossy ravine where a stream cascades beneath yellow maple brush, I come to another open avalanche slide, this one just thick with mountain ash. Tons of red-orange berries are held up like pie cherries for the birds. A Clark's nutcracker, a large gray jay with black wings and tail and a formal military bearing, lands and plucks a mouthful, one-two-three-four-five, and with martial discipline (and cheek pouch bulging) flies up to a high branch in a dead spruce to chew.

Farther on, I win wondrous views of endless spruce forest draping the rounded highlands to the east. Brilliant gold patches of aspen are becoming smaller and fewer the higher I go. Every steep gravel opening is now covered in mountain ash, a veritable scarlet chaparral of the stuff, obviously the perfect ecological niche for the plant. More Clark's nutcrackers arrive, a whole flock skirmishing with precision and daring over the feast, their passionately grating cries—*kraaa! kraaa! kraaa!*—resounding up and down the slopes.

Rounding a point, the trail turns into a deep chasm where another stream rushes, and just as I am enthralled by the lush greenery, the tumbling waters, and the floating mist, a forest falcon flies out through the conifers and lands high up in the spire of one. From the bands of light and dark on the tail feathers, the dark-brown coloration of the plumage, the fierce hooked beak, and white eye line, it has to be a youngish northern goshawk like the one I saw attacking a squirrel in the Jemez Mountains. I watch it fly away with elegant ease, weaving through the trees like a graceful speed demon.

At the stream crossing, a roaring cataract dives downhill through shiny green elderberry, cow parsnip, baneberry, figwort, and columbine, but there are no flowers—only seed stalks with droplets of mist water dangling. The uphill grind becomes steeper and slower. The mountain itself is steeper than 45 degrees, and soon I come to the first switchback in musty old-growth forest hung with spongy bryophytes. It has a rich green hillside of club moss for a slanting floor. Panting under my heavy backpack, I make it to another switchback and slump down to rest. I'm beside the same chute-like cascade that I saw the goshawk fly away from, only higher up, where it roars like a waterfall. A cold wind springs up every time a cloud blocks the sun. I decide to break here for lunch.

Getting up and going on gets harder. At the third switchback, I'm at 10,500 feet, the point at which the trail guide says the trail *starts* to get really steep! Shit. I can't believe how punishing it already is. I keep thinking about the fur trappers back in the 1830s who relayed loads weighing hundreds of pounds over these passes. I'm only carrying thirty-five pounds and yet I find myself seriously considering unloading it and relaying it in two lighter loads. What keeps me from doing it, of course, is the obvious prospect of having to walk back down and go back up this same steep trail a second time. Once is enough. That's what I tell myself, anyway. How can it be this hard?

I lose track of how many switchbacks. At one, right under the bare snout of Chimayosos Peak, I'm at the edge of a deep gorge with the barely visible West Branch of the West Fork Rio Santa Barbara roaring down in rapids. Still no sign of anybody else up here. The only footprints in the trail mud are from wild animals, mainly elk. Chilling mist blows over me on one stretch of trail, then the sun bears down huge and hot on another. Eventually only a few thin wisps of cloud drift overhead. At my first good view back down the canyon, I see Taos Mountain on the distant skyline. Directly across to the east sits *Little* Jicarita Peak, a bare summit with the same shape as the tilted tile roof in the Pizza Hut restaurant logo. Barely visible above timberline, it peeks out like the command bubble on a giant flying saucer that landed on the sierra.

Another switchback. I'm working back and forth between the same two deep cataracts, up blinding-white rock slopes with only a few spare conifers for shade, the mountain becoming nearly vertical. Each switchback is a place to stop and breathe. The roaring chasm of the West Fork soon becomes too deep to see the water anymore, but mist blows up from it continuously. I cross steep talus slopes and more avalanche chutes. Some of the spruce trees knocked down by snow slides are still alive, their tips pointing over the trail with periwinkle-blue cones oozing pitch. A whole flock of grouse flies up, startling me. Wings pounding furiously, they are like chickens fattened for slaughter, bashing around fat and ungainly among the spruce branches, trying to escape with a frantic urgency that makes me laugh. Fool hens, indeed.

Then, unbelievably, the trail levels off and drops gently into a pretty alpine valley. Above the cataract, the stream runs smooth and clear. Giant spruce and fir stand far apart on sloping spring-wet hillsides dotted with flowers of orange paintbrush and purple aster. Mica-flecked maroon rocks with black dots of biotite show in mud with fresh deer tracks—small split-heart hoofprints, perhaps of a yearling or grown fawn. And then, there it is—a young deer browsing the greenery looks up, staring at me with giant mule ears twitching, surprised but still chewing, as if I am the first human it has ever seen. And curiously unafraid until I close to within twenty feet, when it leaps away—*boing, boing, boing*—bounding across the stream in the characteristic four-legged pogo stick bounce of a mule deer.

For just a moment my hours of grinding labor are forgotten, and life seems possible again. Free as a deer, I pass easily through a wilderness meadow at 11,000 feet, the wind rustling gone-to-seed corn lily plants like harvest corn shocks. I'm well into the high hanging valley of No Fish Lake and I can see right up to timberline through a wide avalanche chute on the west slope of Chimayosos Peak. But then the grade gets steep again and I'm right back at it, toiling slowly upward, gasping for air.

The West Branch, when I finally cross it, is a little creek lined with feathery oshá plants gone to seed. The trail winds up onto hills of glacial drift and crosses a large pothole—a perfectly rounded bowl with no outlet, sixty feet across and twenty deep, a weird dip in the forest floor made by a block of ice that sat here after the main glaciers melted around it. Then an even steeper ascent zigzagging up the deep cold ravine where the stream flows down from No Fish Lake brings me finally to a switchback signpost. The sign announces my arrival at the lake, which is, however, nowhere to be seen. I am surrounded by nothing but dark spruce forest. Eventually I glimpse a glimmer of water downhill. Upon investigation, it appears to be little more than a pond in the largest pothole of them all. I'm at 11,500 feet at three in the afternoon, and even in direct sunlight, the wind pouring down from the pass feels freezing. And yet I am suddenly unable to resist the urge to go for a skinny dip in No Fish Lake.

Three

I KEEP EXPECTING people to come by, other backpackers or hunters on horseback, but nobody does. Twenty-four hours have passed and I'm still the only human up here as far as I can tell. At the lake shore a small opening of sky illuminates how shallow and absolutely clear the water is. I was told it has no fish because it freezes solid to the bottom in winter—planted trout cannot survive year to year. Pale underwater areas of solid rock contrast with dark organic muck, and the only spot deep enough to wade in and dunk under is by the back wall, where the mountain comes down almost vertical to the water's edge.

There's no point in testing the temperature of the water. It will be ghastly cold. Then why am I doing it, you ask? Because I'm disturbed by how weak I am, how much I've been suffering climbing this mountain. Once the idea of jumping into the icy lake lodged in my mind, just the audacity—the intrepid willfulness of actually doing it—appealed to me. Even if the shock of it doesn't make me stronger, it will hopefully wake me from my daze of fatigue and prove I'm still tough and daring.

Leaning my backpack against a tree, I strip down and tiptoe naked into the frigid water. Wading toward the deep end, my feet turn numb and I'm all goose bumps. At moments like this I often recall my late father's words urging me into cold lakes as a child: "Don't think about it. Just do it." At waist deep I'm huffing uncontrollably. It takes every ounce of nerve I can muster to take a deep breath and drop down fully underwater. Bursting back up into air with a howl, I thrash back to shore and leap onto a boulder in the sun. I'm shivering but grinning, too, and more alive than I've felt in a long time. Crouched like a naked animal dripping on a rock, heart thudding, lungs inhaling great gulps of sweet mountain air, I feel altered, baptized, purified, wholly immersed in the wilderness at last. Connected to the natural world as never before.

Before I'm quite dry in the chilling wind, I get dressed. My skin feels burned and raw inside clothes as I wander around the shoreline examining the place. The creek pours fully formed from the lake and threads a way downhill through boulders and logs. With no inlet above—no surface water coming into the lake—it must be fed by underground springs. Close to my skinny-dipping spot, I find the spring, a swirling of debris in clear water upwelling from dark holes in the lake floor.

The bark of the spruce trees ringing the lake, a blending of gray and maroon, is smooth and uniform in pattern if not in touch. Rough, resistant, and hard might be the best words to characterize the structural integrity, the woody parts of this tree: the trunks are straight, the heartwood hard, the branches stiff, even the twigs and needles don't bend or break easily. And a positive ID for *Picea engelmannii*, or any spruce, is sharply pointed needles—a prickly character all the way around. Spruces as tall as 120 feet are common in these sierras; the long, drooping, sweeping branches, especially of those that stand alone, are a distant visual giveaway.

The other primary conifer of the highest forests, *Abies lasiocarpa*, subalpine or alpine or corkbark fir, presents a different outline—more compact and forming a distinct spire at the very top. Its bark, smooth and creamy white when young, turns ash gray and deeply furrowed with age. If the spruce is the rigid preacher, the fir is the easygoing backslider: the needles are smooth tipped, flattish, and usually upcurved. When crushed in your fingers they give off a sweet camphor-like scent, which also perfumes the smoke of the burning wood. And the cones, unlike those of spruce, which hang down, stand straight up from the ends of branches like purple cylindrical knobs frosted with pitch.

After something to eat, I fill the jug and go on. The backpack bears down heavily on my shoulders and hips, the altitude makes me gasp, and my thoughts grow muddled. I go by a campsite used by previous hikers at the crossing of another stream and am tempted to stop, but the wind blasts fiercely and uninvitingly through open forest. With still a few hours of daylight left, a dim determination to make it over the divide before I stop for the night drives me onward. Circling around a pothole marsh, I see timberline approaching not far ahead. A sharp peak towers to my right, and it slowly dawns on me it's one of the three crests of the great mountain of the east—North Truchas Peak. I stop and study how the trail I'm on climbs long winding switchbacks across open slopes and rock slides toward the pass. The reality of how far I still have to go to get there suddenly sinks in.

"No way. Forget it," I blurt out loud.

My voice sounds incredulous, dismissive, which makes me laugh. I've reached my limit and that's that. Once I decide, relief is sweet. I realize I've been ignoring how sore my feet and ankles have become. I simply turn around and walk back down the way I came, a stupid happy smile on my face. Back at the campsite by an unnamed creek (the Middle Branch of the West Fork of . . . ?), I drop my pack and hunt for a sheltered spot to set up the tent. The wind still howls, the spruce trees sway and creak. It promises to be a difficult, trying night exposed to the elements.

Once I get the tent pitched by an inadequate screen of small conifers and reinforce the guy lines, I go and gather armloads of firewood. The sun soon sinks behind North Truchas Peak. Everything I do becomes dumbly mechanical, performed in a fog of fatigue. I catch myself at times staring off mindlessly at the windswept beauty of where I am. It takes firm resolve to move on to the next chore. At last, I draw water, a full kettle, and put it to heat over the hissing flames of the gas stove. As the temperature plummets, I add layers of clothing—two tee shirts, a long-sleeve thermal shirt, a jacket, gloves, a wool hat—and yet still feel cold. I make reconstituted freeze-dried beef stew for dinner and with light draining from the sky, eat a hot meal, which finally warms me enough to putter around enjoyably in the solitude of the middle of nowhere.

At dusk, I build a fire with brushy twigs of alpine fir, the smoke scented like perfume, and then build it up bigger with spruce logs and heavy board-like chunks of dead bark. Resting against a rock in the hot blast of a bonfire, I am utterly content. In the last light I see the line of trail going up the white rock wall to the saddle on top. I sit stupefied by dancing yellow flames, stirring only to feed more wood. In time, the world beyond the flickering circle of light goes black, and stars twinkle overhead. The tiny shelf of land high up a mountain grows colder in a ceaseless wind. I am within ten feet of a well-traveled forest service trail but I might as well be alone on an island in the heaving ocean.

In the tent at last, zipped into my sleeping bag with everything tight, safe, secure, I nod off. But as the hours drift past, I don't really sleep well. I feverishly believe I'm still out on the trail, hiking. Then I open my eyes, shivering, freezing cold, and remember where I am. Focusing forcefully on deep breaths until I feel toasty warm again, I drift off. After some unknown period of time, I wake up cold and have to go through it all over again—pant until I warm up and drift off. This happens again and again. In this way I dog nap all night long.

Then I suddenly wake up at sunrise from a vivid dream.

Theresa is dropping me off somewhere in her car. We have stopped and are talking. We see two bluish birds hovering on beating wings outside my window, which somehow join together as one. As if this is not startling and impossible enough, the combined birds then transform into a giant, fat, smiling man who leans down and looks in the window at me. He is enormous, massive—a giant, easily ten feet tall and half as wide—and he gazes at me with hypnotic eyes, smiling with a sort of smug self-satisfaction. I am shocked by the danger of his presence, yet feel certain he has appeared to reassure me. I am convinced I am responsible in some way for awakening him and bringing him forth. He is like a gigantic fearsome protector whom I have unwittingly unleashed upon myself.

The enchanted spell of the dream fades in the grim reality of frigid daylight inside a flapping tent on the side of a mountain. The inadequacy of my sleeping bag to keep me warm at high altitude, even fully clothed, and the low oxygen content of the air have resulted in very little rest. And yet as I climb out into the appalling, empty October air at 11,600 feet, I still feel the warm gaze of the monstrous man in the dream. It kindles a fire inside me. I mumble to myself, "Hmm, so I've awakened the sleeping giant within, have I?"

It doesn't last long. Even after scalding hot coffee and a hot breakfast, I can't fully wake up. Pallid horizontal sunlight shines through tree trunks from the eastern horizon. Wind races full force through the moaning branches of conifers. Stiffly slapping myself with my arms, I sleepwalk through the morning camp routine. It seems so cold I wonder groggily if it might actually snow. I force myself to study the evidence of my senses and think clearly. There's not a cloud in the sky in any direction. Empty blue. At the creek to wash up, I see no sign of ice or frost, so it can't be *that* cold. Near-freezing water splashed on my face finally shocks me fully awake. I strike camp, pack up, and head out. The physical exertion of striding forward under my heavy backpack finally warms me in freezing wind. Squirrels appear, garbed in winter fur on the limbs of trees, chattering loudly at my panting, staggering progress up the trail.

The world of forest comes abruptly to an end. Timberline is sprawling spruce, dead brush, and then nothing but a wall of bare mountain—slopes of white quartzite rock and yellowing autumn tundra. The trail, infinitely easier after a night of dubious sleep, maintains a steep, steady upward grade out into the open. The wide world of the mountains opens up to stupendous views and breathtaking steepness. Looking down the canyon that I hiked up, I see meadows, white-water cascades, and endless forest in clearly focused detail. The faint gold of distant aspen makes me realize there are none here at this higher elevation. North Truchas Peak is huge, an immense pointed height, a cone of rock towering above an exposed world of glacial basins and alpine ridges.

The immediately pressing problem is the trail itself, which becomes narrow and scary, a mere trace scratched in the sheer face of a perpendicular slope. Trying not to peer down too long at what waits below, I scan ahead, desperate not to meet someone on horseback coming down. The wind gusts fiercely out in the open, buffeting me under my massive backpack, making me plant each step carefully. The way leads out onto the stark west face of Chimayosos Peak, then at a switchback heads the other direction toward North Truchas Peak. At a dangerous washed-out spot, a mini-chasm littered with pink quartz rocks, I have to leap across like a pack horse. Then I brace myself and look down. I'm directly uphill from where I came out into the open at timberline, but I'm a quarter of a mile above it, almost straight up a rock slide.

Heart thumping, lungs sucking thin air, head swimming in the blinding glare of sun, I am eager for the summit. The trail crosses a dark granite outcrop with a few scrubby spruce trees. At a long shabby gulch that looks barely free of snow from last winter, I come to the last switchback. The pass is not far ahead—and the rounded summit of Chimayosos, too, which is lined with game trails made by bighorn sheep. As the landscape curves enormously into a broad mountain pass, the ground levels out and turns barren—like the desert, like the moon. Only here and there does a tiny desiccated plant show in the glittering white rocks where the wind roars.

At last, panting, leaning into the wind, I reach the midpoint at a wooden signpost shored up by rocks. I am at 12,000 feet on the Santa Barbara Divide, and despite my elation, my sense of having accomplished something real, I can barely look around. A titanic wind from the south funnels through the gap, trying to knock me down. Blinking, I try to take in, for the first time, the vast view of the very heart of the Pecos Wilderness—the headwaters country of the Pecos River that stretches away to a brilliant horizon—but I get only glimpses before the freeze-drying blast of wind blinds me and turns me away.

Trying to test for cell phone reception, to check in with Theresa if possible, I huddle against the signpost and squint at the glimmering screen. No bars appear. Almost all the places I've gone in the mountains of El Norte have turned out to be cell phone dead zones. Fortunately I'm not a constant contact addict, calling and texting my way through the day like some do. I only use it for basic communication. The truly electronic dependent, teenagers in particular, seldom stray into remote places like this. When they do, they quickly become jabbering lunatics—like Theresa's fourteen-year-old son did while camping with us in Yellowstone National Park, where he fruitlessly checked for reception hundreds of times a day.

The freezing wind drives me off the pass. Facing into it, squinting at the ground before me, I force my way onward, down the other side, searching for an old cutoff trail that forks from the main trail. A quicker, shorter way into the Truchas Lake basin, the older path doesn't appear on most maps of the wilderness, but is reputedly well-used anyway. I find it easily and follow it steeply downhill toward timberline and the promise of someplace to rest out of the wind. In the lee of a gnarled, twisted, wind-sheared thicket of spruce, I finally sprawl in the warm sun. Sheltered from all but a light breeze, I devour a breakfast of beef jerky and trail mix washed down with cold delicious creek water. The fanatic drive that got me over the mountain divide melts away completely in the sloth-like sleepy warmth of dazzling sunshine. Lying back in the grass, I fall quickly and deeply asleep.

Four

THE PECOS WILDERNESS is nearly 350 square miles of raw nature added to the National Wilderness Preservation System for the single purpose of protecting it for its own sake. A fragment of the primordial landscape that once covered the entire earth, it has been withdrawn from any human use that would conflict with the ongoing biological and physical processes that make it what it is—native, natural, unspoiled, untamed.

It was not always like this.

In the late 1800s it was despoiled by vast herds of domestic livestock—millions of sheep, goats, and cattle fed upon the grasslands like locusts every summer. Mining, logging, and unchecked fires closed in on the heartland well into the 20th century. Perhaps only because New Mexico has a long history of colonial backwardness compared to the wealthier states around it—Arizona, Colorado, Texas—did an area this large remain relatively inaccessible into the 1960s. (The Gila Wilderness, in the southern part of the state, is even larger.) Remarkable as it may seem, today the Pecos Wilderness is a place where—in the words of the Wilderness Act of 1964—anybody who comes here is "a visitor who does not remain."

From where I wake up, utterly refreshed at last, and sit lazily admiring the panorama before me, the greater part of the wilderness is in view. Looking out upon the world of light, space, forest, and mountain, I understand at once how lucky I am to be here. The silence is so magnificent, I might as well be the only human being left in the world. Gazing east and south over the rumpled wooded drainages of the Upper Pecos, my eye follows the long broad mesa of the Eastern Divide to Elk Mountain fifteen miles away. In the middle ground, far below, is much smaller Hamilton Mesa, a pale hump of green grassland in a sea of dark timber. Passing over the hazy depths of the Pecos River Canyon and the high hard-rock backside of nearby Pecos Baldy, I am treated for the first time to a closeup view of all three summits of Truchas Peak. Only a mile away and a thousand feet above, they nonetheless look impossibly rugged and steep.

Deepest in the sky stands the sunlit bald of the southernmost peak, my ultimate destination, labeled on maps simply as "Truchas Peak."

Strong again, and ready for anything, I lift my pack and start off. I'm immediately filled with joy to be going downhill for a change! The trail cuts off a mile and a half from the usual route, dropping swiftly down a perpendicular slope. Soon out of the wind and frost zone, I come to boggy ravines with plenty of lush green vegetation, mainly marsh marigold still abloom with creamy-white ray flowers facing the sun. This handsome high-altitude buttercup, *Caltha leptosepala*, has a basal rosette of light-green waxy leaves that are somewhat heart- or arrowhead-shaped, suggestive of the split lobes of an elk's top lip—hence the other common name, "elkslip." Despite the presence of toxic chemicals that can blister the skin and inflame the tissues of the mouth, throat, and digestive tract when the plant is fresh and raw, marsh marigold was once a popular boiled potherb (it tastes like sauerkraut). It was also the main ingredient in certain "love medicine" recipes handed down by elderly Native women in the Rocky Mountain region.

In no time I drop four hundred feet and strike the regular horse trail, called the Skyline Trail, at a rock cairn. Here I turn my boots west, uphill again, heading for the Truchas Lake basin. Back to the grind, but not nearly as steep as before. And now I'm on south-facing slopes, which are much drier and warmer than the north side of the divide, consisting mostly of open undulating grasslands studded with spruce. The trail contours with relative ease even over a broken landscape of alpine parklands dissected by moraine ridges, scree slopes, and deep gulches. And despite the wear and tear of heavy horse traffic on the trail, there are no fresh or even recent tracks showing. I seem to have picked just the right time to experience this high country in complete, lonesome, desolate solitude.

I climb a high ridge, almost level on top, with giant old spruce trees standing in the open, then drop down the other side. A fresh cascade flows tinkling from the heights, crosses the trail in a wet ravine, and spreads out in a corn lily meadow below. The trail skirts the base of rock slides where grand old spruce and pale fragrant alpine fir stand spaced wide apart in the sun. The scenic beauty intensifies the farther up into the lake basin I go. Rocky outliers of the now closer peaks trail out like arms embracing a high bowl. And just like the other side of the divide, there are no aspen trees—only faraway splashes of gold visible at lower elevation.

Higher and higher I go, until I glimpse an unexpected broad, green meadowland in a distant lower basin. Many trees are knocked down across the trail, forcing me to take horse-torn pathways developed around them. The backs of my legs cramp up, but I push on. All summer in the mountains I've been stopping to rest in the shade, but today, in crisp wintry air, I take breaks, standing and panting in full warm sunlight. The trail finally tops out on a wide field of boulders—the same quartzite smoothed like alabaster—and the way through is like walking a cobbled alley where I have to watch my step.

Then in sparse open spruce forest, I arrive, at last, at Truchas Lake, a lovely deep-blue glacial tarn at 11,870 feet. The alpine solitude of the setting is exquisite and at the same time lonely and unnerving. A radiant jewel set amid towering peaks, the surface reflecting an empty blue sky, it seems almost too beautiful to bear. The water is very deep; I could dive in from the shore (but won't). Across the lake a large rock peninsula juts out into wind-choppy waves. I make my way around to it and gaze down where short cliffs plunge into blue-green depths. I find old campsites with fire-blackened rocks back from the verge, but no place in this wilderness has felt more remote and pristine.

Resting on the edge of the sacred lake of the east, I recall that this is where the miraculous little twin war gods of Tewa myth first succeeded in calling up the kachinas to come to the kiva at Yungé, on the Rio Grande. I stare at the troubled waters of "Stone Man Lake" and listen to the sacred waves washing on the shore. I try to imagine how rain gods peeped out from the middle, how they climbed out onto the shore and walked about. How they lifted up their "fog rainbow" and their "cloud flower" and passed over on it, from place to place, all the way to where the people waited at ancient Yungé village, near Ohkay Owinge. In Herbert Spinden's English translation of the myth, the Tewa narrator says of the powerful primordial twins, "Even now they should be made what they will soon be made—universe wanderers in the void!" Cosmic pilgrims, in other words.

On this day, I alone am here to see this wondrous lake and think these rarefied thoughts. The meager oxygen does not permit much articulate consideration. And anyway, I'm distracted by a lone, wary marmot I see foraging along the far shore. The immediate always beckons more strongly in the outdoors. I heave up and push on, following the Skyline Trail as it descends from the lake, southward, down a wide, curving avalanche chute. My legs brush against dead stalks of corn lily, rattling the dry seedpods. Down, down, down I go past many freshly sheared-off spruce trees. The smell of oozing pitch is strong.

At the bottom, at a trail fork, I turn away from one of the streamlets that form Rito Azul ("Blue Creek") and head up into thick shadowy forest again.

The way winds along under the snout of a rock glacier, a creeping living thing sliding stone-slow down the mountain and into the woods. I hear a sharp *peenk!*—the nasal alarm call of a pika, a rat-sized rodent that lives in rock slides. And then a shrill whistle, a different-sounding alarm from a hoary marmot, the woodchuck of the high mountains that also prefers the shelter of the rocks and boulders.

Cruising along a trail churned up by horse hooves (but now dried firm, easy to pass over), I tramp through desiccated meadows and over rumpled bogs with black wet mud holes. In the deep timber are more downed trees blocking the trail, slowing me down. I skirt along beside a large peat bog, once a lake, and beyond that, top a ridge of boulders where a tiny shallow lake appears below. Here I stop for a late lunch and welcome rest before the last push of the day. Then up and across the lake basin I go over angular talus boulders—very tricky footwork under a heavy pack. Crossing another open avalanche chute, I look back: Chimayosos Peak by the pass now looks miles away, and to the northeast are bare ridges and summits, one after another to the horizon. The trail leads out around a spur coming down from Truchas Peak, offering a view to the southeast down into the many tributaries of the Upper Pecos: Azul, Del Padre, Maestas, and Jarosa, lit up with patches of yellow aspen.

Here I begin to see bighorn sheep tracks—the animals obviously use the forest service trail as a convenient highway. Climbing again to 12,000 feet, I arrive at last in a wide-open glacial basin beside Truchas Peak itself, the topmost point shouldering into the sky above. The trail traverses a moraine of white boulders bristling with scattered spruce, and there before me, on the lower slopes of the peak, is a small herd of bighorns. Less than a dozen fat and furry wild sheep, all with curved horns, graze strung out and moving slowly in one direction along an almost vertical pitch. They stop and watch me hiking closer, then resume their aggressive, nose-down tearing at the tough mountain grasses. They all appear to be ewes.

I push on to the very center of the broad bowl scoured by ancient glaciers and see the steep slope I plan to climb tomorrow to reach the top. Bighorn sign is everywhere—hoofprints, droppings, cropped vegetation. I drop into the bottom of a giant pothole, what would have been a lake at one time, perhaps, but now drains out through dank holes in jumbled boulders. Climbing out the south rim, I slow, panting, hilariously giddy and reeling in the thin air.

Searching for a good place to make camp for the night, I follow the trail as it exits the basin through a rock gap and drops down a steep ravine. Picking my way through a maze of huge quartzite boulders, I come to a green bog at the base of rock slides where I suddenly confront two bighorn rams. They stand motionless, right on the trail, staring calmly at me. Each has enormous horns that curl around in a complete arc and point outward at their bulging marbled eyes. They both look terrifically muscled, tough, poised—the kind of bighorn sheep that in wildlife documentaries run at each other and crash their horned heads together. There is a long pregnant pause as we study each other.

Finally I take a few steps forward—they're blocking my way, after all—and both rams amble off the trail uphill about twenty feet and stop again. They watch me with stolid eyes as I walk past. I keep a wary eye on them, but they seem docile, even sleepy.

Then I plunge headlong into another herd of bighorns climbing up the trail toward me, who seem as startled as I am. Ewes and rams both, about twenty of them, scatter quickly to my right and form a line, walking single-file directly across a steep slide of sharp rocks. Every sheep is fat, fit, and thickly furred, brownish gray, with a white rump. Incredibly agile and casual about crossing a vertical rock slide—dislodging rocks that clatter noisily to the bottom—the bighorns seem much more tame and fearless than deer and elk in the high country. Once hunted to extinction in New Mexico, they were reintroduced by the state game and fish department only a few decades ago. I've been told the sturdy sheep crave salt so strongly that some will eat potato chips from a hiker's hand.

The bighorns soon halt and peacefully begin to graze wherever they find themselves on the grassy slope. As I continue down the ravine, I see the bare rounded top of Hamilton Mesa in the distance, much closer than before, and to my right the equally bare flat top of the Trailrider's Wall, a great stone promenade that connects Truchas Peak to Pecos Baldy. At a modest hilltop in old-growth spruce-fir forest, I search around and find what I'm looking for: a flat campsite near a spring. The late afternoon sun still shines down warmly. At just a hair under 12,000 feet, this is the highest altitude I've ever camped in my life.

I get busy. By five o'clock the tent is up, gear is stowed inside, and I've drawn filtered water from the spring. The sun drops behind the mountain, and it turns so cold that gray jays, the opportunistic camp robbers of the alpine heights, float silently to the ground, where they snatch and eat grass-hoppers that have become too stiff to jump away. Tired and cold myself, I climb in the tent and rest. Birds sing and twitter in the twilight. At dusk I climb out and wander around without any thoughts, vaguely at loose ends until I spot lone bighorns grazing above and watch them with complete absorption. As each one beds down for the night and night falls, I don't feel like eating a meal and just snack on things that appeal to me. Eventually it becomes too cold not to be inside my sleeping bag.

Zipped up in my cocoon of nylon and down, I ponder my situation. Two whole days have passed without seeing another human being. It's hard to believe nobody else is up here. Although this last part of my voyage around the horizon has been an isolated, lonely experience, it doesn't really bother me. I've been out in the air and light and silence for so long, the world I came from seems unreal. All I'm certain of anymore is the endless immediate moment and a feeling I've only rarely felt before—a calm sense of well-being—which now seems my permanent state. But I know it won't last. The season is late and I cannot linger up here. If I did, the snow would drive me down. In any event, at least for the time being, I feel I could live like this forever.

Five

I WAKE UP to squirrel chatter and dim light through the tent wall. I don't recall where I am. Then I remember. Truchas Peak, the final ascent.

Another night of dog naps, of waking up shivering, of convulsive deep breathing to warm up and fall asleep again. It must be the elevation, the lowered level of oxygen. Nevertheless, I've been in my sleeping bag, on the ground, around the clock—almost the entire twelve hours of darkness. So I'm refreshed, ready to get an early start, determined to make it to the summit and back down before afternoon storm clouds can gather and make the climb too perilous.

Meanwhile, tree squirrels screech endlessly, celebrating another brightening of daylight on earth, sounding like a series of wind-up alarm clocks going off. When they fall silent, I turn over in my down bag, listening. The air hardly moves. A gust of wind finally blows down the mountain, scours through the tops of trees where my tent is pitched, and then fades away to the east. It is so perfectly still the loudest sound is my heartbeat. Peeking outside, a warm pink alpenglow suffuses the broad wall of mountain above. Thin yellow bars of liquid sunlight shoot through shaggy spruce trees from the horizon. The sudden laser beams of sunrise make me smile. Time to get going.

Stumbling around in the numbing cold, barefoot on the soft duff, I see the world below still in the shadow of night. I am on the shore of an island of light. Only the peaks are bathed in sunshine, like islands in a dark sea. My hands work clumsily at the simplest tasks. Before long, I gulp hot coffee and spoon down hot granola mush. Then I prepare a freeze-dried foil pouch version of hot scrambled eggs and bacon, and, despite a taste that only remotely resembles the original, wolf it down. Bulked up for the physical challenge ahead, I kneel down at the spring where a swamp-like smell hangs heavy in the air. After slaking my thirst, I fill my jug with the tangy organic holy water bubbling from a crack in the earth. Leaving the camp as it is, I load the Scooby-Doo daypack and stow everything else inside the tent or up a tree.

Finally ready, I make my way back up the trail to the basin, the dry glacial cirque I passed through yesterday. Even weighed down with a full jug, food, poncho, coat, survival gear, map, and journal, the daypack feels like nothing. Lugging a backpack like a burro for days up a mountain does have its occasional compensations, and this is one of them: I now feel incredibly light and strong and capable. Free at last, I leap and frolic and dance over boulders.

Up through the gap in the rocks, panting, I see bighorn sheep spread out in brilliant morning light, grazing along the steep open mountain slope I will climb. I hear rocks clattering down as they move along. And right where I fork off from the Skyline Trail to head upward, the same two big rams stand grazing side by side, blocking my way yet again. As I approach, the larger of the two alpha males turns and faces off with me in a threatening manner. He prepares to bellow a challenge at me. Lifting his regal head of massive curled horns, he opens his mouth. But all that comes out is a pathetic bleating *baa-a-a-a!*

I can't help myself—I laugh so hard I have to stop and lean against a boulder. The great beast of the high mountains is begging for a potato chip!

Both rams gaze at me expectantly. "Sorry, guys. I don't have any salty snacks," I say as I pick my way around them. "Don't you know they're not really good for you?"

Then I get down to business. Starting directly up the mountainside with both rams attentively watching, I begin the laborious ascent where boulders stand up from hummocks of frost-nipped yellow grass. The turf is still very green at the base, close to the ground. The bare bones of old Stone Man himself consist of the same white quartzite I've been seeing all along—it appears this whole part of the Sierra is made of this rock. No wonder the Tewa sacred color of the east is white!

When I look back, the two bighorn rams have resumed grazing. I go back to work on the perpendicular slope, choosing a way pretty much straight up the southeast face of Truchas Peak. I have a little over a thousand vertical feet to climb. There is no trail to the summit and no ridge of solid rock to make it easier. Nothing but low mounds of alpine tundra I grab with my hands to help pull me up. I stop and rest every twenty or thirty yards, panting, and look around. The two rams are prone, chewing their cud, idly watching me climb high above them.

I have picked a route between slides of loose sharp rock. From them on each side comes the sharp *peenk!* of hidden pikas. Then I hear the piercing whistle of a marmot. Searching the area where the sound came from, I finally spot the animal sprawled on top of a flat boulder, lazing in the warm sunshine. Not surprisingly called "whistlers" locally, and really a giant squirrel the size of a small dog, marmots are built low to the ground to begin with, and are not often seen during the few months of summer they are abroad, fattening up for a long winter sleep. This species, *Marmota caligata*, the largest in North America, appears dusted with prematurely gray hair over a dark coat, hence the name *hoary* marmot.

More bighorns above me. Climbing steadily, I watch three of them move aside from my line of ascent. I hear rocks rolling downhill from other sheep crossing rock slides out of sight. Then one sits right above me, a ewe with only one horn, the other broken off. She sits chewing her cud in a lazy rhythm, eyes on the two-legged creature climbing slowly up into her thin-air world. Far below, the two alpha rams *baaa*, over and over, for no apparent reason. I choose a route that goes around the resting ewe—she sleepily ignores me as I climb past.

The scramble upward crosses many narrow, horizontal bighorn sheep trails that angle up and down only slightly, making them useless to follow. Nothing will do except continuing to bulldog my way upward. For an ascent like this, a well-oiled machine of heart, lungs, and legs are all that is required. I try not to think too much about how far I've come, or how much more I have to climb. Better to just be wherever I am—live in the now, as they say. Focus on the little patch of mountain that is my only reality at the moment. Ravens drift like black eagles in the wind above, cawing. As I gaze upward at them, I see airliners without contrails crossing the endless blue sky in absolute silence.

I come upon pika nest holes and platforms, the grassy slope as pocked as Swiss cheese, each opening littered with rodent droppings and mounded up with neat piles of snipped green vegetation like miniature haystacks. I assume grizzly bears, before they were all killed off in New Mexico, used to dig out and feast on the fat little pikas, like they still do in Yellowstone and the northern Rockies. I climb up to the level of two more bighorns, resting about forty feet away—young ones, with little spike horns starting to curve back. One gets up nervously but then sits back down. The other ignores me, chewing cud, eyes glazed. I haven't heard any of these bighorns panting like I am.

Farther up, for a moment moving along one of the bighorn trails, I come upon a full-curl ram, another of the kind that crash heads, standing stock-still on the trail, glaring at me. I am infinitely more vulnerable on the steep slope than I was down below. But even the great muscled ram before me simply plunks down on its knees, bored, and watches me angle slowly onward above him. It's hard to believe the state of New Mexico actually allows hunters to come and gun down these amazingly tame, trusting creatures. You couldn't call it actual hunting, could you? The only effort involved is getting to where the bighorns live. The rest would be like walking out into a pasture and shooting a cow!

The wind grows stronger, whipping the tufts of grass into motion. I find matted-down bowls on the slope, which bighorns use as favored resting spots. The air warms and smells of fresh hay and sheep. The declivity becomes too steep to go straight up and I begin to make short switchbacks left and right. At a certain point I guess my position to be about a third of the way to the top, and I can still make out the two big rams, napping on the grass like gray dots on the basin floor far below. At this location I make an amazing discovery—I find a foot-long piece of pure-white quartz in the shape of a giant fang embedded in the soil. Pried out, the glassy stone is semitransparent and smooth to the touch. One end comes to a sharp tip, and though there are no obvious signs of hand working or shaping, I can't imagine this object has occurred naturally. It weighs about four pounds, is flat and sharp along one edge like a knife blade, and resembles museum pieces I've seen made of black obsidian. It is a scary thing to behold, perhaps a ritual object or weapon in the Tewa color symbolic of the east. I hide it on the mountain and go on.

Each higher pause presents a panoramic view to the east. As if just for me, the air is pure and empty, the world visible in stark detail as far as the eye can see—an atmospheric condition known as "severe clear" to men like my father, an Air Force bomber pilot. What I see are rolling ridges of dark forest to a far horizon, broken here and there by patches of golden aspen and mint-green meadow.

I slip and fall twice. Each time is a surprise, a moment of panic and dismay. This is not a place for accidents—I could shoot down the slick grass for hundreds of feet in a matter of seconds. I become extra careful, placing each step just so. There is very little purchase. At least my healed right foot is staying strong.

Reaching an island-like area of solid rock in the midst of tundra grass, I boulder straight up the tilted dark-gray outcrop of schist and gneiss, crossing deep fissures with thick veins of the same white quartz the artifact was made of. Then I force my way up a grassy rubble slope between headlands of country rock. I see no more bighorns—my time wandering alone among them seems to have come to an end. I claw my way through thickets of shrubby cinquefoil. At every vertical rock outcrop, a wind-shorn spruce or slanting copse of alpine juniper hides a pocket of wild oat grass, gone to seed on tall waving stalks.

A five-pound rock I dislodge keeps rolling and sliding downward, so I sit back and watch it. Faster and faster it goes, soon bounding in twenty-foot leaps at incredible speed all the way to the bottom. It could have killed a bighorn like a cannonball! I take it as a warning: "Now, listen here, pilgrim," John Wayne drawls in my head. "Don't you start sliding downhill, ya hear me? You may not be able to stop yourself!"

At last I approach a knife-edge ridge, a long spur coming up from a distant saddle on the south side of Truchas. Atop the loose slabs, shaky-legged in a blasting wind, I look over and down the other side at a totally unfamiliar wilderness spread out to the west beyond. Directly below is an emerald-green lake at the base of a half-mile-long rock slide.

"Omigod! What lake is that?" I gasp aloud.

It has a definite teardrop shape. I drop down in the wind and pull out my topo map. Glancing around at landmarks, at the looming great mountain behind me—the Stone Man still high in the sky—I vector in on a spot of blue on the map called Jose Vigil Lake. The lovely little lake a thousand feet below, one of many scattered around the cluster of peaks, is the source of the Rio Medio, which flows west down a long deep canyon to Cundiyo—where it meets the Rio Frijoles to form the Santa Cruz River. Which empties into the Rio Grande at Española, and so on. All of which I can see as if from an airplane overhead.

The view is magnificent—to the ends of the earth in 180 degrees—a grand sweep from the Great Plains to the sawtooth peaks at the end of the Sangre de Cristos to the dark volcanic Jemez Mountains. Nearby is the Sierra Mosca ("Housefly Range")—no sierra at all but a round wooded mountain—and the miles-long swath of a forest blowdown, hundreds of acres of dead white timber knocked down in a "wind event" a few years ago (that nobody actually witnessed). Through the gap that channeled the prevailing wind that blew the trees down, I see the lowlands beyond Santa Fe, familiar Tetilla Peak like a tiny blip, and the rounded bulk of Sandia Mountain near Albuquerque. To the right, across the wide Rio Grande Valley, I pick out Chicoma Mountain, due west on the horizon. Nearer at hand, the mountain I sit on is surrounded by a vast forested wilderness. And whoever Jose Vigil was, his lake is incredibly beautiful and remote, a gemlike turquoise body of water cradled in a timberline bowl of white rock.

Six

I'VE RESTED TOO long. And maybe eaten too much, guzzled down too much water, but high altitude intensifies such cravings. Just after ten o'clock I make myself stand up and go on. Soon I'm scaling a sharp ridge of rock—straight-up mountain climbing—but then find a trace of trail, a route climbed by others before me, angling off to the left over ground less difficult. Following it at a steady plod, I still sometimes simply can't breathe, or my heart flutters and leaps wildly in my chest and I have to stop. It is exhilarating, but not easy. A good place to die, should it come to that.

The mountain hardens and defies me. Slowly, one step at a time, I clamber over unstable slabs, acutely aware of the straight shot down to the lake below. Rocks I dislodge go bounding down so fast, they simply disappear. So much more physical effort is required as I approach 13,000 feet, I become conscious of my own dwindling ability to think. I notice fresh bighorn tracks and even fresher droppings. The wild sheep come up even here, on top, to graze the low green plants still showing. A chipmunk darts across above me. Tiny grasshoppers leap away from my heavily planted footsteps. One flies away in the wind, swirling upward and outward until only a tiny dot can be seen in the sky.

"Good luck!" I yell at the unfortunate insect.

It could land down there in the lake below, I think to myself. Or hell, it could be buffeted by strong updrafts for miles and miles and come down on Interstate 25, a splatting bullet on a passing car's windshield!

I see a narrowing above, what must be the top, or near it. The route keeps to the left, to the southwest, around a broad shoulder of solid rock. Gasping for air, I pick my way carefully over it and emerge onto the west face, my eyes immediately jumping to the horizon, where the Pedernal stands alone, far away to the northwest. I see Ohkay Owinge at the toe end of Black Mesa, and the collapsed-caldera shape of the Jemez range. Canjilon glimmers at the drop-off of a high forested mesa. And Middle Truchas Peak, only a mile away, floats out in the void at eye level. Spread out below, at the foot of the mountain, are the homes and settled mesa-top farmlands of the town of Truchas. Still plodding upward around the main peak, I glimpse North Truchas Peak—so huge and high when I crossed over the Santa Barbara Divide, but now merely a tip of bare rock off to the north. In the saddle between Middle and North peaks, the Taos Mountains can be seen marching away toward Colorado.

Climbing to the very apex I see above me is like ascending the stone stairs of a pyramid. I skirt a swath of shattered white quartz, grateful there's no lightning, and in fact, no clouds at all, except some growing smudges of white on the southern horizon. Stormy weather is coming but I'm okay for the time being. I force myself slowly onward despite the befuddling lack of oxygen. Jets sail by overhead in the blink of an eye and with no sound whatever of their passing.

Finally, loose rock gives way to the firm rounded dome of the very summit, the last easy steps to the top of the world, marked by a cairn of gray slabs. Here I stand at last on the final peak of my journey. Thoughts are scarce. I am elated to have my home world spread out at my feet below, and the empty alien immensity of violet sky overhead. Surveying the full 360-degree view of the horizon, I am in awe, yet mainly aware of the sharp rhythmic laboring of my heart.

Two glossy-black ravens soar effortlessly on a stiff updraft. Taking an interest in me, they drift closer, croaking, and one dive-bombs me in mock attack, breaking off at the last second. They hang rocking in the wind, watching me with beady eyes. I feel the natural world's awareness of me through the raven's eyes. I wonder if these could be ravens I used to feed at my house down below. Do they know me? Not likely. It's probably just a ploy to get me to cough up a handout.

Idle, useless thoughts.

The view is staggering. I feel blessed just to be here. A pitiful human being is nothing compared to the vastness before me. Here I can see each of the peaks I have circled around on, and all the land between and beyond. Here is the whole world I live in. A few steps farther on I come to a terrifying view down near-vertical slopes, the backside of the peak. Far below, I pick out where I made camp and discern the thin line of the Skyline Trail I followed from one alpine basin to another.

Exploring the summit area at 13,102 feet, there is no wind, only an occasional breeze brushing my face. The air is balmy but not quite tee shirt warm. Eventually I find traces of the old Tewa shrine in a cleft between two promontories. On a flat spot where soil and plants and bighorn droppings and fresh, gopher-dug dirt mounds stand out against the surrounding rocky rubble, I locate a large faint outline of rocks embedded in a horseshoe shape. The open end faces directly westward toward Chicoma Mountain on the horizon. I am standing on the head of the old Stone Man himself—he who stands high above all others in the Tewa world.

At a spot where a deep chasm shoots down the back of the peak, I sing a song, which is not easy—there is no force to my breath at this elevation. Burning some sage, leaving an offering, it occurs to me that I have left a little of myself on each of the peaks of the four directions that I have climbed. I feel a surge of unapologetic pride in my ritual actions. They say to the world: This is me. I am here. Standing in the profound silence on top of Truchas Peak at last, having accomplished what I set out to do, I am at peace.

And then—is that a nail? My goodness, yes it is. A number-8 box, I do believe. Rusty, bent, but a nail all the same. From a wooden cross erected here once? Devout Hispanic Catholics once maintained such crosses on all these peaks, I'm told.

I sit at last and simply marvel at my great good luck to have made it atop such a great mountain. Munching on a light lunch—piñon nuts, carne seca, Snickers bar, Granny Smith apple—I wash it down with the cold, sweet mountain spring water I carried up. The unreal clarity of the air and the sharpness of the noonday light reveal the whole wide world in exquisite detail. I study the distant landscape and pick out a certain faraway landmark: a round wooded hill, barely visible—the mountain next to where I live. Still ahead of me is the two-day journey down and out of this wilderness to reach that far-off home, but for now I simply lean back, resting in the sunlight. It's all downhill from here.

Epilogue

AT DUSK ON the same day I climbed Truchas Peak, in pelting sleet near Pecos Baldy, miles to the south, I finally saw another person. A young tall guy with trailing dreadlocks and a well-worn backpack strode up to me with the same shy smile I gave him. He, too, had seen nobody in days of wandering in the wilderness. The quiet intelligence of his words describing his explorations was remarkable. Human contact never seemed so precious. We sat and talked and made friends, but then parted and went our separate ways.

That night it snowed lightly on my tent pitched in a meadow along Jack's Creek. It all melted quickly away in the first rays of the sun. Elk in great numbers crowded the meadows, the bugling of the bulls echoing all morning. Hiking down the last few miles, I met a man on horseback riding up. He looked like an old Texas cowpoke with his grizzled white beard and eyes squinting from under a Stetson. He asked me if I'd seen his lost blue heeler dog. When I said no, he asked if I'd seen any sign of elk.

"Yeah, they woke me up this morning with their bugling. They're all over the place."

"Like where, exactly?" he said with sudden interest. That's when I saw the rifle in his scabbard and remembered the regular elk season had opened that morning.

"Oh, all up around there," I said waving vaguely (and I hope, unhelpfully) back the way I came.

"Damn! Thanks! Giddy up there!" he cried, spurring his horse up the trail.

One week later a wet Pacific storm swept through and heavy snow fell on the high country of northern New Mexico. On the morning of October 21, all four peaks emerged pure white in the sunrise—the backpacking season was over. Driving from Santa Fe to Española, I stopped at a certain hilltop and got out. I stood gazing at each summit in turn, sensing something different in the fact that I had now been to the top of each. My journey of discovery was over and I had returned in one piece. I felt palpably more at home in this place than I ever had before. And yet I imagined heading off on another walk around some other horizon—soon—to discover some other rare, wild country.

I was fit, after all—lean and hardened and muscled beyond my own expectation. A whole new, wider swath of my surroundings was now a part of my known world. And the adventure, the sheer marvel of what I experienced in the mountains, had whetted my appetite for more.

In a matter of minutes, a leaden overcast spread across the upper world of El Norte and snuffed out the morning sunlight. Each peak in each direction stood pale and indistinct under a lowering sky. Mountains that had appeared proud and invincible moments before slowly dissolved into remote and shapeless points of the compass lost in clouds.

But it didn't matter. I knew they were still there. I had been there—where grasshoppers boldly fling themselves into thin air, where glimpses of the enormity of the wide world await the oxygen-starved wanderer, where the clan of curved horn and cloven hoof thrive among dizzying drop-offs, and where only a few humans have climbed in ten thousand years to sit in wonder at the mystery of where we find ourselves.